Loving Legacy

Ramona Warren

A JANET THOMA BOOK

THOMAS NELSON PUBLISHERS
Nashville

Published in Nashville, Tennessee, by Thomas Nelson, Inc., and distributed in Canada by Lawson Falle, Ltd., Cambridge, Ontario.

Unless otherwise noted, Scripture quotations are from the NEW KING JAMES VERSION of the Bible. Copyright © 1979, 1980, 1982, Thomas Nelson, Inc., Publishers.

Scripture quotations noted NIV are from the Holy Bible: NEW INTERNATIONAL VERSION. Copyright © 1978 by the New York International Bible Society. Used by permission of Zondervan Bible Publishers.

Scripture quotations noted GNB are from the *Good News Bible*, Old Testament © 1976 by the American Bible Society; New Testament © 1966, 1971, 1976 American Bible Society. Used by permission.

Scripture quotations noted KJV are from the King James Version.

Library of Congress Cataloging-in-Publication Data

Warren, Ramona.
    Loving legacy / by Ramona Warren.
        p.   cm.
    ISBN 0-8407-7820-1
    1. Grandmothers—Prayer-books and devotions—English.
2. Devotional calendars.   I. Title.
BV4847.W377   1994
242'.6431—dc20   93–20608
                                                           CIP

Printed in the United States of America

1 2 3 4 5 6 — 97 96 95 94 93

Just about all of us have a grandmother story—a remembrance of something we like or liked to do with her; something she does or did that was special; something about her that we like or liked. The remembrances are funny, sad, touching, joyous, heart-wrenching, poignant, happy, and significant to those who tell them.

As I began writing this book, I thought about my own grandmothers and my mother who was grandmother to my children and my brother's children. I thought of my own experience as a grandmother to six children. I read and listened to hundreds of memories of grandchildren and grandmothers. And I discovered in each memory a common thread: a special bond, that is, between grandmothers and grandchildren, a bond of love that encompasses pain, sadness, sorrow, and loss.

Some grandmothers feel they have another chance to take part in the shaping of a child's life—only this time they aren't as uptight about it. Others gain affirmation of the continuity of families.

Little children get right to the point when you ask them about their grandmothers. When she's around there are usually presents or the prospect of them. Older children and adults have memories of good food and feelings of love and acceptance—basic needs we have all of our lives.

A grandmother's legacy is love. This kind of love comes from knowing that God is love and having a per-

sonal relationship with His Son, Jesus Christ. It is the
love that walks and talks 1 Corinthians 13:4:

> *Love is patient,*
> *Love is kind,*
> *It does not envy,*
> *It does not boast,*
> *It is not proud,*
> *It is not rude,*
> *It is not self-seeking,*
> *It is not easily angered,*
> *It keeps no record of wrongs.*
> *Love does not delight in evil*
> *But rejoices with the truth.*
> *It always protects,*
> *   always trusts,*
> *   always hopes,*
> *   always perseveres.*
> *Love never fails (paraphrase).*

The devotions in this book tell stories of grandmothers and grandchildren that we can all identify
with, then points out a truth or principle from God's
Word for encouragement as we are actively involved in
passing on our very own loving legacy.

Writing 365 devotions was like scaling a mountain,
and I am thankful for the help I had in collecting all
the grandmother memories and stories. My daughter,
Ginnie, and friend, Mitzi Green, win first and second
prizes for supplying me with the most material. Ginnie
asked everyone she met—at work, friends, as well as
others such as total strangers on airplanes; Mitzi asked
relatives at several family gatherings to tell their grandmother memories and wrote down page after page

Friends who live far away, Marilyn Adams and Maralee Stephens sent me letters filled with stories and called to make sure I understood what they had written. Friends nearby—Terri Ferrell, Carol White, Carolyn Hanson, and Deborah Hudgens—who took time to write several of their remembrances and those of other family members and all of these, along with the stories about my grandmothers, my mother as grandmother, and myself as grandmother are included as well as material about grandmothers I've discovered through the years.

Several people encouraged me and prayed with me during the writing of the book and I especially appreciated the support of the small group I belong to and work associates, Diane Norden and Sandy Brotzman.

The devotions also include much of my philosophy of life and is my loving legacy dedicated to the people who made me a grandmother—my two daughters and husbands; my son and his wife:

Bev and Bob Mitchum
Ginnie and Mark Allmendinger
Greg and Deborah Warren

and their children: Jamie, Rob, Becky, Brian, Alex, Angela.

> *. . . from childhood you have known the Holy Scriptures, which are able to make you wise for salvation.* **—2 TIM. 3:15**

*M*y grandson Brian, my son's son, was being dedicated. As I heard his parents promise to teach him about Jesus and begin his Christian education early, I thought about my role in this essential area of Brian's life.

The Bible tells about Lois, a devout Jewess whose family lived in Lystra. Lois taught her daughter, Eunice, and grandson, Timothy. We can only guess at how she taught them, since written Scripture passages did not abound. But she did teach them—probably through Lois's memory of the Word and the way she lived her faith. She taught them so well that when Paul visited Lystra they were ready to hear and accept Jesus.

Lois is the only grandmother mentioned by name in the Bible. Could it be because of her "genuine faith" mentioned by Paul in 2 Timothy 1:5? She certainly walked what she talked.

As my son held his son and publicly expressed his intention to teach Brian as he had been taught, I dedicated myself to continue to live my faith—genuinely.

♥ *My grandchildren notice people who walk what they talk. Help me demonstrate faith that is real.*

GROWING

But grow in the grace and knowledge of our
Lord and Savior Jesus Christ.
—2 PETER 3:18

$\mathcal{M}$y daughter Ginnie keeps detailed baby books for both of her daughters. Shortly after Becky was born, eight-year-old Jamie became especially interested in her own baby book. Jamie often brought out her book to show me her baby pictures and ask questions such as: "Was I as little as Becky is? When did I start to crawl? What were the first words I said? Did you bring me presents, Grandma Mona?"

Jamie continued to study the book, wanting to hear again and again about when she was "little." She even became more observant of her sister's growing and liked to remind her mom to write the new things Becky did in Becky's baby book.

During that time it was so easy and natural to help Jamie identify with Jesus as a baby and as a child who needed to grow and learn as she and her sister were growing and learning. What a privilege it was to be at the beginning of her understanding of the humanness of Jesus, who, being the very Son of God, came to be our Savior and Friend.

♥ *Father, I'm through growing physically, but I desire to continue to grow in knowing You.*

TRUSTWORTHY PROMISES

He has given us his very great and precious promises . . .
　　　　　　　　　　—2 PETER 1:4 NIV

*J*amie was being confirmed. I pondered long about a confirmation gift. She would be delighted with money or a gift certificate, and my gift would include one of these. But I wanted to give her something more—something that would strengthen and enrich her growing faith, something she would use the rest of her life.

I thought first of a Bible. But Jamie had a Bible and would probably own several others during her life. Then I thought about books I read and reread. A book of God's promises is especially worn, and many of the promises are highlighted. The promises of comfort I turned to when my husband died; the promises for help in troubles I know by heart. God's promises are all listed, covering every possible situation. I bought the book for Jamie.

When she opened her presents, the gift certificate received more attention; but God has promised, ". . . My word . . . shall not return to Me void, / But it shall accomplish what I please, / And it shall prosper in the thing for which I sent it" (Isa. 55:11).

♥ *The old hymn says, "Every promise in the Book is mine!" I believe that this is absolutely true!*

TELL THE STORIES

Only take heed . . . lest you forget the things your eyes have seen. . . . teach them to your children and your grandchildren.
—DEUT. 4:9

*G*randma lived with us for many years after Grandfather died. She made wonderful chicken and dumplings and delicious pies. And she always had a bag of peppermint candy in her room. (The candy wasn't necessarily for sharing with grandchildren; it was for her. Grandma had trouble sleeping at night; maybe the peppermints helped.) She had traveled by covered wagon from Indiana to Kansas, where she and Grandfather farmed near the start of the Santa Fe Trail.

I loved my grandma, but I didn't talk with her enough and she didn't talk with me enough. She died at 93, several years after I married and had children of my own. I wish I had talked to her more. There is so much I now want to know about her and her life.

My grandchildren aren't always very interested in the stories I tell them. But I think it's important to talk to them about the past, about what life was like and what I was like, and about my journey of faith. As grandparents we must tell them over and over, creatively and in small doses, until we capture their attention and interest.

♥ *Family stories can knit a warm blanket of security and create hunger for strong faith.*

*A good name is better than precious
ointment.*   —ECCL. 7:1

*M*y grandchildren call me Grandma Mona to distinguish me from the other grandmas in our family. My mother was Big Grandma; my grandmother was Little Grandma because she was very old and seemed to have shrunk.

In Lois Wyse's book *Funny, You Don't Look Like a Grandmother,* the chapter "What Will We Name the Grandmother?" tells an interesting naming story.

> When Josh went to nursery school, he talked continually about his zaide and bubbie. He told of adventures with them, and when show and tell day came, he announced that he would bring in his bubbie and zaide.
>
> When he walked in with his grandparents, Ed and Ethel, his nursery school teacher said, "Who are these people?"
>
> "Bubbie and Zaide," he said proudly.
>
> "But . . . but," she stammered, "I thought they were gerbils."

Whatever we are called (and there's usually a good story behind it), we are challenged by God to have a good name.

♥ *If my grandchildren were to tell what my name smelled like, I wonder what it would be?*

Blessed are those who mourn,
For they shall be comforted.
—MATT. 5:4

I was baby-sitting for Robbie, my three-year-old grandson. He was finishing his dinner and I was washing a few dishes when his parents left. Robbie got down from his chair and ran to the screen door, crying as if his heart would break.

I was surprised at this because Robbie was accustomed to my staying with him. Even more surprising, though, was the strong feeling that I shouldn't rush over and placate him. The crying lasted for several minutes. Then Robbie walked back into the kitchen.

"All done crying," he announced and climbed back into his chair to eat his Jell-O.

I was astonished! Yet I understood. Robbie and his parents often go out together, but this time he was being left behind. Though he was with a grandma who loved him and whom he loved, he felt sad. Robbie needed time to mourn.

When Robbie finished his Jell-O, I picked him up and hugged him. Then we read and rocked.

What a great God we have who understands a little boy's sadness and need to mourn and keeps a grandma at the sink until it's time for comforting with hugs and stories.

♥ *Mourning is sometimes necessary and should always*
 be followed with comforting.

HAPPINESS THAT SHOWS

*A merry heart makes a cheerful
countenance . . .*
—PROV. 15:13

One Sunday, my granddaughter Angie, age four, and I were on the way to evening church service. Angie is a delightful child who is not shy and does not fear new places or experiences. As we walked from the car to the education building, I told her that while I was in the service, she would be with the other children in their special room. As we walked, we talked about how much fun she was going to have with all the kids.

I opened the door, and Angie pulled me toward the children's voices. She burst into the room.

"Hey, kids! I'm here!" she yelled. The look on her face was pure joy! Her happy heart showed all over her face, and the children responded to her like flowers opening to the sun.

I left the room smiling and went into the church sanctuary. I resisted the urge to yell, "Hey, everybody, I'm here!" But I couldn't help wondering what would happen if, when Christians get together, we could feel that same way and have it show in our faces. I think it would make God smile. We might almost be able to hear God say, "I'm here, too!"

♥ *Father, I'd like my heart and face to match so that everyone will see how great it is to know You.*

. . . I have loved you with an everlasting love . . .
                                    —JER. 31:3

*A*s we waited for our food at the restaurant, my granddaughter Angie was busy "writing" in a little notebook.

After a few minutes, Angie slid the paper over to me and said, "I wrote you a note, Grandma Mona."

On the paper was a heart with the words "i Lov vu" printed inside.

This is one of the most precious love notes I have ever received. I keep the note in my office and look at it often. As the song says, "When the dog bites, when the bee stings, when I'm feeling sad, I (look at one of) my favorite things and then I don't feel so bad" (my words in parentheses).

There are other favorite things I look at when things are sad, bad, or whatever. God's love notes to us are sprinkled throughout the Bible. In verses like the one above from Jeremiah, God tells us over and over again, in simple, childlike, yet wonderfully powerful words, I love you. Highlight some of God's love notes to us and mark them with bookmarks so you can read them often—especially when you need to be reminded of His everlasting love.

♥ *Father, I'm so glad and thankful You love me. I love You, too.*

January 8 _____

. . . I will never leave you nor forsake you.
—HEB. 13:5

*D*uring lunch one day, my grandson Brian asked, "Are you ever lonely, Grandma Mona?"

My daughter-in-law, sensitive to my being a widow and living alone, tried to stop him, but I said, "It's okay. That's a good question, Brian. I keep myself busy. I work every day, and I like to travel and read and shop. But yes, sometimes I get lonely. Do you ever feel lonely, Brian?"

The discussion that followed lasted well past the end of the meal. Each of us told about times when we are lonely, how it feels, and what to do about loneliness.

We agreed that we have a choice. We can feel sorry for ourselves and end up really miserable, or we can choose to do something about loneliness. We decided one of the best things to do is to call someone.

We also discussed the fact that we are never truly alone because God is always with us and understands. He means it when He says He will never forsake us. When we tell Him about our loneliness and ask Him to help us, we shouldn't be surprised when He drops the name of another lonely person into our thoughts.

♥ *We don't seek loneliness, but it happens to us. Help us remember Your promise and listen for Your solution.*

TESTING LIMITS

. . . Obey My voice, and I will be your God, and you shall be My people. And walk in all the ways that I have commanded you . . .
—JER. 7:23

*O*ne of the interesting aspects of grandparenthood has been observing how my children discipline their children. I watched with fascination one day as my grandson Brian tested some limits set by his dad.

Brian had been told that he must not disturb some knickknacks on his great-grandmother's coffee table. But he kept moving closer and closer to the table, his fingers itching to reach out and touch. When he was just about to disobey, his father said, "Brian!" and the warning tone of his voice was enough to move the three-year-old to a safer activity.

My son looked at me and said, "You taught me that. I could always tell by the tone of your voice if I was about to get into trouble. I guess I just had to see how far I could go, but your warning voice helped me get back on the right track. It works with Brian, too."

Like the Israelites, we, too, often are like little children, testing God's limits yet needing to obey His loving voice so that our daily walk goes well.

♥ *Dear Lord, help me hear and obey Your voice.*

HELP!

The LORD is good,
A stronghold in the day of trouble;
And He knows those who trust in Him.
— NAH. 1:7

*E*ach year I take as many grandchildren as are available with me on a week's vacation. It's a gift to my daughters, son, their spouses, the children, and me! We go to a cabin or resort and swim, go on picnics, stay up late, sleep late, eat junk food, and play games. We like a game called Life Stories, in which the players share memories of their lives. The game ends with everyone telling a story about or good memory of someone else in the game.

It was granddaughter Becky's turn to remember something about me as we played the game during the second summer after her parents' painful divorce. Becky said, "The night Mom and Dad told Jamie and me they were getting a divorce, I'm glad Grandma was there to help me. We took a walk."

I said, "We helped each other, Beck."

God gives grandparents unique abilities to help and be helped in times of pain, sadness, and disappointment. When we show our confidence in God to take care of us and help us, we find strength and comfort for ourselves and affirm this truth in our grandchildren.

♥ *Lord, I want my grandchildren to know You. Show me ways I can make this possible.*

Rejoice with those who rejoice, and weep with those who weep. —ROM. 12:15

*A*aron, my friend Carol's first grandchild, was born severely handicapped. The family was told there was no hope for normalcy, and he has always lived in a care-giving facility. He does not know or recognize mother, father, grandfather, or grandmother.

When Carol first told me about Aaron I was a new grandmother, too, rejoicing over a healthy, beautiful girl named Jamie. I did all the normal grandmother things such as showing pictures and bragging to everyone I knew, and a few strangers.

Carol had come to visit me and we were taking a walk when she described how she felt as she held her grandchild, knowing he would never know who she was, would never run, play, or go to school. I had no words to try to explain or help to understand. Even comforting words seemed somehow useless and inappropriate. So I cried. We cried together for Aaron and for his grandmother, and we found comfort in our shared tears. Years later, Carol told me that our shared tears helped more than anything else during that difficult time.

♥ *Help me to exemplify Your characteristics, Lord.*

NEVER FORGET

*And these words which I command you
today shall be in your heart; you shall teach
them diligently to your children . . .*
— DEUT. 6:6–7

$\mathcal{I}$ was playing Life Stories with my grandchildren Jamie and Becky and their mother, Ginnie. When it was Becky's turn to tell a memory or story about me, she said, "I like it that when Grandma Mona comes to visit; she always brings me a book or game or something to help me learn more about Jesus and how He wants me to live."

I thanked her and inwardly thanked God for affirming my part in her spiritual growth. (I admit to wondering at times if it made any difference to include gifts with RSQ (redeeming spiritual qualities) along with the toys and clothes.)

When God told His people to teach their children about Him, I'm sure grandparents were to be part of the process. The verses following the passage above explain the when and how the children of that time were taught. The how will probably be different. (Verses 8 and 9 tell the people to tie the words to their arms, wear them on their foreheads, and write them on the doorpost.). But the when will be the same (repeat them when at home, when away, when resting, and when working).

♥ *Lord, it's a privilege to tell grandchildren about You as many ways as I can.*

MODELING

*. . . walk worthy of the Lord, fully pleasing
Him, being fruitful in every good work and
increasing in the knowledge of God.*
—COL. 1:10

*W*e were playing Life Stories again, Jamie, Becky,
Ginnie, and me. Jamie was fourteen, an age when her
mother often felt that most of her words and the example she set were ignored. But Jamie surprised us when
it was her turn to say something positive about her
mother. She quoted, word for word, advice her mother
had given her!

And what she said about me brought tears to my
eyes. Jamie said, "Grandma is a model for me. If I
don't get married or if I ever get a divorce or my husband dies, I know I can make it on my own because
Grandma does!"

Jamie never knew Grandpa Warren. He died before
she was born. She did know that I worked and lived
alone, and that through the years there have been difficult times. I would have never guessed, though, that
this was something that my granddaughter had
watched and admired.

We need to constantly let God transform our view of
life, even when we don't understand what happens to
us. Our grandchildren are watching; we are their
models, good or bad.

♥ *Help me live a worthy life for You and for my grandchildren.*

*When hope is crushed, the heart is crushed,
but a wish come true fills you with joy.*
—PROV. 13:12

I periodically send cards and notes to my grandsons Brian and Alex in California because I don't see them as often as my Illinois grandchildren. I don't send notes as frequently as I should, but when I do I send each boy a card addressed to him personally. The only problem with this is that the post office doesn't always deliver both cards the same day.

One day there was a card for Brian but not for Alex. My son, without thinking that he could have held the card until the other arrived, delivered the single card to Brian. The next day Alex's card arrived. When he saw it, he said, "Oh, good. I was so worried that it got lost and wouldn't get here."

The incident reminded me how much children love to get mail, and I determined to do a better job of communicating with my grandsons. It also reminded me that while I would never intentionally crush the hope of my grandchildren, I am not always able to make their wishes come true. Only Jesus can do that. I can keep helping them to place their hope in Him for their ultimate joy.

♥ *Jesus, I'm glad that my and my grandchildren's hope and joy is always satisfied in You.*

THINK ABOUT IT!

The LORD is my shepherd;
I shall not want.
            —PS. 23:1

*T*he New International Bible says, "The Lord is my shepherd. I shall not be in want." The Living Bible says, "Because the Lord is my Shepherd, I have everything I need!"

A grandmother overheard her small grandson praying, "The Lord is my Shepherd, and that's all I want."

This beautiful psalm of trust has comforted, encouraged, and reaffirmed confidence in God for millions since it was written by Godly inspiration through a shepherd boy, somebody's grandson, who knew the importance of the shepherd to the sheep. The picture of tender care and constant watchfulness portrayed in the verses of the psalm describe a personal relationship with a loving Father. The Bible tells about this wonderful Shepherd in other places, too—Jesus the Good Shepherd (John 10:11), the great Shepherd (Heb. 13:20, 21), and the chief Shepherd (1 Peter 5:4).

I think God would like the small grandson's paraphrase. We do, indeed, have everything we need. It should be all we want.

♥ *Lord, everything I really want, I find in You.*

THIS IS THE DAY

This is the day which the LORD has made;
We will rejoice and be glad in it.
—PS. 118:24

We are all readers in our family. From the youngest to the oldest, we love to read—especially in bed before going to sleep. Grandchildren staying overnight can always talk me into extending their already later-than-usual bedtime so they can read for just a little while longer.

As usual, when it was time for my grandson Rob to go to bed, he asked for just a half an hour to read. I was worried that he might be tired and crabby without enough sleep, but Rob said, "I promise I'll wake up happy, Grandma. And I'll get right up!"

I smiled at his optimism and kissed him goodnight. "Only half an hour," I reminded him.

The next morning I went into the bedroom to wake him. With an almost wide-awake smile, Rob immediately sat up in bed and said, "It's going to be a terrific day, Grandma!"

God wants us to recognize that He gives us each day. He asks that we be happy about it and during it, being glad from the minute we open our eyes.

♥ *Heavenly Father, help me to remember to rejoice in each terrific day first thing every morning.*

NEW HOUSE

*And I will dwell in the house of the LORD
Forever.*
—PS. 23:6b

*E*veryone called her Grandma. She was a plain woman, born and raised on a farm, married to a farmer. In her early 50s, her husband died and she had to support herself by working as a maid at a hotel in town.

Her three daughters were grown and had children of their own. All too soon those grandchildren grew and had children, and she was a great-grandma.

She was always active. Though in later years she required hip and knee surgeries, she still loved working in her flower and vegetable garden.

When she was ninety, her eldest daughter, who lived in another state, died of brain cancer. Grandma arrived the day of the viewing at the funeral home. She walked up to the casket, put her hand on her daughter's face, and said, "Lord, if only it could have been me."

How hard it is for us when children and grandchildren die before we do. It isn't the way things are "supposed" to happen. "It isn't right! It isn't fair!" we cry out to God—until we let His Word remind us of who our loved one is with.

♥ *Dear Lord, it helps to know the one I love is with
You.*

*And let us not grow weary while doing good,
for in due season we shall reap if we do not
lose heart.*   —GAL. 6:9

*B*obbi was seven when her mother abandoned her
and she went to live with her grandparents. Bobbi says,
"They supplied my every need. Grandma kept a marvelously clean, well-organized home. She made my
clothes, baked, and canned food from her garden.
They took me to church, and even made sure I took piano lessons."

But Bobbi was never hugged or told she was loved.
She didn't understand how much love her grandparents' actions showed and felt unloved. She became re-
bellious, and at fifteen was out of control. She married
at nineteen and continued to make many wrong
choices.

"Then," Bobbi says, "at thirty-seven I found a relationship with Jesus. The hatred, anger, and rebellion I
felt toward everyone began to dissipate. I began to think
about my grandparents. Though I hadn't accepted their
values then and hated every part of my youth, their example helped bring me to Jesus. Now, at fifty-six, I look back
and praise the Lord for my home with them."

We must never underestimate the influence we have
on the lives of our grandchildren.

♥ *Dear God, my grandchildren are Your children, too.
Help me show them how much You love us.*

The LORD is near to all who call upon Him.
—PS. 145:18a

*I*t was "Grandma and the grandchildren week" at a cabin in Wisconsin. All six of the grandchildren, ages five through thirteen, were with me and having a great time. The swimming pool was just a few feet from the back door, and they spent hours playing in the water. My job was lifeguard, encourager, and food provider.

Even though the children were busy nearly every moment, I noticed that they would find time, in ones or twos, just to be close to me for a few minutes. Then off they'd go to rejoin the group.

Grandson Rob put it best one day when he came over to the deck chair where I was sitting, put his arms around me, and said, "I need a Grandma hug!"

As I hugged him back and thanked God for him, I realized this was a picture of the relationship we have with God. He is our lifesaver, encourager, and provider. We spend our time here on earth busy with many people, but every so often we need to get away from the crowd and be alone with God. We need a God hug— the reminder and comfort of His presence in our lives.

♥ *Dear Father, I'm glad You are always there when I need You.*

WINNING

For whoever finds me finds life,
And obtains favor from the LORD.
—PROV. 8:35

*G*randson Rob is competitive and wants to win at whatever game or activity he pursues. One day when he was small we went to the park to play miniature golf.

Miniature golf is one game I can play fairly well. That day we hadn't played too many holes when it was evident that I was winning. Rob started to get upset, and tears of frustration were near. We needed to take a break.

I talked about it being just a game that should be played for fun, then said, "I'm not very good at many games, but miniature golf is a game where I usually do well. Why does this upset you so much? You don't want me to lose on purpose so you can win, do you?"

Rob shook his head, "No," he said, "but I should be able to beat you because you're so old!"

I hid a smile and said, "Well, that's another reason I'm doing so well—I've had years of practice!"

Rob is older, now, and still competitive. I am trusting God to help him temper his discouragement and frustration when he loses so he will understand that winning isn't the only point of games or life.

♥ *God, belonging to You is the ultimate of winning.*

Assuredly, I say to you, whoever does not receive the kingdom of God as a little child will by no means enter it.
—MARK 10:15

*W*hen I go to visit my grandchildren, I almost always take them some little thing. More often than not, it's a book. I had taken six-year-old Angie a little picture book showing and telling about God's love for children, moms, dads, aunts, uncles, grandparents, and several other categories of people.

I read the book through once. Then Angie and I read the book through together several times until, finally, Angie "read" the book to me.

When she finished, she looked at me and said, "I just love God."

Hearing over and over, again and again, the simple but profoundly true words that God loved us spoke to both Angie and me. Angie's response was immediate in expressing her love for Him. No wonder Jesus uses children as an example of the kind of faith required for entering into His kingdom. Children recognize God's love as absolutely authentic and accept it without reservation. We adults need to take note and learn from them about being trusting of God's love and grace.

♥ *Dear God, I just love You, too. Thank You for loving me.*

GRANDMOTHERS ARE GREAT!

Whoever receives one of these little children in My name receives Me; and whoever receives Me, receives not Me but Him who sent Me.
—MARK 9:37

*I*t's a long day for small children who are brought to a day-care center early in the morning. One little boy, nodding off into his lunch plate said, "I'm too little to go to school."

Our hearts ache when even little children know they should be cared for at home. They ache as well for parents who know this, too, but who must work. This is one reason Grandma Barrett visits the two-year-old class of the day-care center in the church where I work. Her daughter, the teacher of the class, asks her mother to visit the children periodically as "Grandma." She says the children love to have Grandma Barrett come to visit and are better behaved during her visits than at almost any other time. Other classes say that a feeling of calmness settles over the children as they group around "substitute grandmas" who visit.

When Jesus had a little child stand in the midst of the disciples, He was giving them a recipe for greatness. They needed to willingly take the humble position of service, even to children.

Grandmothers have years of experience in service. Maybe that's one reason we eventually are called great-grandmothers.

♥ *Lord, how easy it is to serve You by caring for my grandchildren.*

OUR WORTH

But the very hairs of your head are all numbered. Do not fear therefore; you are of more value than many sparrows.

—LUKE 12:7

*W*hen I was very young, probably four or five, I spent a marvelously free and unstructured summer with my grandparents in a small, one-street town in North Dakota. I remember getting up on my own and leaving the house early each day to roam the little town, returning only to eat and go to bed.

The other town children and I broke into the school/church building to play school. We played with farm animals and climbed trees. On rainy days I played on Grandma's ivy-covered porch or in the attic, where I had discovered boxes of old toys that had belonged to my mother.

When my mother came to visit one Sunday, she saw a dirty little girl with uncombed hair, mismatched clothes, and no shoes walking down the road. She was shocked to discover that girl was me. That was the only bath I remember at my grandma's.

I probably didn't have as much freedom as I thought. The town was so small Grandma could probably see wherever I was by looking out the window. Certainly God knew what I was up to, just as He does now. It's good to remember that He still knows the number of hairs on my head—and yours. And that we are worth more to Him than anything else He created.

♥ *Thank You for telling us how much we mean to You.*

January 24 _____

*How much better it is to get wisdom than
    gold!
And to get understanding is to be chosen
    rather than silver.*   —PROV. 16:16

*W*hen Robbie visits her grandmother, she always hopes her grandmother will make her special chocolate cake. The cake is just a regular chocolate cake; it is the frosting that Robbie says makes it special. This frosting frustrates her grandmother and delights Robbie. The frosting is thick and heavy, and when Grandmother pours it over the cake, the cake cracks in several places and the frosting runs down into the cracks, making the whole cake taste absolutely wonderful.

Robbie says that her grandmother is always upset about the way the cake looks. Robbie doesn't care about how the cake looks. The scrumptious taste of frosting in the middle of cake is exactly what makes the cake special to her.

Life seems to be full of these chocolate cake experiences. Situations often have a way of not turning out the way we expect. It is then that we have a choice. We can fuss and fume because things aren't the way we want them to be, or we can enjoy the specialness of the turn of events. We can model for our grandchildren wisdom in understanding who God is and that He is always in charge.

♥ *Lord, help me to make the best choice in my next chocolate cake experience.*

ROYAL GRANDMA

Children's children are the crown of old men.
                                    —PROV. 17:6a

$\mathcal{L}$isa flew in from her home in Montana to attend her grandmother's funeral. She was the only grandchild. After the service, Lisa talked about her best memory of her grandmother, "When I was a little girl, Grandmother taught me to sing, 'You Are My Sunshine.'

> You are my sunshine, my only sunshine. You make me happy when skies are gray. You'll never know, dear, how much I love you. Please don't take my sunshine away.

"Whenever Grandmother and I sang the song, she would cry and cry. I never understood why. It is one of the first songs I taught my children, and whenever we sing it, I cry. And now I understand why she cried."

Grandparents cry over their grandchildren for all kinds of reasons—the things they say, their hugs and kisses, when they make us proud, when we are worried about them. Happy and sad tears.

The crown God has given us is sometimes light and sometimes heavy. Perhaps one of the reasons we cry is that we know that in this imperfect world the sunshine of their lives just might be taken away—the last line is sung as a prayer.

♥ *Dear God, thank You for my crown of grandchildren.*

CONTENTMENT

*. . . for I have learned in whatever state I
am, to be content.*
—PHIL. 4:11

I read a letter to Dear Abby from a grandmother
who had lost her foot at the ankle. Her grandson wants
to take her to his school for "show and tell." He wants
Grandma to show the class how she can take off her
foot.

Applause to this grandma who says she learned
early that something positive can always be found in a
bad situation. With her happy disposition (and a good
sense of humor), she shows that although she has what
people call a disability, she will not allow it to disable
her in the more important ways.

This is a grandma who understands what Paul was
talking about in the verses following the quote above.
"I know how to be abased, and I know how to abound.
Everywhere and in all things I have learned both to be
full and to be hungry, both to abound and to suffer
need. I can do all things through Christ who strengthens me" (Phil. 4:12–13).

Grandma plans to go to her grandson's kindergarten
class and, along with the foot removal, talk about taking care of their bodies with exercise and good food.
She won't need to say a word about having a good attitude!

♥ *Dear God, help me to share Your wonderful secret
of contentment.*

DID JESUS HAVE A GRANDMA?

*And the Child grew and became strong in
spirit, filled with wisdom; and the grace of
God was upon Him.*   —LUKE 2:40

*M*any people believe Jesus' grandmother was a
woman named Anne, whose story is found in the apo-
cryphal book of James.

The following poem was written by Carol Sherbondy
White for her grandchildren.

For Jesus' Birthday Party

Did Jesus have a grandma?
I never thought about that before.
Did Jesus have a grandma
Who came knocking at the door?

Did Jesus have a grandma
Who made cookies by the score?
Did He have a grandma
Who gave hugs and kisses galore?

If Jesus had a grandma,
Did they play blocks upon the floor?
Did they take long walks and talk
About outer space and stars—and more?

If Jesus had a grandma,
She would have prayed for Him each night
That He would grow to please His God
Just like your grandma will tonight!

♥ *Dear God, hear my prayer for my grandchildren.*
Help them to please You.

ONLY ONE THING

But one thing is needed, and Mary has chosen that good part, which will not be taken away from her. —LUKE 10:42

*A*my's family enjoys weekly dinners together at Grandmother's house, where they catch up on what everyone is doing and have lively discussions on a variety of topics.

One evening after dinner, Amy disappeared into her grandmother's bedroom and stayed there for some time. When she returned, her grandmother apologized for the mess the room was in; she hadn't expected it to be visited. Amy said she hadn't noticed any mess. She had been enjoying the room and the things in it, touching the pictures and knickknacks, remembering the notes she wrote and placed on the pillows, finding comfort in the lingering scent and sights that made Grandmother so precious to her.

Rooms, food, and clothing do not need to be absolutely perfect at all times. What others notice about where we live, the food we serve, the way we look— what they notice about us—is the presence or absence of our warmth and acceptance.

In the story of Mary and Martha, Jesus commended Mary's choice of what is most important. What's most important to us will live in our grandchildren's memories.

♥ *O Father, when I make choices, help me remember their effect on my grandchildren.*

*. . . for he who comes to God must believe
that He is, and that He is a rewarder of
those who diligently seek Him.*

—HEB. 11:6

*J*im Townsend, Bible editor, teacher, preacher,
and author, tells about his grandmother who never attended church with the family and was never observed
reading the Bible. Nevertheless, she did teach him
something that he believes profoundly contoured his
entire life. Grandma taught him this prayer:

*Now I lay me down to sleep;
I pray the Lord my soul to keep.
If I should die before I wake,
I pray the Lord my soul to take.*

According to Jim, "That simple childhood prayer
contains in it the seeds of vastly important issues that
formed my life. First, that there is one called the Lord.
The poetic prayer also informed me of the stark reality
of death. Death could visit me. Finally, the last line in
that simple prayer bred in my consciousness the awesome reality that the Lord might not take my soul."

Yes! What grandmothers teach grandchildren can
have a profound and permanent effect!

♥ *Lord, I want the things I teach my grandchildren to
make a difference in their lives.*

God is our refuge and strength,
A very present help in trouble.
—PS. 46:1

*L*ooking at a picture of Grandmother Stockton, one might think of a Napoleonic field general. A photo does not display her as a person a shy child would sidle up to affectionately. Photos picture her as a staunch, no-nonsense person, even overbearing. She might have weighed over two hundred pounds.

Grandma Stockton never went to church. She always had roast beef, mashed potatoes and gravy, green beans, iced tea, and lemon meringue pie on the hardwood table when her grandson Jim, his three cousins, and his aunt and uncle arrived home from church for their Sunday meal.

Despite her lack of church connections, Grandma taught Jim one Bible verse his memory has enshrined—Psalm 46:1. Jim feels it was to that verse his grandma was anchored when her beloved Mary (his mother) died of cancer when Jim was three years old.

As we age, our anchors-of-soul can cling evermore to the truth of Scripture that never ages.

♥ *Dear God, Your ageless Word has become more precious to me.*

ADOPTED GRANDMOTHER

*This is My commandment, that you love one
another as I have loved you.*
—JOHN 15:12

*W*hen Richard was small, his family lived next door
to Mrs. Setchell. One of his first memories is of Mrs.
Setchell sitting on her porch watching him roller skate.
She told him what a good job he was doing and encouraged him to try again when he fell. This support continued during all the years they lived there. She attended
his Cub Scout activities, helped with homework, and
was always there to talk to.

They played table games together, and Mrs. Setchell
taught Richard practical things that continue to help
him. She taught him how to hoe weeds and prune
roses; to play games for pleasure and enjoyment and
not just for winning; and to know the peace of Christ.

Richard remembers, "She was a special individual
who touched my life. Through her continual support,
unconditional giving of time, and practical teaching,
Ethel Setchell etched a deep impression in my memory. I hope some young person will be able to say about
me, 'He helped to build me into the person I am
today!'"

♥ *Lord, is there someone in my neighborhood who
needs an adopted grandmother?*

PICTURE OF LOVE

Let all that you do be done with love.
—1 COR. 16:14

The kindergarteners had these things to say about their grandmothers:

"She lets me use her pillows to make a fort." Brandon.

"We go out for pizza and she reads me stories when I sleep over." David.

"She plays games like pinball with me and makes chicken, my favorite food." Andrew.

"My grandma lives a long ways away but she likes me very much, plays Candyland with me, and takes me to church every Sunday." Zackery.

"She plays trucks with me and I help her water the garden and pick the fruit." Jeff.

"She plays trucks with me and makes good oatmeal." Kevin.

"She gives me ice cream before I go to bed." Benjamin.

The things children remember most at this age are the activities we participate in and the food we fix. When we help to supply these basic needs, we are also helping lay a foundation that can lead to trust in God, whose love and care for us is shown through the love and care of family. We are meant to be pictures of God's love.

♥ *Help the picture I present of You to my grandchildren be clear and true.*

STRENGTH

The LORD is my strength and my shield;
My heart trusted in Him, and I am helped.
— PS. 28:7

I sat next to her on the airplane. We talked about where we had been and where we were going. Then we exchanged information about our sons, daughters, and grandchildren. She had five grandsons; one was adopted. Her daughter, his mother, is a nurse. She had adopted the boy after he was abandoned at birth because he was born with several handicaps. The little boy was now five and attending school.

She said, "It has been difficult for everyone. He takes so very much care. I know it has put a strain on their marriage. I've often wondered if it was a good decision to adopt him."

I appreciated her honesty. I could tell her love for this grandson was as strong as her love for her other grandsons. There was concern, too, but it was her acceptance of the situation that impressed me most. A decision had been made—perhaps without her input, maybe despite her input—but now he was her grandchild and she loved him.

Our children often make decisions that affect us. Remember we do have God's promise of strength and help.

♥ *I count on Your strength and help in situations I accept but sometimes feel overwhelmed about.*

February 3 _____

A GOOD THING

It is good to give thanks to the LORD,
And to sing praises to Your name, O Most High.
                                    —PS. 92:1

A two-year-old was watching his grandmother bake cookies. His eyes grew bigger each time she took a sheet of cookies from the oven and replaced it with another. He followed every move she made as she placed the cookies on the table to cool and then in the cookie jar.

Suddenly, unable to hold his enthusiasm any longer, he blurted, "Grandma, sit down and let's thank the Lord right now for all these wonderful cookies!"

How God must rejoice over that kind of immediate recognition of His goodness! There are so many things each day that I should sit down right now and thank the Lord for—the day itself, food, clothing, a place to live, family, friends, God's Word, things to do. And there are all those serendipitous pleasures—visits from family and time you experience God's goodness and blessing. Sit right down and thank the Lord!

♥ *Dear God, I love the hymn "Great Is Thy Faithfulness" because it is absolutely true. Thank You.*

But I will sing of Your power;
Yes, I will sing aloud of Your mercy in the morning;
For You have been my defense
And refuge in the day of my trouble.

—PS. 59:16

*J*im's mother died when he was three years old. His grandmother raised him. He remembers a time as a lonely preschooler when he scoured the house, yelling for Grandma. He was frantic when he had run through the house twice and was unable to find her. He tells how he was in tears before he finally discovered she had made a rare trek out behind the garage and was talking with a neighbor in the yard.

Jim looked to his grandmother as an emotional anchor and mainstay in a scary and sometimes lonely world, which had robbed him of his mother. She was God's chosen refuge for him.

Perhaps you, too, have been chosen to be a refuge—part- or full-time—for your grandchildren because of death, divorce, or other family crisis. Maybe continuing to deal with diapers, chicken pox, homework, and teens is not the way you intended to spend your grandmother years. We don't always know or understand why things happen the way they do, why you may be in a situation like this. But we do know what we need to do for our grandchildren. It is good to remember that God is our ultimate refuge.

♥ *Sing with the psalmist, "I will praise you, my defender. My refuge is God, the God who loves me.*

February 5 _____

*Beloved, let us love one another, for love is
of God; and everyone who loves is born of
God and knows God.* —1 JOHN 4:7

*M*y sister-in-law's granddaughter, Heidi, was listening to her teacher define words for a spelling test. The children were puzzled by the word *apron.*

The teacher said, "It's what your grandma wears when she cooks."

Heidi said, "Not my grandma. She wears jeans!"

I'm sure that apron production for grandmas in the United States is in a slide. And whether I wear jeans, slacks, a skirt, or a dress when I cook, I never even think of putting on an apron. I don't think I even own an apron anymore.

Whatever the reason or reasons for the decline in the use of aprons, grandmothers can no longer be stereotyped by clothing. We can, however, be stereotyped in a more important way. We love our grandchildren.

This ability to love may be our best characteristic—a characteristic endowed by God and further enhanced as we continue to grow in our love for Him.

♥ *I want the characteristic of love to be obvious in my
life—for You and my family and friends.*

In everything set them an example by doing what is good.
—TITUS 2:7a NIV

*M*y son-in-law Bob remembers his grandmother as his only baby-sitter. He stayed with her often, and she always had a plentiful supply of quarters to give him for good grades or just for being a good boy.

Bob loved Grandma's house, especially the attic where his uncle's toys were stored. One day he must have been playing up there for a long time because he was suddenly aware that his grandmother was calling him as she rushed through the house and out into the yard.

Bob sauntered to the attic window, waved, and yelled, "I'm here, Grandma." It wasn't until years later that he understood her look of relief when she saw him at the window.

But his best memory of her is, "She taught me to hug. The rest of the family wasn't particularly demonstrative, but Grandma hugged me a lot. I learned to hug from her."

What a wonderful privilege it is to teach a grandchild to hug! I'm sure Bob's grandmother didn't even realize what she was teaching. As the old adage says, "More lessons are caught than taught." It's what God has in mind. His Word tells us we should live so that others will know who He is. The emphasis is on the actions.

♥ *Are my actions the ones I want my grandchildren to catch?*

February 7 _____

HIGH QUALITY TEACHERS

*Blessed are the people who know the joyful
  sound!
They walk, O LORD, in the light of Your
  countenance.*
                                    —PS. 89:15

*B*ev and her sister Ginnie stayed with Grandma
Long in the Ozarks for a month each summer. A highlight of the stay was that Grandma let them take turns
cooking. The girls admit now that it might have been
that she made them feel like they were cooking when
they were actually helping her. In any event, she taught
them to cook.

Grandpa cleaned the fish they caught, and
Grandma showed them how to cook them. The vegetables were grown in Grandma's big garden. Meals were
eaten on a screened porch overlooking the lake. Cleaning up was part of the cooking privilege, but Grandma
didn't expect perfection. Everywhere, a feeling of re-
laxation prevailed.

I wonder how many grandchildren have learned
some useful skill such as cooking or sewing from a
grandmother.

Whatever we are teaching, we must remember that
we are also teaching our grandchildren about God and
how He wants us to love by the way we live.

♥ *Dear Lord, the old hymn says, "Teach me, Lord,
that I may teach." I echo those words.*

COMEDIENNE GRANDMA

A merry heart does good, like medicine.
—PROV. 17:22a

$\mathcal{G}$randma White was widowed in her sixties. For most of her adult life, she had lived in the shadow of her husband, and as Grandma began her widowhood we worried about how she would get along without him. After all, he had paid the bills, decided when and where they should go, and was generally in charge.

We needn't have been concerned. It was as if Grandma had come into her own. She took charge of her life, and her personality blossomed. In fact, much to the surprise of her family, she became a stand-up comedienne!

We began to hear how she had her peers holding their sides laughing at the stories she told at church potluck dinners and other social gatherings. At her eightieth birthday party, after the toasts and accolades from family members, she stood and told several of her favorite jokes to the delight of one and all.

One of God's great gifts to us is a sense of humor. We could not laugh if He had not given us the ability to be cheerful. His Word indicates that it is for our benefit.

♥ *I need to remember each day to take my medicine of cheerfulness with a large dose of laughter.*

*Your will be done
On earth as it is in heaven.*
—MATT. 6:10

*G*randma Rose and her fifth-grade grandson Patrick were discussing the Lord's Prayer. She asked him to think about what might be the most important part of the prayer. Patrick wasn't exactly sure, so he asked Grandma what she thought was most important.

Grandma opened her Bible and pointed to the phrase that said, "Your will be done. . . ." She explained that when we do what God wants us to do (follow His will), we feel at peace, even when we are not in a peaceful situation.

But sometimes it is so hard to do what God wants us to do! Our humanness gets in the way and we are unloving and unforgiving; we lose patience; we don't speak out against wrong. That might be why "And forgive us our sins" was included in the prayer.

The prayer expresses our total dependence on God. When we do His will, it is because we trust Him to help us; when we fail, we acknowledge our need of the forgiveness only He can give.

♥ *Jesus, thank You for saying, "Thy will be done," to Your Father and making His forgiveness possible for me.*

TIME WISELY SPENT

Remember how short my time is.
—PS. 89:47a

*W*hen Beth and her daughters were visiting her mother, they went to the kitchen for gingersnap cookies and milk. Beth was disappointed to see a package of store-bought cookies on the table.

"I thought you meant homemade gingersnap cookies from Grandmother's recipe," she lamented.

Beth's mother laughed, "Grandmothers don't have time to make cookies today!"

Today's grandmothers have kitchens filled with state-of-the-art appliances designed to make life easier. Yet most of us eat out more, entertain less, and purchase quantities of packaged foods that often require little more than opening the container to serve.

Before you start getting angry, I acknowledge that many of us have full-time careers or volunteer obligations that keep us out of our kitchens and prevent us from doing "grandmotherly" things like making cookies, writing a note of encouragement, or teaching something only you know how to do.

God's Word reminds us about the shortness of life. And grandchildren take time. But it can be time well spent as God uses us to help shape their lives through the things we do with and for them.

♥ *Help me to use time with my grandchildren wisely.*

> *Love never fails. But where there are*
> *prophecies, they will cease; . . . where there*
> *is knowledge, it will pass away.*
> **—1 COR. 13:8** NIV

*W*hen Maryell and her cousin graduated from high school, they each received a card with some money and a lace handkerchief from Grandmother O'Melia. What surprised the girls about their presents was that their grandmother had been dead for six years! She had gotten the gifts ready for the girls years earlier and told the family where they were in case anything happened to her before graduation. She didn't want her granddaughters to think she had forgotten them. Talk about planning ahead!

Another grandmother bought Christmas presents all year, wrapped and tagged them, and put them in the closet where they would be found if anything happened to her before Christmas. The family tells how special it was to receive a gift at Christmas the year Grandma died in July.

First Corinthians 13 is called the love passage. In the New International Version it begins, "And now I will show you the most excellent way." It then tells what love is and what love is not. The best part is that when everything else fails, love goes on and on. Our bodies won't last, but the love we have for others lives on in the special memories we leave.

♥ *Thanks for telling us about "the most excellent way"*
You want us to live and be remembered.

INHERITANCE

The wise in heart will be called prudent,
And sweetness of the lips increases learning.
                                    —PROV. 16:21

*G*innie is a quilter like both her grandmas were. She has only seen quilts that Grandma White made, but she and Grandma Taylor talked a lot about quilting. Whenever Ginnie would take one of her finished quilts to show Grandma Taylor, Grandma would say, "I wish the ladies in the quilt circle could see this." But no amount of urging could convince her to keep one to show off to the circle. She was afraid something might happen to it.

Grandpa Taylor would say, "Imagine someone your age being interested in making quilts!"

Ginnie has a Grandmother's Flower Garden quilt that Grandma White made. She'd like to have one made by Grandma Taylor as a remembrance of the common interest they shared. In many ways it would be an inheritance to treasure.

The inheritance our grandchildren receive from us comes in many forms. Something of monetary value— a family recipe, photo albums—is often accompanied by wisdom gleaned from daily reading of God's Word served up in loving, pleasing ways.

♥ *Your wisdom is a wonderful inheritance I want to share with my grandchildren. Help me to do it right.*

*And whatever you do, do it heartily, as to
the Lord and not to men, knowing that from
the Lord you will receive the reward of the
inheritance. . . .*
                              —COL. 3:23–24

Sometimes I've wondered if my grandchildren wish
I had a different job. When they come to spend the
weekend, we have to get up early and be at church before
anyone else since Sunday is a working day for a
minister to children. Sometimes they even have to help
sharpen pencils, make juice, and count cookies to help
me get ready for Sunday school and other programs.

One day my grandson Rob was blowing up balloons
for a special children's activity when he commented,
"I like having a grandma who is in charge of Sunday
school!"

I enjoy my work and am glad when I hear that my
grandchildren think it's a good occupation, too. I want
to continue working at something until I am taken
home to be with God. Work has been with us since the
beginning. God told Adam to work the Garden of Eden
and take care of it. Other verses in the Bible aren't so
much about what kind of work we do as about how we
should work. Since God has given people work to do
ever since He created them, work must be part of His
plan for our lives.

♥ *Thank You for the work You give our hands to do.*

ENCOURAGING GRANDMA

. . . warn those who are unruly, comfort the fainthearted, uphold the weak, be patient with all. —1 THESS. 5:14

I teach speech to college students. One assignment was an impromptu speech about their grandmothers.

Christine's grandmother had nine children and lots and lots of grandchildren, but always had time for each of them, and she was patient. Juan's grandmother died when he was in first grade, but he remembers the time she spent telling him stories.

Michelle hated that her grandmother smoked and once hid a carton of cigarettes in the dishwasher right before her grandmother turned it on. Grandmother understood her concern and wasn't upset.

When Robin stayed with her grandmother, they'd go to the store and buy malted milk balls. When the family went to the lake fishing, Grandma defended the children when Dad got upset.

These college students talked easily about their grandmothers and how they felt encouraged by them. God's instructions to encourage others can be found throughout the Bible, including 1 Thessalonians 5, where Paul specifically names ways we can encourage people.

♥ *Dear God, let the many ways You encourage me inspire me to be an encouraging grandma.*

> *Be anxious for nothing, but in everything by*
> *prayer and supplication, with thanksgiving,*
> *let your requests be made known to God.*
> —PHIL. 4:6

*Y*ou've heard the old saying, "If Mother says no, ask Grandma!" We grandparents seem to have the reputation of being more indulgent of grandchildren than we ever were of our children—even to the point of reversing a parental decision.

Sometimes it's okay to ask Grandma, maybe for a toy, clothes, or other desire that a parent might have denied because of lack of money. But we need to be careful when a child petitions us to overrule a parental decision the child doesn't like—eating another cookie right before dinner when Mom said no more, or taking part in an activity parents have denied. Even if Grandma is sympathetic to the grandchild's request, it's best to support parents when the child asks you and then talk with the parents privately on the child's behalf.

We continue to parent all of our lives, but as our sons and daughters become adults and have children, there usually isn't as much "hands on" involvement. There is plenty of opportunity for continued prayer involvement, though. God wants us to talk with Him about everything. Our grandchildren need to be a priority on our prayer list.

♥ *Thank You for my grandchildren. Guide my involvement in their parenting.*

JESUS LOVES ME

In this is love, not that we loved God, but that He loved us and sent His Son to be the propitiation for our sins.

—1 JOHN 4:10

*T*hree-year-old Wesley and Grandma Sandy were watching television. When the people on the program began to sing "Jesus Loves Me," Wesley joined in. To the delight of Grandma Sandy and everyone else in the room, Wesley continued, "Jesus loves Grandma, this I know; for the Bible tells me so."

How easily small children accept as absolute truth that Jesus loves them and everyone else, especially the people they love. A great theologian once said that the message of God's Word is summed up in that simple song.

God not only told us of His love, He showed it when He sent His Son to die for us. The sacrifice of Jesus makes it possible for us to become part of God's family. Think of the glorious family reunion that will take place when we all get to heaven—sons, daughters, parents, grandparents, great-grandparents, generation upon generation. It will take forever to talk with everyone we're related to and to praise our great God for His all-encompassing love.

♥ *I do know You love me, Jesus. Thank You.*

. . . for it is time to seek the LORD.
—HOS. 10:12

*C*heryse spent a lot of time with Grandma Iona and has many happy memories. Grandma used to take her shopping and buy her a complete outfit. One summer, Grandma got front row tickets for a concert by a teen idol and took Cheryse to see him. Years later Cheryse realized her grandmother went to a lot of trouble (and expense) for her.

Grandmothers love to do things for their grandchildren. Some things cost effort and money, things we may have more of in our grandmother age. And what better way to spend both?

The time we spend with them, especially, is what grandchildren remember. That time gives important messages. As we play Uno for the hundredth time, read books we have memorized, sing songs our grandmothers sang to us, tramp around zoos when we'd rather be home with our feet up, and sit in theaters with hundreds of screaming kids, we're saying to our grandchildren, "I care about you; you are important to me."

The time I spend with God is important, too. His Word tells me that He wants to spend time with me. What messages am I giving God? Does He know I care for Him?

♥ *You are important to me, Lord, and I love You. Help me to show it in the time I spend with You.*

Better is a dinner of herbs where love is,
Than a fatted calf with hatred.
—PROV. 15:17

Child-friendly was the way Sally described Grandma Ackemann's house. There was a basket of toys in one of the bedrooms—nothing fancy, just blocks, cars, balls, dishes, and dolls—ordinary toys kids like to play with. And she sat on the floor to play with the children, who knew they could build and knock over the blocks again and again.

Grandma Ackemann also took her grandchildren to lunch. Again, nothing fancy, but it wasn't the place but the activity that was special.

Grandmas are supposed to have child-friendly homes. That doesn't mean that we rearrange everything for the convenience of children; it does mean that when children visit there is an atmosphere of acceptance, belonging, and care. We all create that atmosphere in our own way—with a basket of toys, or special books to read or music to listen to, or activities we do together.

We might liken this atmosphere to the fellowship we seek when we meet with God to read His Word, talk to Him, and listen for what He has to say to us. It's knowing that the person wants us to be there, enjoys our company, and loves us no matter what.

♥ *Lord, I want my fellowship with You to be the guidelines for fellowship with my grandchildren.*

CHERRY PIE AND MERCY

*Blessed are the merciful,
For they shall obtain mercy.*
—MATT. 5:7

Grandma Kyte always made Richard a cherry pie when he came to visit. Richard was a picky eater—his daily diet consisted mostly of peanut butter sandwiches—but he liked cherry pie, too, and Grandma knew it.

As Grandma grew older, she moved from a farm to a small house and then to an even smaller apartment. She couldn't see as well anymore, and her cooking suffered.

Richard was grown by this time, and his diet included more than peanut butter sandwiches, though he was still a picky eater. When he visited Grandma Kyte, a cherry pie was ready for him as usual. The problem was it didn't taste the same. In fact, it wasn't good at all! But Richard ate every bit of it!

Why did picky eater Richard eat that terrible pie without a word? Because for years Grandma Kyte had demonstrated God's continual love by making one of the things he would eat—just for him. He returned that love when she needed it most.

The lessons grandmothers teach are mostly silent ones. And God leads grandchildren's responses to these lessons.

♥ *Help me to demonstrate Your mercy in a silent lesson to my grandchildren.*

GOD'S PRESCRIPTION

My son, give attention to my words;
Incline your ear to my sayings. . . .
Keep them in the midst of your heart.
  —PROV. 4:20–21

*G*randma Brown wasn't feeling well. She didn't have any specific aches or pains, just a general overall not-up-to-par feeling, so she went to the doctor for a check-up. He said, "That's what happens when you have an eighty-year-old body." Grandma said, "I'm not eighty, I'm ninety-two!"

This says much about her attitude toward life. The way we think affects our health; positive attitudes, humor, and good expectations help us live longer. Proverbs contains much wisdom about how we should live our lives.

Put away from you a deceitful mouth,
And put perverse lips far from you.
Let your eyes look straight ahead, . . .
Ponder the path of your feet, . . .
Remove your foot from evil. (Prov. 4:24–27)

This is God's prescription. It warrants passing on to the next generation.

♥ *Dear God, help me to follow Your prescription beginning today!*

FUTURE GENERATIONS

*Telling to the generation to come the
    praises of the LORD,
And His strength and His wonderful works
    that He has done.*
                                    —PS. 78:4b

*A*shley, age five, calls her grandma "Meemaw."
One day Ashley asked Meemaw, "Do you know that
Jesus is with us all the time? He's sitting on our laps all
the time. He loves little children, and He holds our
hand. He loves moms and dads, too. They were little
children once."

Meemaw told this little story with tears in her eyes.
She said, "I wasn't raised in a Christian home, and to
hear my granddaughter talk about Jesus' love is a
blessing. I guess I was successful in instilling a love for
God and Jesus in my children that they are nurturing
in their children—and possibly to unlimited future
generations."

This grandmother is a transition person. She has
stopped the transmission of negative or destructive tendencies so that they do not pass to the next generation.
She stopped a pattern of faithlessness and started a
pattern of faith building.

♥ *In what ways do I help build my grandchildren's
    faith for future generations?*

IMPORTANT STORIES

*And beginning at Moses and all the
Prophets, He expounded to them in all the
Scriptures the things concerning Himself.*
—LUKE 24:27

*L*inda's grandma became engaged to a soldier just before he left for World War II. Several weeks later she received a letter from her fiance. Also enclosed was a letter to another girl—he was engaged to her as well! Linda's grandma broke up with the soldier and soon married someone else. The soldier married the other girl. Years later Linda's grandfather died and the soldier's wife died. You guessed it! Linda's grandma and the soldier met again and married.

Our grandchildren don't usually view us in romantic relationships or situations unless we tell them those stories about ourselves. My brother has reminded me that our parents had lives before we were born—lives we didn't know very much about unless they told us or we asked about them. But we needed to know about them, because their stories would help us understand them.

God wants us to know Him better and He has given us His stories: in the Bible, churches, and study books.

♥ *Lord, I want to know You better. Keep me reading
and asking about You.*

So also will be the word that I speak—
it will not fail to do what I plan for it;
It will do everything I send it to do.
— ISA. 55:11 GNB

*J*ill's Grandma Tennison loved the movies, and Jill remembers waiting for the bus at the bottom of the hill three or four times a week as she and Grandma went to the movies.

Jill also remembers her grandmother's Bible. The pages had handwritten notes all around the edges and felt as smooth as silk. The leather cover was soft and worn from constant use.

Here was a grandmother who loved stories—the wonderful pretend stories portrayed on film (in the less violent and explicit '40s and '50s) and the great, true stories of God's Word.

The simile in the verse preceding the one stated above gives a vivid picture of one of God's promises: "My word is like the snow and the rain that come down from the sky to water the earth. They make the crops grow and provide seed for planting and food to eat" (Isa. 55:10 GNB)

A grandmother's Bible is often a valuable legacy. It is one way that God's Word is snow and rain to water and nurture the spiritual growth of future generations long after her physical presence is gone.

♥ *In what ways will my grandchildren know that I love*
and believe Your Word?

For to me, to live is Christ, and to die is gain.
—PHIL. 1:21

*G*randma Alice was an unconventional grandma. She shaved Jim's full head of hair at three weeks, played games with him and other grandchildren under the table at formal dinners, and was a country western singer on the Stuart Hamblin show. She taught Jim how to play the guitar when he was in second grade.

Jim says, "Grandma Alice taught us how to die. When she was very ill and knew she was going to die, she asked for her guitar and made a tape to play at her funeral. The tape included a message that told us not to be sad for her, but happy because she was in Heaven with Jesus. She asked the people present to comfort her family and one another."

Before her death she also talked to each of her grandchildren and helped them understand. She asked them if they knew where she was going and assured them that she would see Jesus soon.

What a testimony of how to live and die! Her grandchildren had no doubts about her faith and were given a marvelous example of trust that they, too, could have as they believed and accepted the same free gift of salvation through Jesus Christ.

♥ *O Lord, I want my life and death to be examples of the faith and trust I have in You.*

WISE GRANDMA

My son, do not walk in the way with them,
Keep your foot from their path.

—PROV. 1:15

*A*drienne's grandmother, Momee, was short and roly-poly. She drove her car everywhere, sometimes causing minor accidents of which she was completely unaware. Momee carried a huge purse, bulging with all sorts of things, including mints that she sometimes distributed to her grandchildren. She was talented at decorating china, and for most of her life ran a tourist home.

After her children were grown, Momee decided she wanted a college education. And so it was that she and her daughter (Adrienne's mother) attended college at the same time. They both majored in child psychology. Momee was a popular person on campus. However, she maintained a B average in grades while her daughter received straight A's. This seemed unfair to Momee because, "I proved I knew the subject because I had successfully raised my daughter!"

Grandmothers who continue to learn throughout their lives are rich examples for grandchildren. God's Word advises us to listen and add to what we know. There are no age restrictions.

♥ *Help me to keep on learning, especially when I'm*
tempted to think I know it all.

OUR BEST EXAMPLE

For I have given you an example, that you should do as I have done to you.
—JOHN 13:15

$\mathcal{G}$randma O made an afghan for each of her grandchildren, but they couldn't have the afghans until they had their own homes. What a special way to be part of grandchildren's lives as they set out on their own. The warmth and comfort of the afghan is a reminder of her love for them in times when they might be tired, afraid, or discouraged. No matter how capable, independent, and self-sufficient our grandchildren may seem, they need reminders of our love and care as they make their way in the world.

God is our best example of someone who gives continual reminders of love and care. We feel warmth and comfort as we read His Word and talk with Him. We are surrounded and covered with God's invisible afghan, knitted with indestructible strands of love.

We follow God's example when our reminders of love and care include writing encouraging words and notes, visiting, making afghans, baking, or anything else we enjoy doing. Whatever you do, you will have the privilege of being a part of your grandchildren's lives and memories.

♥ *Dear God, help me to follow Your example of love and care.*

. . . As He sat at the table with them, that
He took bread, blessed and broke it, and
gave it to them. —LUKE 24:30

*J*ennifer and her family were going to visit Great-
grandma Green in Kansas. Jennifer wasn't happy
about this trip because it meant she would be away
from home on her birthday.

When Jennifer and her family got to Kansas, Great-
grandma asked Jennifer what kind of cake she wanted
for her birthday. Jennifer wanted angel food cake with
strawberries, the cake that Great-grandma *only* made
for Great-grandpa. But she made one for Jennifer's
birthday. Jennifer and Great-grandma even picked the
strawberries for the cake. It was the best birthday cake
ever!

Grandmothers and food seem to go together as naturally as sunshine and flowers. We are often involved in
making or baking food for grandchildren or taking
grandchildren out to eat. Some of our best times together are while we eat. It is called fellowship.

We read about fellowship in the Bible—Jesus and
His disciples; Jesus with Mary and Martha; Jesus and
the two going to Emmaus; Christians in the New Testament—many of their times together were around the
table.

♥ *Thank You for the fellowship we have with our*
grandchildren.

MARVELOUS RELATIONSHIP

The LORD God formed man of the dust of the ground, and breathed into his nostrils the breath of life; and the man became a living being.
—GEN. 2:7

*F*ive of my grandchildren and I were driving home from a day at a cousin's house on the lake. We started talking about family relationships—the similarities and differences in brothers, sisters, cousins, aunts, and uncles—and soon found ourselves deep in a discussion about creation and God. We debated some of the theories taught in school and agreed that we believed the biblical account of God forming man in His image from the dust of the ground and breathing life into him rather than the theory of man's evolution.

The discussion lasted even after we reached our vacation home, donned pajamas and were enjoying a late-night ice cream treat. Once again, I realized how much children like to talk with adults who will listen to what they are thinking about and questioning. And when we are receptive to hearing their opinions, they are much more willing to hear ours.

♥ *Father, thank You for allowing us time to share with our granchildren.*

SHINE!

Let your light so shine before men, that they may see your good works and glorify your Father in heaven.
—MATT. 5:16

*M*itzi called her grandmother Granny. When Mitzi was in junior high, she needed to go to the hospital for several days for some tests. Her mother was unable to leave her job, so Granny came to the hospital to stay with her every day, calming her fears and reading her stories.

Granny was always there to help others—at church, in her neighborhood, in the family. One of her sons was an alcoholic, and while others in the family gave up on him, Granny continued to take care of him when he needed care.

Granny became one of Mitzi's models, her life's example shining brighter than that of any famous star. Granny was one of God's lights in the world, showing the way God wants us to live.

Years later, when Granny was ill, she came to live with Mitzi. Mitzi sat by her bed day after day, listening to stories of her childhood and calming her fears. Mitzi's light shines brightly, too.

♥ *O Lord, I want my life to shine so brightly that people can't help but see You.*

QUESTIONS, QUESTIONS

*If any of you lacks wisdom, let him ask of
God, who gives to all liberally and without
reproach, and it will be given to him.*
—JAMES 1:5

*G*randchildren ask questions—sometimes funny,
sometimes serious, and often a delight and challenge.

Once Tony asked his grandmother, "Just what kind
of being is God, anyway?" Another time, when she was
tucking him into bed, Tony asked, "Who are your he-
roes, Grandma?"

Grandma, an artist, mentioned some artists she admired and said, "Jesus is my best hero."

Tony said, "He's a good hero, Grandma."

Preschool children ask "why" thousands of times
each day. How privileged we are to be among those
who can give them the answers to their questions! A little boy trying to learn who God is and who is important
to his grandmother is searching for answers on which
to build his values.

God puts us in the question-answering position for a
number of reasons: we have experience in life, our
faith is strong, we are often able to spend time listening
and answering, and we are often more patient. But God
hasn't left us without support. He will give us the wisdom we need to answer our grandchildren's questions.
We just need to ask Him.

♥ *Lord, get me ready for when those questions come.
I want my grandchildren to know and love You.*

But it is good for me to draw near to God.
                                        —PS. 73:28

*B*ette Lou has eight children and many, many grandchildren. Some live in distant states, so she doesn't see them as often as she or they would like. One way Bette Lou communicates with her grandchildren is by sending them books with tapes she makes of herself reading the book.

One day a grandson was listening to the tape his grandma had sent when his mother came into the room. The boy looked at his mom and said, "Could you leave us alone now, Mom? This is my time with Grandma."

Gone are the days when grandmas live in the same house, town, or even the same state. This means we need to be creative in thinking of ways to be part of their lives. Our grandchildren need to see us and hear our voices. Today's technology can help. The cassette tape idea above is one possibility. Or have you ever considered making a video of yourself talking to your grandchildren?

The way we get to know and love people is by spending time with them however we can. That's true of God, too. We know and love Him by spending time with Him as we pray, read the Bible, and worship Him.

♥ *Lord, my time with You is precious. I'd like to duplicate that feeling with my grandchildren.*

REMEMBER WHEN?

But the word of the LORD
endures forever.
—1 PETER 1:25a

*C*arolyn's Grandma Skala likes to tell stories on herself. One favorite is about when she was nineteen and she came from Czechoslovakia to Chicago to work as a maid. She could not speak English, and many things were new to her. For example, she had never seen ice cream before. One evening, after serving ice cream to the family she worked for, she took some home and put it under her pillow to save and enjoy later. Of course, the next morning she woke to a mess!

Everyone loves stories, especially those about family members. That's what family reunions and holiday get-togethers are all about. Someone will say, "Remember when . . . ?" and off we go. Have you ever noticed what your grandchildren are doing during this storytime? Usually they are sitting very close to the teller, listening intently.

The Bible is a book of stories about people. Someone has said, "The great biblical narrative of God's love for man runs from Genesis through Revelation, encapsulated in tiny story segments from the lives of His people."

♥ *Dear God, help me to be a good storyteller of Your*
great and wonderful stories.

Blessed be the . . . God of all comfort, who comforts us . . . that we may be able to comfort those . . . with the comfort with which we ourselves are comforted by God.
—2 COR. 1:3–4

*W*hen Dorothy was four, her Grandma Lucy sent her a rose from the florist when she was sick in bed. This was special because Grandma lived only a few houses away from Dorothy.

When Dorothy was five she had to go to the hospital in another town because she had pneumonia. Grandma came to visit one day and found her granddaughter lonely and sobbing. Grandma Lucy immediately ordered ice cream.

Grandmothers are great comforters. With extraordinary God-given sensitivity we know how to stop the flow of tears, quell fears, and hasten the healing of hurts. Favorite words and phrases include: I know, I know; it's okay; you'll be fine soon; Grandma's here; and I love you. Of course, all are accompanied by liberal doses of hugs, pats, and kisses.

Our grandchildren are never too old for these words and actions of comfort. God reaches out to us through words of the Bible and through the loving and helpful words and actions of family and friends. No one is ever too old to need the comfort He readily gives.

♥ *Dear God, I have been the recipient of Your comfort so often. Thank You for helping me to pass it on.*

NEIGHBORHOOD GRANDMA

But do not forget to do good and to share,
for with such sacrifices God is well pleased.
—HEB. 13:16

*O*ne woman who lived in a neighborhood with many young children became the neighborhood grandma. She decorated the tree in her front yard with hearts for Valentine's Day, eggs for Easter, flags for Fourth of July, pumpkins for Halloween, turkeys for Thanksgiving, and ornaments for Christmas. She also was known to feed anyone who came near—plates of cookies, sacks of candy, piles of fruit, and other assorted goodies were readily available. Hers was a "sure bet house" for trick-or-treating and Christmas caroling. She could always be counted on for items needed in scavenger hunts, or bandaids when your supply was out.

Talk about ministry! Here was a grandma who was using her gifts to the fullest. Like Dorcas (Acts 9:36–42), she looked around for a need and set about to meet that need by doing the things she knew how to do.

♥ *Dear God, is there a need in my neighborhood that I can meet?*

The heart of the wise teaches his mouth,
And adds learning to his lips.
> —PROV. 16:23

*W*hen Willie was a little girl her grandparents lived on one bank of the river and she and her family lived on the other. In the winter, Willie would go to her grandparents' house to visit, and she and her grandfather would get on the sled, fly down one bank and across the frozen water to the other bank. Willie would always get soaking wet from landing in the snow, and Grandma would dry her off before her mother, who worried about colds, came to get her.

Willie said, "When Mother asked Grandma if I had gotten wet, Grandma would say, 'She's not wet now.'" Her mother always looked at her and Grandma a little suspiciously, but never pursued the matter. Grandma and Willie never talked about it, either.

Wise parents and grandparents know the boundaries, which include the way we say things to one another. Our words and the tone of our voices can cause tempers to flare.

The Bible gives us advice about what we say and how we say it. (God knew that would be one of the areas that would get us into the most trouble.) The verse for today gives us a good guide to follow. It's God's way to do things.

♥ *Help me, Lord, to take time to listen to my heart before I speak.*

ENCOURAGING WORDS

Let no corrupt communication proceed out of your mouth, but what is good for necessary edification, that it may impart grace to the hearers.
—EPH. 4:29

*M*y friend Bette designs and creates the gorgeous flower-laden floats in the Rose Bowl parade. It's a year-round job. Bette is a grandmother with several "natural" grandchildren and crews of "borrowed" grandchildren who help put the flowers in place on the floats in those hectic last few hours before the parade.

The children are from various institutions and facilities that care for abandoned and abused children. They need short-term goals to help them feel successful. Putting flowers in place under the patient and encouraging direction of a substitute grandmother helps them meet that goal.

Of course, the way Bette talks to the children helps: "Oh, honey, that's just perfect!" "Darling, let's put some more of these here." "Sweetie, I really need your help." "Precious, you do such good work!"

Bette calls everyone honey, darling, sweetie, and precious. She means the endearments, and the children know and love it. The way we talk to one another is important. God has given us guidelines for how we should speak. He also gives us examples in the loving, encouraging way He speaks to us.

♥ *Lord, I want to think before I speak so that, like You, I communicate love and encouragement.*

CONFIDENCE

Now this is the confidence that we have in Him, that if we ask anything according to His will, He hears us. —1 JOHN 5:14

*B*ecky remembers that her grandmother spent hours playing games with her and her brothers and sisters—games the grandchildren always won while Grandmother exclaimed, "Oh, you won again. How did you do that?" Years later they realized that Grandmother had let them win.

There are those who don't feel that adults should let children win when playing games with them. There are as many good reasons to let them win as there are not to let them win. Winning at games is a fun way to learn confidence. Becky appreciates her grandmother's generous spirit; it did a lot for her self-confidence. Obviously, Grandmother felt it was important for the children to win. Perhaps she saw the need for some confidence building.

We need to demonstrate to our grandchildren the confidence we possess, especially our confidence in God and in our relationship with Him. They need to see us as people whom God loves and equips to handle each day. Watching us is another way they learn how they, too, can be confident.

♥ *Dear God, does my confidence in You show?*

JOY

But let the righteous be glad;
Let them rejoice before God;
Yes, let them rejoice exceedingly.
— PS. 68:3

Once when my brother Richard was staying at Grandma Kyte's, a friend of hers came to visit, bringing her granddaughters. The two little girls always dressed in frilly dresses and wore hats with ribbons.

Richard wasn't happy about having them around, and one day decided to have some fun with them. First he made a large mud puddle in the driveway. When the girls came out to see what he was doing, Richard jumped across the puddle and nonchalantly commented that this was something that girls couldn't do. The girls immediately tried to do it and fell into the puddle. Grandma and her friend rushed out to rescue the screaming girls; Richard was banished to the back porch. After they left, Grandma laughed about the whole incident.

Our grandchildren are wonderful sources of joy and laughter. The things they do and say delight us, sometimes to the dismay of their parents who often fail to see the humor in the pranks.

There are dozens of verses in the Bible about gladness, happiness, and rejoicing. As Christians, the ultimate joy and happiness of our salvation should spill over into all areas of our lives.

♥ *I rejoice in the grandchildren You have given me, Father.*

REUNION

A friend loves at all times. . . .
—PROV. 17:17

*W*e were four grandmothers having lunch together during a fortieth high school reunion weekend. We commented that all of our classmates had seemed friendlier at this reunion than at the others. Some classmates were balder, grayer, heavier, thinner, shorter—but all of us were definitely friendlier. It was as if there was less need for competition in how well we were doing and more acceptance of one another and the troubles we had gone through. Some spouses had died or been divorced and some were remarried. More than a few classmates had died or were too ill to attend.

As the four of us talked of the past, laughing and sighing over boyfriends, antics, and dreams, we shared present concerns and future goals. We exchanged addresses and promised to keep in touch.

It is good to be with people who knew us early in our lives, people who "know all about us and like us anyway." These real friends are usually people who can talk with us almost as if there had been no intervening years between conversations.

The book of Proverbs has many verses about friends. They describe our greatest Friend of all—Jesus!

♥ *What a Friend I have in You, Jesus. Help me to be a friend like You.*

WALKING IN THE LIGHT

But the path of the just is like the shining
*   sun,*
That shines ever brighter unto the perfect
*   day.*
                              —PROV. 4:18

*R*oger's grandmother, Mary Moore, was born the year the Civil War ended. She was raised on the Iowa prairie, and her stories included those of being told to give Indians whatever they wanted if they came to the house. Mary was a pioneer mother, rearing her family in the days before electricity, radio, telephone, cars, and the many other conveniences we now have. She raised and canned the vegetables and fruit for the household, baked the bread, sewed the clothing, crocheted and knitted, and helped with the out-of-doors work. She was also an active fifty-year member of the church.

Grandma Mary died at ninety-eight. Roger has a copy of her funeral service, which quotes the verse above and tells how, early in life, Mary set her feet on the path of the righteous as she gave her life to God. The longer she walked on this path, the brighter the light became, because she was moving toward the source of light.

For her, as for other believers, evening was not a forerunner of darkness. The colors of sunset were beautiful anticipation of eternal dawn.

♥ *Lord, the idea of limitless life with You is delightful to think about as I walk in Your light.*

And we know that all things work together
for good to those who love God, to those who
are the called according to His purpose.
                                              —ROM. 8:28

*T*he following is an excerpt of a poem a grandson remembered his grandfather wrote about his grandmother who died while still young. It begins with grief
and ends with hope.

> *So brief the years*
>   *So short the time*
> *When I was yours*
> *And you were mine*
> *When hand in hand*
>   *Along this way*
> *We walked together*
>   *Day by day, . . .*
> *Shall I despair?*
>   *No! Thou didst teach*
> *And by thy living*
>   *Always preach,*
> *That all things work*
>   *For good not ill*
>   *For those who try*
> *To do God's will.*

This is a keepsake to treasure, giving witness of a
grandfather's love for his wife—and their love and trust
in the One who loved them both.

♥ *What will the things I leave behind tell my grand-*
children about me?

For with God nothing will be impossible.
—LUKE 1:37

*G*randma Ollie had twelve children, twenty-five grandchildren, and ten great-grandchildren. Each Christmas she bought one gift for each of them!

Granddaughter Cheryl tells that her parents provided very well for her and her sister—they had all they needed and many extras. But one year at Christmas, what she really wanted was a set of day-of-the-week underpants. When Cheryl opened her gift from Grandma Ollie, there they were! Cheryl remembers being amazed and pleased that her grandmother knew exactly what she wanted.

Often grandmas are listeners and noticers. While other family members are talking, we listen with our ears and our hearts. We notice wants and concerns that are hidden in words and actions.

The best part is that we know what to do about the things we hear and notice. Many times we can take care of, or help to take care of, concerns and thank God that He makes it possible. But the overwhelmingly large desires and needs that are beyond our physical, mental, and financial abilities we can take straight to God. He will help us and our grandchildren know how to handle whatever it is.

♥ *Keep me from worrying and fussing about those concerns that overwhelm me. Keep me talking to You.*

Open my eyes, that I may see
Wondrous things from Your law.
—PS. 119:18

*W*es was having a busy day with Grandma Sandy. But it wasn't a good busy day. It was a bad busy day, with Wes taking from everyone and wanting more and more. His attitude needed adjusting quickly.

Finally, Grandma asked Wes to come and sit on her lap while she read him *The Giving Tree.* The story tells how a boy came every day to eat the tree's apples, swing from her branches, and slide down her trunk. This made the tree happy. As the boy grew older, he wanted more and more from the tree, and the tree gave and gave and gave, at great cost to itself. Even at three, Wes understood the message of the story and, at least for the rest of that day, changed his attitude.

Congratulations to a grandma who thought of a creative way to help a grandson work on, minimize, and perhaps eliminate an undesirable behavior.

We all need attitude adjusters of one sort or another at times. One of God's creative ways to help us is His Word. If we listen closely when we have an attitude that needs fixing, we can hear Him say, "Sit down with Me. Open My Book. I want to tell you a story."

♥ *Dear God, when I sit down with You and Your Word,*
I learn and my attitude is great!

Let not mercy and truth forsake you;
Bind them around your neck,
Write them on the tablet of your heart.
—PROV. 3:3

J recommend *The Grandmother Book* by Jan Stoop and Betty Southard; it should be required reading for all grandmothers. The authors state, "Each of us has a grandmothering style, a special way of giving loving support and nurture that fits us perfectly. Our challenge is to find that particular style and work from within it."

The four main styles they identify are the doer, the discoverer, the dreamer, and the director. No one style is better than another; each brings with it specific strengths and abilities as well as potential pitfalls. If you know your style, you can maximize the strengths and avoid the pitfalls.

I'm sure we all agree that our grandmothering is very different from the way we were grandmothered or the way our mothers were grandmothered. It's not necessarily better or worse; it's just different. The basic principles of grandmothering still apply. They all stem from the word *love*.

♥ *Father, Your love is the foundation on which my love for others can build and remain strong.*

HANGING OUT TOGETHER

Sow for yourselves righteousness;
Reap in mercy. —HOS. 10:12

$\mathcal{E}$very St. Patrick's Day since Dugan was eight months old, Grandma and Grandpa have taken their little red-headed Irish grandson out to dinner, complete with green-colored 7-Up. (They take along green food coloring and now, at age nine, Dugan reminds them to bring it.)

Grandma calls Dugan on January 2, when she is filling in her calendar for the new year, to invite him to the St. Patrick's Day treat, and he is eager to add it to his calendar. It's their time to talk, listen, and hang out.

A University of Missouri study several years ago asked students who was important in their lives. A good number responded, "grandparents." When asked what they remembered most, they answered, "Not big events, just hanging out together."

There's no getting away from the importance of time we spend with people, is there? The time we spend with God in reading His Word and talking to Him is valuable, too. It needs to take precedence over everything else on our daily calendar. Maybe we could put it on our schedules as "hanging out with God."

♥ *My time with You is always well-spent, Lord.*

*. . . The Lord is risen indeed, and has
appeared to Simon!*
—LUKE 24:34

*P*astor Dave and his wife bought a bread machine
for Easter. The machine mixes, kneads, and bakes
bread, all the while wafting the aroma of freshly made
bread throughout the house. It was that wonderful
smell, which reminded Pastor Dave of his Grandmother Lillian's house, that sold the machine. The
aroma triggered the feelings of well-being and security
he had felt as a child.

In a sermon about what he called the first supper,
Pastor Dave suggested a similar trigger that helped the
two people on their way to Emmaus recognize the Person who walked with them. The Bible says that as He
sat at the table with them, "He took bread, blessed
and broke it, and gave it to them." When they saw this,
"their eyes were opened and they knew Him" (Luke
24:30, 31). The breaking of bread was a trigger to remind them who Jesus was and what He said was true.
He was alive!

We still need triggers to remind us who Jesus is and
that what He says is true: He lives! It can happen any-
time, anywhere as we read God's words, listen to the
testimony of others, and experience His presence in
our lives. Suddenly our eyes are opened and we recognize Him.

♥ *Dear Lord, keep my eyes open to see and know You
better.*

Whoever receives one little child like this in My name receives Me. —MATT. 18:5

I am starting a campaign in my church, a campaign to motivate grandmothers (and grandfathers) to care for babies in the nursery.

Through the years, when recruiting nursery help, I've been told, over and over again, "When my children were babies, I took my turn and did my part. Now it's those young mothers' turn."

I used to accept that as a good reason. Not anymore. The only good reasons for grandmothers not to work in the nursery are that they have health problems, don't like babies, or have a ministry in another area of the church that would make it impossible to spend one Sunday every three months in the nursery.

We've been wrong to feel that the people who use the nursery need to staff it. The nursery is a ministry— a ministry not only to babies but to their parents as well. Parents need the support of their church family as they raise families. We can help build whole, healthy families by caring for their babies while they receive spiritual direction and guidance. And cuddling, holding, and rocking babies is an ideal ministry for grandmothers.

♥ *Dear God, am I involved in a ministry of serving or have I become musty?*

Sing to the LORD, bless His name;
Proclaim the good news of His salvation
from day to day.
                                        —PS. 96:2

*M*y daughter and I finished shopping and went to pick up Angie at the baby-sitter's. As we were leaving, the sitter came out to the car and leaned into the car window to say, "So you're Angie's Grandma Mona. I wanted to meet you because she talks about you all the time!"

I was surprised and pleased to hear this. Angie's family doesn't live too far from me and I get to see them fairly often, but I didn't realize until then the important place I have in her life and how much she loves me.

Sometimes it's interesting to find out what kind of witness our lives are to people we know. This incident has made me reassess the place that Jesus has in my life. Can people tell by the way I live and talk how important He is to me and how much I love Him? Does my life reflect Him so consistently that one day the people I know might say, "Tell me about Jesus. I want to meet this Person you talk about so much!"

♥ *Dear Jesus, help me to introduce You to people who*
  don't know You by the way I talk about You.

CONSISTENCY

Jesus Christ is the same yesterday, today, and forever.   —HEB. 13:8

*A*mong my family members I have the reputation of moving quickly to get where I am going. For example, when the grandchildren and I get ready to leave for our week together, I usually tell them to be sure to have gone to the bathroom and packed everything they need to keep themselves occupied in the car, because we won't be stopping before lunch unless there's an emergency.

Granddaughter Becky, explaining this procedure to someone, said, "You know Grandma, when she's driving she just goes!"

It's a good idea for grandchildren to know we mean what we say. That's one way we can support their parents in their efforts to be consistent.

Our best example of consistency is our Heavenly Father. Just think of some of His characteristics: the everlasting Father (Isa. 9:6); gentle (Matt. 11:29); loving (John 13:34); patient (Rom. 15:5); forgiving (Col. 3:13); honest (Eph. 4:15). Add to the list by thinking of an attribute for each letter of the alphabet; turn it into a prayer of praise for a God who we can be absolutely sure means what He says.

♥ *Father, thank You for being a consistent God who I can trust thoroughly.*

. . . Know the God of your father, and serve Him with a loyal heart and with a willing mind; for the LORD searches all hearts and understands all the intent of the thoughts.
—1 CHRON. 28:9

*D*orthea's Grandmother Sternweis did all her own baking—bread, cookies, pies, cakes. Dorthea remembers her family driving to see Grandmother Sternweis and arriving very late at night to find a table laden with delicious goodies Grandma had baked. She also remembers that her grandmother went to church daily and always spent time in morning and evening prayer.

The two things her granddaughter most remembers are interesting: the way her grandmother showed her love for her family through baking, and the way her grandmother showed her love for God by worshiping Him each day. The two activities are related. The time we spend with God should motivate us to love others in practical ways.

What do you enjoy doing most? God has given you that interest or talent for you and for others. Are you using it to show love to others? If not, how could you?

If we do the things we are interested in and enjoy doing for others, we will find ourselves having much more energy and enthusiasm for ministry. It's the way we find joy in serving God.

♥ *Dear God, help me not to be selfish with my interests and talents and to use them in loving others.*

. . . The joy of the LORD is your strength.
—NEH. 8:10

J asked the women in the church office to tell me some grandmother stories. Kathleen showed me that she was wearing Grandma Eickelkraut's engagement ring, the one that is always handed down to the youngest daughter. Kathy told me about her daughter Tracy's Grandma Praff who one time worried that Tracy wouldn't have anyone to play with on Christmas Day and so came and played dress-up with her. Theresa remembered her grandmother putting on cat's-eye-shaped glasses at night, settling in bed, and telling them it was time for her devotions.

After a few minutes of discussion, Kathleen said, "Just look at the smiles you brought to us. You asked about our grandmothers and thinking about them, we're all smiling."

What a great comment about grandmothers! Thinking about us should make people smile and be happy. We should be people with joy. God has much to say about the kind of people He wants us to be. He tells us how to live so that we can be happy and so that others will see that happiness and want it, too.

♥ *I want my grandchildren to think joy and happiness when they think about me. Help me to have real joy that comes from knowing You.*

> *In My Father's house are many mansions; if it were not so, I would have told you. I go to prepare a place for you.* —JOHN 14:2

$\mathcal{S}$ometimes Diane would try to get out of going to school by saying she had a scratchy throat so she could go to Grandma's.

Often Grandma's house is the next best place to home for grandchildren. Children need places where they are assured of safety and comfort, where they feel welcomed and accepted. The more places like this in their lives, the better able they will be to face the places that are intimidating.

Diane tells how Grandma Ruth always went on vacation with her family. During one of those vacations Grandma Ruth became very ill and died. When Diane's father came to tell her, Diane ran and hid.

It's hard to lose someone who has provided love and security, and it's natural to try and hide from the truth of that loss. But it was because of the time she spent with her grandmother that Diane could eventually accept her grandmother's death and go on to share her memories with her children.

Our houses here on earth need to be the next best thing to our eventual home in Heaven. As we provide love, security, acceptance, and comfort, we are experiencing just a sample of what it will be like when we hear Jesus say, "Welcome home, children."

♥ *Make my home what my grandchildren need giving them a glimpse of Your home.*

Seek the LORD and His strength;
Seek His face evermore!
    —1 CHRON. 16:11

*P*hone calls to and from grandchildren can be very satisfying. You can hear the pleasure in their voices as they greet you with, "Hi, Grandma!" Their greetings do so much to lift our spirits. We should call them frequently for that reason alone. What's so wonderful about all this is that they feel the same way when they hear us!

One young woman feels closer to her eighty-five-year-old grandmother as an adult than she did as a child and calls her every week. A grandmother says her phone calls become family visits because they live far apart; she considers it money well spent. Another family gives Grandmother a long-distance service as a gift so she can call family members as often as she likes.

We don't have a phone hook-up to God, but talking with Him often is one of the principles of a satisfying Christian life. A visit with God about our families can give us peace. Certainly prayer draws us closer to Him. And we can talk to Him whenever and wherever. The cost is our time. God's gift is His constant availability to hear us.

♥ *Thank You for being glad to hear my voice when I talk with You.*

HAND WORK

And let the beauty of the LORD our God
be upon us,
And establish the work of our hands for
us. —PS. 90:17

*T*he only thing I really remember about my grandmother," Barbara began, "is how hard she worked. She had eight children, and all she ever did was work; when she finished her work each day, she went to bed. She didn't read to us or play games with us; we didn't even really talk with her much. But she did make each of us a quilt and gave them to us when we graduated from high school."

Some grandmothers are not able to show love for their grandchildren in words or in actions like hugs and kisses. But somehow and in some way, grandmothers will let their grandchildren know they love them, as Barbara's grandmother did with the quilts. This grandmother gave her love in the best way she knew how—the work of her hands.

The psalm the verse above was taken from is a prayer of Moses as he and the Israelites wandered in the wilderness. The request in this final verse of the Psalm is that we will do something of value in life before we die. It challenges us to concentrate on using our lives for eternal good—like the love sewed into every square of a grandchild's quilt.

♥ *Dear Lord, I want the work of my hands to be valuable now and for eternity.*

March 26 _____

IMPORTANT TIMES AND PLACES

For what great nation is there that has God so near to it, as the LORD our God is to us, for whatever reason we may call upon Him?
—DEUT. 4:7

*W*hen Tena was seven, she and Grandma Hetrick spent nearly every summer day sitting in the front seat of an old 1957 Chevy, coloring in her coloring book. Tena says there were seven people living in their small house and the Chevy was where she and Grandma went to be together—it was their special time. A 1957 Chevy is still one of Tena's favorite cars. She remembers the year of the car because it's the year she was born, and because that time with her grandma was so meaningful to her.

Extended families living together was normal in times past, and some feel it is becoming necessary again. Whether or not our grandchildren live with us (or we with them), we need to establish a special time and place to be with each grandchild.

We also need to establish a special time and place to be with God, and keep it even though it is not always easy. God longs to meet with us regularly—daily. The time and place are up to us.

♥ *Help me to keep my time with You each day.*

KEEP UP THE GOOD WORK!

Therefore comfort each other and edify one another, just as you also are doing.
—1 THESS. 5:11

I remember lying on the couch in my grandmother's living room (I was supposed to be taking a nap) and listening to my two grandmothers talk about me in the kitchen. What I remember most about their conversation was their agreement that they must not tell me I was a pretty little girl; it might make me think too much of myself. What I heard and remembered was that they thought I was pretty. They just weren't going to tell me.

There was a time when people thought it best not to praise or compliment children. It was thought not to be good for their character. It might "turn their heads," which meant we might become proud and think more highly of ourselves than we ought.

We've gotten past that kind of thinking, and it's a good thing. Now we are concerned about a child's self-esteem and look for ways to build it so that children grow into healthy, whole adults.

Our Heavenly Father has given us the pattern to follow. We are constantly assured of His unfailing love, forgiveness, and acceptance. They depend solely on accepting Jesus as our Savior.

♥ *Father, You created us with good self-esteem. Help us not to harm or diminish what You made.*

CREATIVE COMFORT

By purity, by knowledge, by longsuffering, by kindness, by the Holy Spirit, by sincere love, by the word of truth, by the power of God . . .
—2 COR. 6:6–7

*W*hen Jerry was four years old he needed surgery on his hands because he had webbed fingers. He doesn't remember much about the hospital stay except that following the surgery his grandmother came to see him and brought him a teddy bear with bandages on his paws. The bandages were just like the ones he had on his hands. At that time, hospital visitation times were limited even for families, and Jerry, now a surgeon, remembers the comfort of the teddy bear in the long hours alone. In fact, he still has the bear.

I wonder if every teddy bear grandmothers have bought were laid end to end how many times we could circle the globe. Teddy bears are comforting. They can even be a kind of substitute when a grandmother isn't available.

When the Apostle Paul needed comforting, God sent a person to encourage him and bring him good news. God knows what we need. He is the God of all comfort who will comfort us with His words, the feeling of His presence, good news, other Christians, and even teddy bears from grandmothers.

♥ *Lord, thank You for Your comfort that sometimes comes in surprising and unexpected ways.*

NO GREATER LOVE

*Greater love has no one than this, than to
lay down one's life for his friends.*
                                    —JOHN 15:13

*T*racy calls her Grandma Queen (short for
McQueen) her second mother. She says her grandma
is always there for her and would do anything she
could for her. Grandma sends her cards with comforting
messages when she knows things aren't going well
at school or she's had a disappointment. She tells
Tracy that she's praying for her every day and makes
special efforts to find specific presents Tracy wants.

Once, when Tracy was very young, Grandma Queen
was worried that Grandpa wouldn't remember to pick
Tracy up at school on his way home from work.
Grandma walked several blocks to be there when Tracy
got out.

Tracy says she would do anything for her grandmother.
Her grandmother has given her a good picture
of the kind of love Jesus was talking about when He
said we should love each other as He loves us.

The passage in John 15:9–17 begins and ends with
a command to love one another, and it includes a definition
of the greatest kind of love there is—love that
proved Jesus was willing to do anything for us when He
gave His life so that we might live eternally.

♥ *Thank You for your wondrous love. Help me to be
willing to love as You do.*

_____

March 30 _____

HUMOR TRYOUT

The light of the eyes rejoices the heart,
And a good report makes the bones healthy.
          —PROV. 15:30

As Gary and his grandparents passed a large cemetery during a car trip, Gary asked, "Did you know they won't let anyone living in Chicago be buried in that big cemetery?" Grandma said, "No, why not?"

Gary said, "Because they're still living, Grandma!"

They traveled several miles and passed another cemetery in another town. Gary asked his grandma the same question using that town's name. To this day Gary says, "Grandma fell for the same joke twice in one hour!"

It may be that Grandma didn't fall for the joke even once, but it says a lot about the kind of grandmother she was that her grandson still thinks she did. Telling silly jokes and singing funny songs are part of childhood. And grandparents make wonderfully receptive audiences for grandchildren to try out their senses of humor without ridicule.

There aren't too many references in the Bible about laughter or humor, but there are dozens about joy and happiness. Most of those verses remind us that true joy and happiness come from knowing God.

♥ *Dear God, thank You for the joy and happiness You give me.*

UNCONDITIONAL LOVE

Behold what manner of love the Father has bestowed on us, that we should be called children of God!
—1 JOHN 3:1

They were all gathered for Grandmother's eightieth birthday. As one of her grandsons and his wife handed her a gift, Grandmother said to him, "You've always been my favorite grandchild."

His wife, noticing several granddaughters sitting within hearing distance, quickly said, "You mean grand*son*, don't you, Grandma?" (The grandson later said his wife's sensitivity is only one of the reasons he loves her so much.)

Sometimes grandparents do have favorite grandchildren, but we try not to say so or show it (unless, as my mother once said when she was in her eighties, "Now I'm old enough to say anything I want").

One of my favorite Erma Bombeck columns is about a woman who wrote a letter to each of her children. Each letter began, "I've always loved you best." There are reasons for us to love each of our grandchildren best. With some grandchildren we may have to look harder or longer for the reasons, but they are there. Or we can simply do as God does with us—love them unconditionally.

♥ *Let the security of Your unconditional love for me cause me to love others the same way.*

GUARDIANS OF MEMORIES

Wisdom is with aged men,
And with length of days, understanding.
                                        —JOB 12:12

A grandmother named Mildred Meyer wrote this for her grandchildren and ours:

Sometimes younger people look at us older people and they have not seen us—they have seen their idea of us.

They see our wrinkles and think wrinkles subtract from our appearance. But wrinkles are the maps of our character. Gnarled knuckles, raised veins, and new twists in the direction of our fingers are just pages in the history we represent. Our eyes and ears no longer distinguish all the finer sensations.

Despite the invasion that time has made on our faces and bodies, we are still whole and vital. Age is not a place, it is a time. We are not relics but guardians of memories. If they would look at us very carefully, they would see more than our past—they would see their future.

God gives us the gifts of wisdom and understanding. They will help us prepare our children and grandchildren for taking our place.

♥ *Dear God, I want my grandchildren to look forward*
   to their future through knowing me and You.

*O righteous Father! The world has not
known You, but I have known You; and
these have known that You sent Me. And I
have declared to them Your name, and will
declare it, that the love with which You
loved Me may be in them, and I in them.*
—JOHN 17:25

*M*y daughter-in-law Deborah remembers visiting
her grandmother and great-grandmother in Newfoundland when she was six years old. They lived in a large,
beautiful home surrounded by a fence.

Great-grandmother, grandmother, and Deborah
slept together in a huge brass bed. After grandmother
went to sleep, she and great-grandmother ate peppermint candies until they both went to sleep. Now Deborah receives peppermint from her grandmother each
Christmas in memory of that special time.

Grandchildren watch adults to see how they act and
react in a variety of situations. It's one of the ways they
learn what to do when faced with similar circumstances. They need to see us act courageously, and will
love to observe us doing something childlike such as
furtively enjoying candy. These actions make us more
approachable and easier to talk with.

God sent His Son, Jesus, to earth to give us a better
idea of who God is and what He is like. When we look
at Jesus' life, read and listen to His words, we find it
easy to approach and talk with God.

♥ *Thank You, God, for sending Your Son, Jesus, to help
us know You.*

GOOD FROM BAD

*For our light and momentary troubles are
achieving for us an eternal glory that far
outweighs them all.* —2 COR. 4:17 NIV

Grandma White liked to talk about the good old days
when she lived with her parents on the plains of North
Dakota. In 1907 her father filed on a claim for 160
acres. He was a carpenter and built a five-room house
for his family.

Grandma was fifteen months old when she experienced her first bad prairie fire. The table had just been
set for supper, with a big layer cake in the middle of it.
Her mother had to help fight the fire, and so had put
the family dog in the house and told him to watch the
little girl. When Grandma's mother and father finally
came in from the fire, Grandma was standing at the
window chewing on half of a broken plate while the
dog, very contentedly, lay at her feet. She had crawled
up on the table and fed him the whole cake!

Even some of the bad times in our lives make good
memories. Maybe we learned something during that
time that helped us later. If we believe that God is with
us in everything, He can use all our experiences to
teach us things He wants us to know.

♥ *In good and bad times, help me to learn what You
want me to know.*

THANKS AND WILL

*In everything give thanks; for this is the will
of God in Christ Jesus for you.*
                              —1 THESS. 5:18

*M*y grandchildren have not yet met their grandfather; he died before they were born.

The church we attended at that time asked the con-
gregation to memorize a verse each week. The verse
for the week my husband died is the one above. The
night he died, we went to a fundraising dinner. As we
crossed the parking lot to the banquet room, my husband asked why I was walking so fast. That should have
been my first clue that something was wrong. We sat
down on a bench; my husband put his hand on his
chest, turned to say something to me, and was dead.

The next morning I looked in the bathroom mirror
and said, "I don't like this, God."

Immediately, the verse we had memorized went
through my mind. I said, "All right, I will thank You in
this circumstance. But I don't like it."

His answer was clear in my mind. "I know. I will
help you." And He has through the years, in more ways
than I have room to tell about here.

I tell this experience to my grandchildren to help
them recognize God's faithfulness in their lives—they
have seen it in my life.

♥ *The old hymn says, "Trust and obey." It's one of Your
principles for happiness.*

*I love the LORD, because He has heard
My voice and my supplications.
Because He has inclined His ear to me,
Therefore I will call upon Him as long as I
    live.*
                                    —PS. 116:1–2

*O*ne of my grandchildren's favorite stories about the time following their grandfather's death is the one about the deposit box key.

My husband's insurance papers were in the box, and I could not find the key to open it before the bank sealed the box until the estate was settled.

My husband died on Saturday; on Monday morning we needed to go to the bank as soon as it opened. The family searched the house. We looked through my husband's clothes, in the closet, and through every dresser and desk drawer. I personally removed everything from the top of our dresser in the bedroom more than once. No key.

Family and friends prayed throughout the day as we looked. We went to bed praying on Sunday night when there was nowhere else to look. On Monday morning, when I woke up, the key was lying on the edge of the dresser—the one I had personally searched several times.

God does, indeed, answer prayer. We don't always understand the reasons or His timing. And sometimes we refuse to hear or just don't recognize the answer. But He always answers!

♥ *Thank You for answered prayers, even for those I'm still waiting for.*

April 6

And whatever things you ask in prayer,
believing, you will receive.
—MATT. 21:22

*M*y grandchildren know that I believe in prayer. The year following my husband's death I kept a small notebook, which I titled, "Fantastic Answers to Prayer in 1976 and 1977." Each day when I prayed, I wrote my requests and concerns on a separate line in the notebook with the date. Every time I received an answer, I wrote that date next to the request.

Years later I came across the notebook and discovered two amazing things. First, nearly every request had been answered—some in ways far beyond my expectations. Second, many things that I thought were so crucial and important then, I had forgotten all about or could barely remember when I read about them years later.

I haven't stopped praying, but I don't always keep a record of answered prayers like I did that year. Perhaps I should; it is such a visible reminder of the many, many times God does hear when I call on Him—and answers in ways that are always best and often more than I dared ask for. It also illustrates that most of the things I get so frantic about aren't really all that world-shaking; certainly they are not too big for God to handle. I think it's time to start another notebook.

♥ *How good You are to me, God. My prayers include praise for who You are.*

April 7 _____

Then Naomi took the child, laid him in her lap and cared for him.

—RUTH 4:16 NIV

*L*ydia Maria Child's famous poem "Thanksgiving Day" says,

> *Over the river and through the wood,*
> *To grandfather's house we go*

But I wonder why nearly everyone who quotes it says "grandmother's house." Is it simply because home and Grandmother seem to go together so naturally? It does seem that when we think in terms of warmth, comfort, and family, grandmothers automatically come to mind. I think God ordained it that way. We are not usually or necessarily the primary caregiving mothers for our grandchildren, but we can be if necessary. And most of us enjoy their short-term visits as much as they do.

It was different in Bible times; grandmothers usually lived in the same house as their grandchildren. The Bible gives us the example of Naomi, who was Obed's grandmother. Obed was the father of Jesse, the father of David. It's interesting to imagine what of her influence, love, and care for Obed found its way through the genealogy of David to Jesus.

♥ *Heavenly Father, I want the love and care for my grandchildren to be passed on generation after generation.*

Get wisdom! Get understanding!
Do not forget, nor turn away from the words
of my mouth.
—PROV. 4:5

I was shopping for a particular toy that my granddaughter Angie had asked for when I saw a T-shirt that said, "The only person who understands me is Grandma!" It brought a smile to my face as I paid the cashier and left with the stuffed toy that I had gone to store after store looking for.

Grandmas do understand grandchildren. They can tell from the tone of a voice or a look on the face whether a child needs a cookie, a hug, or both. They know the difference between cries of pain and temper tantrums, and they know what to do about both. They've learned to listen first and ask questions later, sometimes not talking at all but simply patting a hand or giving a hug.

God has gifted most grandmothers with understanding. Those who don't have it can get it. They just have to remember what it was like when they were children and needed someone to love them without conditions, just for being who they are. Better yet, they need only to think about God's love for us. He loves us just the way we are—unconditionally. And His love comes with absolute understanding.

♥ *Thank You for loving and understanding me. Help me follow Your example in my family.*

DO YOU GET IT?

I love those who love me,
And those who seek me diligently will find
me.
—PROV. 8:17

I was having dinner with my daughter and son-in-law and their children Rob and Angie. Angie wanted to tell a riddle. She asked, "Why did Rudolph carry an umbrella?"I dutifully asked, "Why?"

"Because," Angie said, "he's a reindeer. Do you get it, Grandma? Do you get it?"

Our laughter was more in delight at her recent discovery of play on words than the joke itself. I love to be around children when this happens—when they discover something that has become commonplace to me and other adults. For a moment or two we are able to share in the wonder of their revelation; maybe we even recapture the feeling of when we were the discoverers.

Reading the Bible should be a time of discovery for us. Every time we read a passage or a verse, there should be a discovery—some new way that God speaks to us that we haven't seen or read or heard before. We should be finding out who God is. I wonder sometimes if God is looking over my shoulder as I read asking, "Do you get it, Ramona? Do you get it?"

♥ *Lord, as I read Your Word, I want to get it. I want to know You better and better.*

*. . . the older women likewise, that they be
reverent in behavior, not slanderers, not
given to much wine, teachers of good things.*
　　　　　　　　　　　—TITUS 2:3

*D*orothy had agreed to teach the two-year-old Sunday school class. She hadn't taught for several years but volunteered because she knew there was a need. The class turned out to be larger than expected, and each week Dorothy and her helpers welcomed at least sixteen two-year-olds!

I heard Dorothy explain to a parent, "Yes, there are a lot of children, but I love them. They remind me of my grandchildren; I have a lot of them, too!"

I'm thankful for Dorothy and other teachers like her who are willing to spend time telling Bible stories, preparing activities, singing, and loving children at church.

One day Dorothy told me, "We just couldn't seem to get to the lesson. We just got through the morning!" But they got through the morning with background music of Jesus' love, a simple verse showing God's care, hugs and smiles, and laughter.

Dorothy's two-year-olds know she loves them. She's laying a good foundation for an understanding of God's love for them, too. The lesson is always being taught.

♥ *In what ways am I teaching others about You, Lord?*

GRANDMA'S WALK THROUGH THE BIBLE

*Heaven and earth will pass away, but My
words will by no means pass away.*
—MATT. 24:35

Terrie says her Grandma Alice was everything you
ever imagined a grandmother to be. She remembers
vacations in Canada with her parents, aunts, uncles,
cousins, and grandparents. The men fished, the
women cooked, and the children set off firecrackers.
Firecrackers were illegal in their state, and the children knew their grandfather wouldn't try to take some
home because their luggage might be checked at the
border. But when they got home, they discovered that
Grandma had hidden some firecrackers in her suitcase!

Terrie also remembers Grandma Alice's funeral.
The pastor walked everyone through Grandma's Bible.
He read all the underlined verses and the things she
had written in the front and back of her Bible. Her children and grandchildren heard what was important to
her—the very same things they had seen in her life.
Perhaps that's what Jesus had in mind when He said
the words quoted above.

♥ *Dear God, I love Your Word. Show me ways to share
that love with my grandchildren.*

PRIVILEGED STORYTELLERS

For I gave them the words you gave me and
they accepted them. —JOHN 17:8 NIV

*W*es and his parents went to the airport to pick up
Grandma and Grandpa Brotzman. As they loaded the
luggage into the car, Wes asked, "Why is your suitcase
so heavy, Grandma?"

Grandma said, "Because my Bible is in there."

"What's in the Bible, Grandma?" Wes asked.

"Stories of Jesus," Grandma said.

Wes said, "Tell me a story about Jesus."

Grandma told Wes the story of Baby Jesus. When
she finished, Wes said, "Tell me another one,
Grandma."

So, all the way home in the car, Grandma told Wes
about Zaccheus, Jesus and the children, and the little
boy who gave his lunch to Jesus. She also promised to
tell him more every time they were together.

We are privileged to be the storytellers. Repeating to
children, grandchildren, perhaps even great-
grandchildren God's wonderful words of life in exciting
stories that can bring about life-changing results.

♥ *Lord, Your stories are wonderful to hear and tell.*

*I thank my God, making mention of you
always in my prayers.* —PHILEM. 4

*T*he Girl's Club spent the whole meeting talking about their grandmas. Annette talked about sleeping over at her grandma's, visiting the lake to feed the ducks, and watching television. Marilyn showed pictures of the day she and her grandmother went to an old-fashioned craft fair. It was the day Marilyn slipped and broke her arm; she remembers it was her grandmother who caught her as she fell.

Tracy's grandmother always takes her to the movies on her birthday. Then they visit the toy store and go out to eat. Karin helps her grandmother cook foods that are part of their heritage.

Joy spoke with concern about a grandma who is losing her sight. Katie brought a pillow that her grandma had made; Marcia showed a bookmark from her great-grandmother. Amy told about the lady who lived next door who was just like a grandma to her.

None of the memories were of world-shaking events; they were all simple expressions of the love and faith of their grandmothers. These memories of Grandma would stay with them and help shape the memories they make with their own grandchildren.

♥ *Help me remember that in simple expressions of love
and faith You are most evident.*

PICTURE OF CONTENTMENT

But godliness with contentment is great gain.
—1 TIM. 6:6

Carol came from a large family that didn't have much money. Her grandmother had a huge garden and fruit vines and trees, from which she sold the produce for a living. Carol and her siblings were told not to eat the raspberries, grapes, and cherries. But the children would sneak out and help themselves anyway. (Grandma always really knew what they were doing.)

Grandma always made them a big dinner of chicken and dumplings and fried apple pie. Carol can still picture her grandma and grandpa sitting in their rockers, side by side, reading their Bibles after that Sunday dinner. Even as a child, she felt their peace and contentment.

In *Thru the Bible with J. Vernon McGee,* Dr. McGee states, "It is important that the child of God find satisfaction with his position in life." When a grandmother and grandfather are able to portray that satisfaction for their grandchildren, they are a powerful witness for their Heavenly Father.

♥ *Dear God, You are the reason I am content. How can I best make it known to my grandchildren?*

COURAGEOUS GRANDMA

*See then that you walk circumspectly, not as
fools but as wise, redeeming the time,
because the days are evil.*

—EPH. 5:15–16

*W*hen I asked Libby to tell me something special
she does with her grandchildren, she said rather nonchalantly, "Oh, we just rollerblade together."

Do you know what rollerblading is? It's roller skating
on ice skates that have wheels. Libby is a courageous
grandma! This is nothing new to her grandchildren.
They watched Grandmother Libby courageously and
victoriously battle cancer that left her without a voice
for several months. Her testimony of faith in God during this siege helped strengthen and sustain her and
everyone in her family.

I wonder how aware we are of our grandchildren's
careful observation of us at crisis times. Consciously or
unconsciously they are checking us out to see if what
we say we believe is true.

The Bible is all about how we should live. Dozens of
verses give God's instruction to us about what our lives
should be like—not only because it's best for us, but
also because of its worthy witness to others.

♥ *O Lord, help me to let You use my crisis times as a
worthy witness especially to my grandchildren.*

*. . . therefore choose life, that both you and
your descendants may live.*
—DEUT. 30:19

*G*randma Orcutt lived with her son's family for a
while after her stroke. But she recovered so well that
the family felt she would be happier living in her own
apartment in a retirement community than sleeping on
the hide-a-bed in their den. Grandma wasn't so sure;
she didn't want to leave the security of the family.

The first night after moving her into a brand new facility, her son and granddaughter Beth went to visit her.
Beth said, "My dad gave Grandma a lecture. He told
her she could choose to sit in her room and be lonely
or she could find some new friends and be happy."

The next night when Beth and her dad stopped to
see Grandma, she had met some people and joined a
pinochle group. The group eventually grew into a major interest and filled her life with friendships. Moving
to the retirement community was the best thing for
Grandma. Her response to the lecture was a life lesson
about choices for Beth.

Like the Israelites who had to make a choice to obey
God and continue to receive His blessings, God lets us
decide whether to follow Him or go our own way. This
life or death decision is a daily choice as we face each
new situation in our lives.

♥ *Dear God, help me to continue choosing to follow
You for the rest of my life.*

You will show me the path of life;
In Your presence is fullness of joy;
At Your right hand are pleasures
forevermore. —PS. 16:11

I read recently about a grandmother whose baby grandson had AIDS. Her heart was broken when it was necessary to have him live with a foster family during the week. The grandmother picked him up and cared for him most weekends. Then, as the baby neared death he just stopped eating; this was very hard for her because she is a grandmother who loves to feed her grandchildren. During this unbearable time, she says it is only God who keeps her from ending her own life.

Unbearable pain is part of many lives. It devastates those who must watch helplessly as their grandchildren suffer from diseases or handicaps that have no cures. The natural response is anger and frustration toward God. But when we know God, when we become part of His family and belong to Him, He accepts and deflects the anger and frustration that threaten to overwhelm us to the point of harming ourselves with His comforting presence. When we seek His presence we find peace and hope.

♥ *It is only in Your presence, Lord, that I find what I really need.*

Your word I have hidden in my heart,
That I might not sin against You!
          —PS. 119:11

T love to give books for birthdays and Christmas, and giving Bibles to grandchildren is one of the best privileges of being a grandmother. As I was filling out the presentation pages in the Bibles I was giving my grandsons for Christmas, I remembered what my father had written in one of the first Bibles I received:

> *This Book will keep you from sin,*
> *or sin will keep you from this Book.*

I remember thinking at the time that it was nice and made sense, but it was no big deal (I was in junior high). Funny thing, though, the phrase often comes to mind as I review my life, and it has proved to be absolutely true. Regular Bible reading and absence of sin definitely correlate; the teachings of the Bible become "hidden in my heart" when I read and memorize them.

As I finished writing the presentation pages in my grandsons' Bibles, I closed with the little couplet. My prayer is that they will realize exactly how much sense it makes and that God's Word is the biggest and best deal there is.

♥ *Father, help me to realize and draw on the power of Your Word.*

That the generation to come might know them,
The children who would be born,
That they may arise and declare them to their children.
    —PS. 78:6

𝒟r. Robert Strom, chairman of the elementary education department of Arizona State University, teaches a course in grandparenting. An article about the course states that the experts agree grandparents always have been important and always will be, and that the ways grandparents contribute are unlimited. They include vocabulary development, self-confidence and, most important of all, by giving a child love that doesn't have to be earned.

Dr. Strom says grandparents "have to be able to relate on both their children's level and their grandchildren's level." It seems that grandchildren know more earlier and grow up faster today, and communication is a real challenge.

Think of all the ways God communicated with His people in the Bible, from meeting with them daily in the Garden of Eden to giving John the Revelation vision. Then, think of all the ways God continues to communicate with us. Ask yourself, "What can I learn about communicating with my grandchildren from the One who so clearly communicates His love for me?"

♥ *Father, when You are communicating, help me to listen and learn so I can communicate with my family.*

TRAINING GROUND

Train up a child in the way he should go,
And when he is old he will not depart from
it.
                                    —PROV. 22:6

*W*hen Pat was a young girl she visited her Grandma
Barnes in the hospital and read Bible stories to her.
Grandma always thought Pat would grow up to be a
missionary. Pat says, "She was pretty close. I grew up,
married a minister, and have spent 18 years working
with him in the church."

I suppose we all daydream a little about what our
grandchildren will do when they grow up. One of my
granddaughters wants to work with children, another
has an artistic bent, and a third would make a good ac-
tress. My grandsons' ambitions range from sports an-
nouncer, to scientist, to baseball player. Like every
other grandmother in the world, I want them to do what
they will enjoy.

I think God puts that desire in our hearts because
that's His desire, too. He has given each of our grandchildren gifts and talents to be developed and used all
of their lives. Their gifts and talents can be used in
such a wide variety of ways that they can't even begin
to be listed. Enjoyment and happiness come when they
see their gifts and talents in these jobs as the ministry
God has given them.

♥ *Dear God, I want to be part of helping my grand-*
children develop their gifts and talents.

*Beloved, now we are children of God; and it
has not yet been revealed what we shall be,
but we know that when He is revealed, we
shall be like Him, for we shall see Him as
He is.* —1 JOHN 3:2

*M*y granddaughter Angie was spending the weekend. As she was putting on her dress for church, I
commented that her mother had one like it when she
was a little girl. I told Angie that I might even have a
picture of her mother in the dress. Angie was eager to
see the picture, so I promised we would get out the picture albums after church and lunch.

That afternoon we spent a long time looking through
the picture albums that showed her mother from an in-
fant to adult. All the time we looked, I could almost
hear Angie's mind processing what she was learning—
that we were all babies once, that her mother has sisters and a brother just as she has a brother, that they
all went to school and grew just as she is growing.

Picture albums help children make connections.
They often explain the "what happens next" of life better than words can. They help introduce children to
family members they never knew. There are also a
wealth of family stories that pictures bring to mind!
Looking through family picture albums should be a
regular habit with grandchildren.

♥ *Father, the family is a way You picture Your relationship to us. I'm glad I'm in Your family.*

WRITTEN HEIRLOOM

*And these things we write to you that your
joy may be full.*   **—1 JOHN 1:4**

*W*hen Lissa was eight, Grandma Ferrell gave her a
book called *Grandmother Remembers*. The cover of the
book calls it "A Written Heirloom for My Grandchild."
Inside, each page is a treasure of memories in words
and pictures. It includes a family tree, remembrances,
and family stories. It also includes a letter to Lissa,
which gives advice, talks about values, and describes
feelings and emotions involved in being a family.

When we make a written record of our lives, with
our feelings, values, and advice for our grandchildren,
we are truly following a model that God has given us in
the Bible. When we become members of God's family,
the Bible becomes a treasure to us as we read it to
learn more about who God is, what He has done, and
what He wants us to do. The Bible is God's story to
generations of His children.

♥ *Dear God, thank You for telling me Your story so that
I can know You better.*

*And those who know Your name will put
their trust in You;
For You, LORD, have not forsaken those who
seek You.*
—PS. 9:10

*G*randma Bloomfield worked in the church's preschool as part-time bookkeeper. One of her grandchildren, Kerri, attended the school. Each day Kerri came in to visit her grandma when her mother picked her up to go home. After kisses and hugs, Kerri would open Grandma's desk drawer to find a treat—cookie, candy, gum, or a small toy. There was always something there.

Grandmas usually can be counted on to do the little things that make their grandchildren happy. One reason is that making grandchildren happy makes us happy (and we love all those hugs and kisses). When our grandchildren can count on us, we are helping them learn about trust. It is from these first little steps of trusting that children can move to the bigger and more important steps of trust that can lead them to place their faith in Jesus Christ as Savior.

God can use a grandma who tries hard to show her grandchildren an example of an all-mighty God who can be absolutely counted on!

♥ *Father, thank You that I can count on You—no matter what!*

To everything there is a season,
A time for every purpose under heaven.
—ECCL. 3:1

I have a "holiday policy" to propose to all grand-mothers: When your sons and daughters grow up, marry, and have your grandchildren, give them the freedom to stay home on Christmas. You go to visit them (if you are able) so that they can begin making their own traditions. (Before we go any further, I must tell you that this proposal receives almost a standing ovation in every young women's workshop or seminar where I speak—they all want me to tell their mothers about it!)

Why do I propose this idea? Because I remember when I was a young mother and how difficult it was to separate the children from the toys on Christmas morning and get everyone ready and in the car to go to Grandma's. Trips out of town at Christmas with children were a nightmare. Also, I really do believe young families need to begin making traditions of their own.

As we grow older, we must be willing to let the things that need to change, change. While our role in the family structure is still vitally important, it needs redefining. God's Word speaks about change and often equates it with growth.

♥ *Help me to know if my role in the family needs redefining, Lord.*

GOD'S NEARNESS

Draw near to God and He will draw near to you.
                                     —JAMES 4:8a

*T*hree-year-old Mike was visiting his grandmother. She was washing dishes and Mike had to go to the bathroom. Grandma lived in the country, and the bathroom was an outhouse across the backyard. She told Mike to go ahead and she would be right there in a minute or two. Mike took a few steps outside and came back, saying it was dark and he didn't want to go alone.

Grandma said, "You won't be alone. God will be with you."

Mike answered, "If God is with me, why won't He say anything?"

Indeed, there are times when we have all asked Mike's question—especially when we have felt alone and scared and wanted to know by the sound of His voice that God is with us. But we can know His presence. We are told that fact and faith equal feeling. It is a fact that God is real, and His Word tells us He is near to all who call on Him. If we have faith in those two facts, we feel God's presence. And sometimes, when our minds are very, very still as we think about God we can almost catch the timbre of His voice.

♥ *Dear God, thank You for the comfort of Your presence.*

Therefore be followers of God as dear children.
—EPH. 5:1

*W*hen Jen was about two years old she received a toy piano for Christmas. Her grandmother recalls that she quickly learned to play "Jesus Loves Me" with one finger. She would play the tune for a little bit and then stop and say, "Now everybody. Everybody sing." Later, they learned that Jen was imitating her Sunday school teacher, who urged her class during music time, "Now everybody, everybody sing."

Children are great imitators. The younger they are the more obvious and often humorous the imitations. As they grow older, they become more subtle and serious. Our challenge is to make sure what we show them is worthy of imitation.

The Bible tells us to be imitators of God. We are told one characteristic we should imitate is love. God's love is the most admirable of God's attributes because it is so all-encompassing. First Corinthians 13:13 reminds us that faith, hope, and love are all excellent, but love is the greatest of all three.

♥ *The Bible says, "God is love." I want to be like You.*

A GOOD NAME

*A good name is to be chosen rather than
    great riches,
Loving favor rather than silver and gold.*
    —PROV. 22:1

$\mathcal{T}$he names for grandma around the world are varied.

Afrikaans: Ouma	*Hebrew: Savta*
Arabic: Sitt	*Hungarian: Nagyanana*
Bulgarian: Baba	*Irish: Mama, Scanmhathair*
Chinese: Zu-ma	*Italian: Nonna*
Danish: Oma	*Japanese: Oba-San*
English: Grandma	*Korean: Hal Mo-ni*
Norwegian: Farmor	*Polish: Babcia*

If we asked the children what they call their grandmas, there'd be a whole new list because children take the name of Grandma and give it a unique twist that has a special meaning just for them.

When the Bible talks about having a good name it means having a good character and reputation. When we say the names of people we know, we think about what they are like. The importance God places on a good name is clear: No matter how it is said, *Grandma* needs to be a good name.

♥ *I like the name of Grandma. I want it to be a good name for me.*

THE BEST GIFT

. . . You shall love the LORD your God with all your heart, with all your soul, and with all your mind.   **—MATT. 22:37**

*B*rian and Alex and their parents met me at the airport. They could hardly wait for me to get to their house; they had a surprise waiting for me. As the car pulled into the driveway and we got out, the boys raced to the front door and opened it with a flourish. A huge computer banner was strung across the entry way wall: WELCOME GRANDMA!

It was truly a spectacular surprise that spoke of hours of painstaking decorating and coloring. The boys assured me it was all their idea and work because they were so happy I was coming for a visit. As we took it down and folded it so I could take it home, I considered hanging it in my office or home to remind me of their love and joy.

Ask any grandmother and she'll tell you about some simple item a grandchild made that means more to her than the most expensive gift she's ever received. This helps us understand a little bit about how God feels about what we give Him. The God of all doesn't need or want anything we can buy. God longs and desires only what we can freely give—our love.

♥ *God, I want my life to be a banner that welcomes You because I love You so much.*

Who gives food to all flesh,
For His mercy endures forever.
—PS. 136:25

*M*any grandmothers are known for their good cooking, or at the very least are remembered for always serving food to their grandchildren. In many families, recipes handed down from generation to generation are known as Grandma's Overnight Bread or Grandma Smith's Sugar Cookies. In other families, inheriting Grandma's cookbook is a great honor.

Food is one of the basic necessities of life. Making and serving it is often thought of as an act of love and care. The verse above is from a psalm that may have been a responsive reading in Bible times. The repetition of the phrase "For His mercy endures forever" helped the people understand the lesson. We can know that God will never run out of love because His lovingkindness comes from a bottomless source.

♥ *I praise You, God, for Your lovingkindness in all areas of my life.*

CONFESSION

Let the words of my mouth and the meditation
of my heart
Be acceptable in Your sight . . .

—PS. 19:14

I admire the way my children and their spouses are bringing up my grandchildren. For one thing, the fathers are much more involved from birth now than when I was raising children. And I feel today's mothers are more relaxed and able to give children more freedom in some areas than I did.

One morning while visiting my grandsons Brian and Alex (they were eight and ten years old), I watched as they prepared their own breakfast. They quite ably assembled and cooked bacon, scrambled eggs, and made toast while their mother and I drank coffee and read the morning paper. After they ate, they cleaned up. The fact that the preparation was messy and the clean-up less than absolutely spotless didn't bother my daughter-in-law at all. I silently applauded her. Her ability to let them learn by doing was much more important than an immaculate kitchen.

The things we say and do have a long life. God cautions us to be careful both in our actions and in our conversation. We can be sure that when these are acceptable to Him they will be acceptable to everyone else.

♥ *Place Your hand gently over my mouth when I speak unwisely, Lord.*

May 1 _____

TOTALLY COOL GRANDMA

Even to your old age, I am He,
And even to gray hairs I will carry you!
—ISA. 46:4

*L*ydia, a teenager, says her Grandma Veldt is "totally cool and treats me like the age I am." She said, "I like to talk with her. She talks to me about my boyfriend and asks me how school is going. She doesn't talk down to me."

When I asked her if her grandmother had given her any good advice, her face lit up and she told how her grandma had taught her how to walk like a model. Grandmother had watched a television show where models demonstrated how to walk tall and straight, and then she and her granddaughter practiced together.

The key phrases here are "treats me like the age I am" and "doesn't talk down to me." We grandmothers do sometimes forget that our grandchildren grow up. We may unconsciously desire to keep them young, maybe so that it will seem that we do not age. But if we want our grandchildren to talk with us and enjoy our company, it's important to remember Lydia's words.

The path that leads to talking with grandchildren about things spiritual begins with a sincere interest in who they are and what interests them.

♥ *God, help me to know my grandchildren as individuals just as You know me as an individual.*

GRANDMA KNOWLEDGE

When wisdom enters your heart,
And knowledge is pleasant to your soul,
Discretion will preserve you.
                                    —PROV. 2:10–11

*W*hile Grandpa drove on the long trip, Grandma entertained Jenny with sayings and songs. After some time, Jenny said, "You sure know a lot of those things, don't you, Grandma?"

Grandmas have a wealth of material to use in entertaining grandchildren in cars, while baby-sitting, in hospitals and doctors' offices, and in sick rooms. We draw on what our mothers and grandmothers taught us, what we learned while raising our own children, and on our creativity. And what we don't have in our minds we can supplement with books and games that we have been collecting for years. There is no grandmothers' manual; the knowledge is just there when we need it, as is the ability to produce even more as necessary.

I believe that God equips grandmothers to be able to do this. The Bible tells us we are created in His image. I take that to include the marvelous capacity of the wonderful minds He gives us. Minds that always have room to learn more—especially about Him.

♥ *Thank You for the ability to learn. Help me never to stop.*

LIFETIME POSITION

Let my teaching drop as the rain,
My speech distill as the dew,
As raindrops on the tender herb,
And as showers on the grass.
For I proclaim the name of the LORD.
—DEUT. 32:2–3

*D*anielle's grandparents had moved to Florida and Danielle, a preschooler, was visiting them for the first time. Danielle watched intently as her grandmother used a hand juicer to squeeze oranges for fresh orange juice. After several moments, Danielle asked, "Wouldn't it be easier to just get it out of a can?"

This is a good illustration of one of the purposes of grandmothers. As technology advances, we are the preservers of other ways of doing things. Grandchildren need some knowledge of "old-fashioned ways," and who better to give it to them than grandmothers? This is good to remember as we spend time with our grandchildren and they have the opportunity to observe just how we do the commonplace things of life.

All grandmothers are teachers. We became teachers with our children and continue to the end of our days. There is no such thing as a grandmother emeritus. This is a lifetime position. And part of the job description is to introduce them to the Person who makes whatever we do possible.

♥ *Teach me, Lord, so that I may teach.*

GOD'S IDEAL WOMAN

She also rises while it is yet night,
And provides food for her household.
                                    —PROV. 31:15

*M*y dentist's grandmother came from another country and didn't speak English very well. When his family visited her, she got up early and walked several blocks to buy crullers (donuts) for breakfast. He remembers her giving them to him saying, "Eat, boy, eat."

John's grandma always had a big crockery bowl full of huge sugar cookies. Bob remembers his grandma working hard on the farm—always cooking and canning.

It's interesting how many times our memories of Grandma are tied to food. These days memories may not be of Grandma cooking; they may instead be of Grandma taking grandchildren out to eat. Whichever way, it's not bad to be linked to providing one of life's basic needs. Grandmothers know that food is necessary for health and growth and a good way to help people feel loved, comforted, and cared about.

It is no surprise that being a provider of food is one of the characteristics that God lists for the ideal woman. While it would be impossible to imitate the woman described in Proverbs 31 in every detail, she is an inspiration to us.

♥ *Along with the food I provide grandchildren, help*
  them to feel generous helpings of Your love and care.

GOD'S PERFECT PLAN

For by one offering He has perfected forever those who are being sanctified.
—HEB. 10:14

A preschooler was on his way to church with his grandmother. As they walked along, Grandma pointed out all the things God made—the trees, flowers, birds. The little boy listened intently, then asked, "But Grandma, who made the weeds?"

It's easy to point out and talk about the things God made and gives us that we like. Things such as weeds, poisonous bugs, and violent weather are harder to deal with. It's possible that we are still struggling with the answer ourselves.

The fact is God does allow weeds and bugs and violent weather to be a part of our world. It wasn't part of His original plan, but when those first people, who had everything they needed, accepted the temptation to disobey God, they opened the door to imperfection—theirs, ours, and the world's.

Ever since then God has been giving people the opportunity to live with Him in His perfect home. God even sacrificed His perfect Son, Jesus, to make it possible for us. He's the only way that we can become perfect, too.

♥ *Help me look beyond the weeds to my home with You.*

If we confess our sins, He is faithful and just to forgive us our sins and to cleanse us from all unrighteousness. —1 JOHN 1:9

Crystalynn and Tim and their parents were visiting Grandma's house. When it was time for eighteen-month-old Crystalynn to take a nap, they put her in Grandma's bedroom. All was quiet for more than an hour. Then big brother Tim, who was four, ran into the kitchen shouting, "Emergency! Emergency! I've just seen her face, and Crystalynn is in deep trouble!"

Everyone rushed to the bedroom, where Crystalynn had gotten into Grandma's purse and discovered lipstick. It was all over her face, her clothes, and the carpet. Before cleaning up, someone ran for the camera to get a picture to show Crystalynn when she got older.

The fact that the emergency was funny rather than tragic removed Crystalynn from the deep trouble her brother had predicted. Some things are easy to forgive.

The freedom we have as adults can sometimes plunge us into deep trouble. When we realize it, or have a good friend to call out "Emergency" and warn us, we can turn to God and ask Him to forgive us. He forgives us all things.

♥ *God, thank You for the assurance of Your forgiveness when I am in trouble of my own making.*

*Go therefore and make disciples of all the
nations. . . .*   —MATT. 28:19

$\mathcal{A}$ grandmother told me about her grandson
Brandon, who was born with a heart defect. When he
was about eight months old his diet was restricted and
he could only eat a little at a time. When he was fed
something he didn't like, he would grunt and eat it; but
when he was given something he liked, he would just
eat it.

Isn't it fascinating that even at such an early age children can communicate with us? It should encourage
us to pay attention to the kind of communicating we are
doing with them—beginning the day they are born.

Telling babies about our love and God's love in song,
words, and prayers can and should begin from the very
first moment we hold them in our arms. God means for
us to be His witnesses to everyone. That surely includes our own grandchildren. We usually have more
opportunities to talk and sing about God when they are
babies than we will have at any other time in their lives.
We need to take advantage of it.

♥ *Thank You for every opportunity I have to tell my
grandchildren about You.*

Your kingdom is an everlasting kingdom,
And Your dominion endures throughout all
generations.

—PS. 145:13

*T*he following is an excerpt of a letter I received from friends who are missionaries:

Joy, sorrow, forgiveness and new life is the summary of our daughter's year. With joy she experienced the completion of her college career. Ahead she faced a different world than she or the family had anticipated when she came to us and told us that she was pregnant. At this time we do not know all that God has ahead, nor do we have all of the answers, but we do covet your continued prayers for all of us. Our grandson was born on September 29 and has in a short space of time brought more love and joy to our whole family.

The encouragement we can share is that God is truly faithful and His love is truly enduring. He is able to take every situation and teach us more about His love and forgiveness.

God has blessed this grandson with grandparents who know God and His life-giving message to all who believe in Him.

♥ *Father, Your love is too wonderful not to tell.*

Now also when I am old and grayheaded,
O God, do not forsake me,
Until I declare Your strength to this
generation. . . .

—PS. 71:18

*G*reat-grandma lived with Grandma when Brandon
was little. Great-grandma had become childlike, and
one day she and Brandon engaged in a tussle over the
broom that was on the patio. They both wanted to use
it to sweep. Great-grandma won because she was bigger, but as she swept in one direction, Brandon came
along behind her and threw dirt to cover where she had
just swept. She would turn around and sweep again,
while he would throw dirt where she had just been.
They kept it up for a long time; Grandmother watched
but didn't stop them. It had become a game for
Brandon, and perhaps for Great-grandma, too.

Generations aren't together as much as they once
were. We seem to have lost something there with all our
"progress."

Have you ever wondered what God thinks of our
homes for the elderly? Do you think they are what He
had in mind when he designed the family structure? I
know that in many situations they are the only answer
and thank God for the dedicated people who minister
in them. And we can be thankful for the assurance of
His presence no matter what our age or where we live.

♥ *Lord, as I grow older help me to praise You even*
more.

RETIREMENT

And let the beauty of the LORD our God be
upon us,
And establish the work of our hands for us.
—PS. 90:17

*R*etirement is not in my vocabulary. That doesn't mean I intend to stay in the job I am presently in until I die (unless God has that in mind in the near future). I do hope that my next job will allow me a little more freedom and flexibility so I can try some different kind of work I'm interested in.

Larry Burkett, author and speaker on Christian finances, states that God never meant for the Christian to stop working. He feels that if we don't need to work for financial reasons, we should work as volunteers.

I agree with Mr. Burkett, and the statistics bear witness to the fact that those who continue to keep working at something are happier, more content, and healthier, and live longer than those who retire to play and do nothing.

There's always a place for us in doing God's work. It has no age restrictions.

♥ *May the work I do now and later honor You.*

*For whatever things were written before
were written for our learning, that
we . . . might have hope.* —ROM. 15:4

The family camping trip included everyone from preschool-age Bryan through two great-grandmas. One afternoon Bryan climbed a steep hill with the big boys. Grandma and the great-grandmas sat at the bottom of the hill to watch. At the top of the hill, the big boys disappeared and Bryan didn't quite know how to get back down the hill. He yelled out, "Grandma, come and help me. I can't get down!"

The grandmas looked at each other. Then Grandma called out encouragement, "You can do it, Bryan." Eventually, with her encouragement, Bryan was able to scoot on his bottom down the hill.

Grandmas are good encouragers. They may have given up climbing hills, ice skating, playing basketball, and horseback riding, but they are more than willing to stand by and give encouragement to grandchildren who do all those things and more.

God calls us to a ministry of encouragement. Some are better at it than others, but with practice we can all do better. Think about all the ways God encourages you. How might you duplicate that encouragement in the lives of your grandchildren?

♥ *Your Word encourages me, God. Help me use Your
words along with my own to be an encourager.*

For the LORD Most High is awesome;
He is a great King over all the earth.
—PS. 47:2

*T*he beautiful children's picture book *When Grandma Came* by Jill Paton Walsh and Sophy Williams tells the story of a grandmother who travels to see the wonders of the world and returns to assure her beloved granddaughter that she is the greatest wonder of all.

Sandy's grandma was like that. "Grandma traveled a lot and brought us neat things—like grass skirts from Hawaii." When Grandma went to Italy, all the grandchildren went to Chicago's O'Hare airport to give her a surprise send-off.

Many grandmas do get around more these days. But the pull to return is always there and very strong. God gives us that bond between young and old. He helps us continue to make it stronger with each passing year and experience we share. The wisdom we gain with God's help is for sharing, too. How it must delight God when we share with the grandchildren, who are more wonderful than anything else, the knowledge that He is even greater than the greatest wonder of all!

♥ *Lord, I will tell of Your wonder and greatness to my grandchildren.*

*And above all things have fervent love for
one another, for "love will cover a multitude
of sins."*
　　　　　　　　—1 PETER 4:8

*D*ana spent much of her growing up time with her
Grandma Ward, who told her stories about Grandpa,
who died before Dana could meet him, and taught her
German words and phrases and how to cook. Dana especially remembers her grandma saying, "Never forget German" and "Always have your tools ready when
you cook." Grandma Ward called Dana "Heartzkind,"
which means child of the heart.

Our grandchildren are children of our hearts. We
love them simply because of who they are—from the
moment we lay eyes on them. Our blindingly strong
love for our grandchildren sometimes causes their parents to make amusing comparisons that begin, "How
come you never let me do that?"

I like to think that God helps grandmas to have a
slightly different view of discipline; it doesn't interfere
with parental rules but has layers and layers of love and
forgiveness learned from the years of our relationship
with Him. There's also the natural aging God takes us
through. We now see some things aren't as worthy of
discipline as we once thought they were. It's amazing
the things that love covers!

♥ *Father, I'm glad I'm a child of Your heart.*

PRIORITY ONE

But as for me, I trust in You, O LORD;
I say, "You are my God."
My times are in Your hand. . . .
—PS. 31:14–15

A letter to Dear Abby from a grandmother told the gifts she would like to receive for Christmas. The list included time, postage stamps, a writing tablet with lines, plain envelopes, a ballpoint pen that works, long-distance telephone coupons to make calls to friends, payment of one month's heating bill, small home repairs, and visits.

There may be some things we can think of to add to the list. In fact, it made me wonder if maybe we should make a list for Santa to circulate among the family.

Did you notice that the list began and ended with a request for spending time with her? That is the most precious commodity.

I believe God wants us all to take a look periodically at how we spend our time. God is our first priority. When we recognize this and put God first, the other priorities of family, work, and pleasure seem to fall into line so that there is time for what is important in our lives.

♥ *Dear God, You are the most important person in my life. Help me to keep You in first place.*

Trust in the LORD with all your heart,
And lean not on your own understanding;
In all your ways acknowledge Him,
And He shall direct your paths.
—PROV. 3:5–6

*W*hen friends of mine learned their daughter-in-law had miscarried their first grandchild, they were grief-stricken. Everyone in this family had a strong faith, faith which gave them peace and comfort to believe in God's permissive will that allows sad and heart-breaking things to happen.

Friends of the young couple, who were not Christians, found it hard to understand the family's peace and calm during this time. Hardest for them to accept was how it could possibly be God's will that a child die.

Some theologians say that if we were to understand all of God's purposes, we would not need Him. This family knew they needed God and trusted Him completely. And even in their deep sorrowing, they trusted that their faith in God would help bring these non-Christian friends to Jesus. They felt that their unborn child had a worthy purpose.

♥ *The old hymn says, "Trusting Jesus—that is all."*
Keep me trusting You, Lord.

LOVE STORIES

*And now, O Lord GOD, You are God, and
Your words are true, and You have promised
this goodness to Your servant.*
                                   —2 SAM. 7:28

Grandchildren like to hear about how we met their grandfathers. Grandma Ferrell wrote about it to her granddaughter Lissa.

> I met your grandfather when I was twelve. It was at church. He had his arm around a girl and I tied a piece of string around his suit coat cuff button and to a nail on the bottom of the pew. Then I yanked his button off! Your grandfather liked me because I was pretty and good. He told me when I was twelve that he was going to marry me when I grew up and he did—five years later!

Our personal stories of love interests that didn't blossom and the one that did sometimes help grandchildren understand their relationships. Stories about people and their lives are one of the best ways to learn things. It's no wonder the Bible is always on the best-seller list.

♥ *Dear God, Your stories help me understand my story.*

*Continue earnestly in prayer, being vigilant
in it with thanksgiving.*   —COL. 4:2

*I*n her book *What Happens When We Pray for Our
Families,* Evelyn Christenson writes:

> I have grandchildren, but God does not. He only
> has children. We only can become the children—sons
> and daughters—of God, not His grandchildren. My
> prayers for the ultimate salvation of my grandbabies
> started before they were born, and mingled together
> with their own parents' prayer. So prayers for these
> precious little ones entrusted by God into my chil-
> dren's families multiplied and multiplied until one by
> one they have received Jesus.

I hope the above encouraged and inspired you to
begin praying or keep on praying for your grandchildren as much as it did me. One grandma I know
even asks her grandchildren on a regular basis what
they would like her to pray about for them. Then she
checks back to see how things are going.

God instructs us to pray for ourselves and for others.

♥ *God, to know that You hear my prayers is wonderful,
that You should answer them is astounding!*

*Remember those who rule over you, who
have spoken the word of God to you, whose
faith follow, considering the outcome of their
conduct.*
                                        —HEB. 13:7

$\mathcal{T}$he lead sentence in a travel magazine reads,
"More grandparents than ever are gathering their
grandchildren for a vacation together." There are even
travel agencies that specialize in grandparent tours.
We've come a long way from spending the week with
Grandma at her house.

The consensus is that intergenerational travel is
good for everybody. One grandmother told how the
grandchildren cheered as they drove off on vacation.
At the same time, she saw in the rearview mirror her
daughter and son-in-law dancing a jig as they waved
them off.

Traveling with grandparents gives grandchildren the
opportunity to see the world with people who want to
share the world with them and who will include daily
hands-on demonstrations of living faith. It also gives
grandparents the opportunity to pass on the faith that
was modeled for them in their lives. There's no better
way to invest your time and life.

♥ *Dear God, thank You for every opportunity You give
me to share my faith with my grandchildren.*

A wise man will hear and increase learning,
And a wise man of understanding will
attain wise counsel.
— PROV. 1:5

*V*icki is raising her grandchildren. When her daughter's marriage began its slow descent to dissolution and she needed to go to work, Grandma Vicki knew what was important for her to do. She offered to share her home with her daughter and grandchildren so that she could be the primary caregiver of her grandchildren.

The reasons she gives for this decision are worth noting. She felt her grandchildren needed a good family structure in which the values she and her husband feel are important would be taught. Vicki feels strongly that this would not happen in a day care situation or in someone else's home.

There was no other possible decision for Grandma Vicki, so she traded her empty-nest freedom and returned to full-time motherhood. Her daughter lost the independence of her own home and shares her position of mother with Grandma. For them what's best for the children matters most.

God expects us to choose what is best in every situation in our life. The decisions and choices you make may not be the ones someone else makes. That's all right when you are letting God help you make the right ones for you.

♥ *Lord, I want You to be part of every decision I make.*

ANGER REMEDY

*"Be angry, and do not sin": do not let the
sun go down on your wrath.*
                                        —EPH. 4:26

*R*ob and Angie were staying with me for the weekend. When they are at my house, Rob usually takes
over the loft for watching sports on TV, reading, and
playing games. One day I was fixing lunch and called
to Rob to ask if he would come down to eat with us or
wanted to eat upstairs on a tray.

Rob answered, "I'd like to eat up here if it doesn't
make you mad."

Before I could answer, Angie told him, "She doesn't
get mad at us; she loves us."

Of course, grandmothers do get angry at their
grandchildren, though probably not as often as their
parents or others do.

The Bible tells us, in the verses surrounding and including the one above, how to handle our anger so that
we don't hurt people or our relationships with them or
keep it all inside, hurting ourselves. Paul advises us to
take care of our anger right away to keep Satan from
having the chance to use it and cause problems. Love
is always a good substitute for anger.

♥ *Help me to turn my anger to love that seeks to work
things out.*

*And this is the promise that He has
promised us—eternal life.*

—1 JOHN 2:25

A grandmother I met in the beauty shop was showing pictures of a new grandchild. I asked what she liked most about being a grandmother.

She said, "I think it's being so much wiser about children now. I don't think I was any great shakes as a mother. I made a lot of mistakes. I don't feel that my grandchildren were dumped on me. I really enjoy them and look forward to being a part of their lives. They won't have to wait until they're grown to learn about Jesus, like I did. He's going to be introduced to them early in life. I want them to know how much He loves them so they will want to be part of God's family."

God's design for families includes the extended family and all that they bring to enhance family life. We each have a God-given privilege and challenge to influence the lives of grandchildren in positive ways. His plan gives us the opportunity of being a family together forever with Him.

♥ *I accept the challenge, Lord. The privilege is worth it.*

*Therefore, as the elect of God, holy and
beloved, put on tender mercies, kindness,
humbleness of mind, meekness,
longsuffering.*

—COL. 3:12

*O*ne afternoon while I working on this book, my grandson Rob was asking questions about the book and reading over my shoulder. I asked him if he wanted to read what I had written about him. When he finished, he asked, "Could I make a suggestion, Grandma?"

I nodded.

"Maybe it would be better if you didn't keep identifying me as Grandson Rob or my mom as Daughter Bev. It wouldn't be so awkward to read."

I told him why I thought it was necessary to do it that way, and he made a suggestion for how he might do it. We agreed that the editor would make the final decision. It was a good discussion. What pleased me most was that he felt free to offer his advice and ideas.

Listening to and talking with grandchildren is a big part of being a grandmother. It isn't a skill that comes quickly; it takes years of in-service training that emphasizes time and patience. Our Heavenly Father is a good model for us. The Bible tells us He is always there for us. His patience is unfathomable.

♥ *Dear God, help me to learn from You how to be the best grandmother I can be.*

*Out of the mouth of babes and nursing
   infants
You have ordained strength . . .*
                              — PS. 8:2

A moving illustration from *The Ministry of the
Child* by Dennis C. Benson and Stan J. Stewart tells the
story of a preschooler who stopped in front of a man
who was moaning softly while waiting in a doctor's office. The illustration says:

> The waiting room becomes silent. All eyes focus on
> this child-adult encounter. What will the child do to
> this man who should be left alone? She toddles to his
> knees. Her hand reaches out to his face, and she
> wipes the tears from his cheeks.
>
> "All right, all right, all right," she says gently. The
> man opens his eyes. The shape of his mouth changes
> slowly. He gazes as the littlest one in the room contin-
> ues to roughly wipe his face. He gently catches her
> hand between his wrinkled fingers and kisses it.

As grandmothers we often minister to our grandchildren. They can also minister to us, too, because of
their wonderful ability to trust God so completely.

♥ *Dear God, I need to be more childlike in my relationship to You.*

Let us hold fast the confession of our hope without wavering, for He who promised is faithful.
—HEB. 10:23

*M*any grandmothers are raising grandchildren, some by choice and some by accident. Census Bureaus statistics tell us that 3.2 million children live with a grandparent.

One grandmother told me that her daughter died of cancer and left an eight-year-old daughter. The father disappeared. The grandmother needed to make a major adjustment in her life so that she could raise her grandchild.

Our churches must become aware of their multigenerational families and offer help for grandparents, including classes to help grandparents understand how their grandchildren's culture is different from when they were raising their children.

The best thing multigenerational grandmothers have going for them is that they are in a great partnership with God. He loves their grandchildren even more than they do and is interested in their growth and development right along with them. God's promise to supply what we need in every circumstance is an ironclad guarantee for all of our lives.

♥ *Thank You, God, for the promise of Your supply for my need.*

COMPLETE LOVE

No one has seen God at any time. If we love one another, God abides in us, and His love has been perfected in us.

—1 JOHN 4:12

*M*arilyn has had what she calls the biggest honor of being a grandma—that of leading four of her grandchildren to know Jesus as Savior. She always tries to include Jesus in terms of things that happen at school and with friends. She does wonder at times if she has done too much spiritual programming; she doesn't want to be pushy.

The results speak for themselves, though. Three of her grandchildren accepted Jesus as they sat on her lap and she prayed with them. The fourth was riding in the car with her and they were talking about heaven.

Marilyn said, "You can go to Heaven if you want to. When I stop the car, we can have a talk with Jesus about it." The little boy said it was what he wanted to do, and Gram and he prayed together as they sat in the car.

Telling grandchildren about Jesus is a priority on God's agenda for grandmothers. We are the ones who usually have known Him longer than others in the family. We can testify to the wonder of His grace, the strength of His power, and the peace of His presence. Our lives can be a picture of His love.

♥ *Dear God, what kind of a picture of You do I give my grandchildren?*

OOPS!

Confess your trespasses to one another, and pray for one another, that you may be healed. The effective, fervent prayer of a righteous man avails much.

—JAMES 5:16

*M*arilyn's teenage grandsons were getting ready to drive back home after visiting her. Marilyn prayed with them before they left, and during the prayer, asked God to help them give up smoking. Marilyn's prayer made the grandsons angry.

And after thinking about it, Marilyn decided she needed to write an apology to them. Here's an excerpt from her letter:

> I know I made a mistake asking God to help you stop smoking (in front of you). That was a prayer I should have kept between God and me. I'm sorry.
>
> Grandpa and I were both smokers when we were young, and we know quitting is hard, but we stopped when we realized it was an unhealthful habit. But that is a decision you have to make for yourself.

God told us what to do when we make mistakes and sin. When we follow it, sometimes amazing results are set into motion. At the very least our relationship is right with God again because we know we have His forgiveness.

♥ *Dear God, when I make a mistake, help me to put it right as soon as possible.*

> *. . . I praise You, Father, Lord of heaven*
> *and earth, that You have hidden these*
> *things from the wise and prudent and*
> *revealed them to babes. . . .*
> **—LUKE 10:21**

*W*hen Joyce's grandchildren come to visit her, their favorite thing to do is to walk the trail along the creek that starts in her backyard. During their hike, they pick the tiny strawberry-like thimble berries, see wild raspberries, find deer tracks, and look at the polliwogs in the creek. At one point the only way to get to the bottom of the hill is to slide; grandmother and grandchildren slide down it together.

Joyce uses this time to talk about the wonder of God's creation. She explains to the children as simply as possible how God makes plants, provides food and shelter for animals, and turns polliwogs into frogs.

Back at Grandma's house, the children request a story about Jesus. This thrills Grandmother Joyce because she and Grandpa are the children's only exposure to God.

Sometimes we worry about how to tell our grandchildren about God, especially when they aren't being taken to church or hearing about Him at home. God understands this. He wants our grandchildren to know Him, too.

♥ *Help me to recognize and take advantage of the natural ways that can lead to talking about You, God.*

PICTURES

*For now we see in a mirror, dimly, but then
face to face. Now I know in part, but then I
shall know just as I also am known.*
—1 COR. 13:12

One day Marilyn's grandson, Jay, laid down on the floor and used the dog as a pillow. It was a picture moment. On her way to grab a camera, Marilyn said, "Don't move, Jay. Grandma wants to take a picture."

But Jay, being two years old and not understanding what she was talking about, got up and toddled after her.

When he saw the camera in her hand, Jay ran back to the dog, and posed in the exact same place.

Every self-respecting grandmother has a camera and takes lots of pictures. Give a grandmother a picture of grandchildren for her birthday, Mother's Day, and Christmas, and you've made her day. Some walls in houses are held up by a gallery of grandchildren's pictures. I keep mine in my bedroom so they are the first faces I see when I wake up.

They start my day with a smile.

Pictures are almost like having the people we love with us in person. I suppose that's why even though we don't know what Jesus looks like, artists have always painted pictures of Him. We long to see the Person we love so much. One day we will!

♥ *The old hymn says, "Face to face in all His glory, I shall see Him by and by."*

CREATIVE PRAYING

Let my prayer be set before You as incense,
The lifting up of my hands as the evening
*   sacrifice.*
                                    —PS. 141:2

 $\mathcal{D}$ o you pray with your grandchildren? Prayer together can be a source of great joy for you and them. For all grandmothers, everywhere, here are some suggestions for praying creatively with your grandchildren:

1. Have a special indoor and outdoor praying place.

2. Sing prayers to well-known nursery rhymes and songs. For example, to the tune of "Happy Birthday," sing the following words:

    Dear God, we love You. (repeat)
    We love You and praise You.
    Dear God, we love You.

3. Begin a prayer sentence and have the child/children finish it. Example: Dear God, please help _____.

Use these ideas as "creativity starters" and add some of your own.

As our grandchildren join us in experiencing different ways to talk with God, they will begin developing a lifelong practice that will become as helpful and meaningful to them as anything else you could possibly teach them. It will please God too.

♥ *I want talking to You to be as interesting and as much fun as talking to my best friend, because that's who You are.*

HEAVENLY WISDOM

But the wisdom that is from above is first pure, then peaceable, gentle, willing to yield, full of mercy and good fruits, without partiality and without hypocrisy.
—JAMES 3:17

Grandma Bettie's face glowed when she spoke to me about her first grandchild, Amanda. Her eyes sparkled and sometimes had the hint of tears as she told me, "Everything she does intrigues and delights me. I enjoy being with her so much. We go shopping, dance, and play school. She means the world to me."

One of their favorite activities to do together is look through catalogs. As they look, Grandma explains whatever is pictured. Grandma explains about everything, including Santa, the Easter Bunny, and God.

The day Grandma Bettie's dog died led to questions about Heaven. She explained about that, too, and spoke with Amanda about her loving Heavenly Father.

The statistics tells us that preschoolers ask hundreds of questions every day. It's one of the ways God has given them to find out the things they need to know. It's also part of God's plan that grandmothers help to answer those questions. He is the One who gives grandmothers wisdom and understanding.

♥ *Dear God, thank You for the availability of Your wisdom.*

FIRST LOVE

We love Him because He first loved us.
—1 JOHN 4:19

*R*obbie met Grammy Bell when he was her paper boy. It didn't take him long to discover that she was a grand, neat lady he could talk to about anything. Robbie says, "For a kid who didn't see his grandparents very often, she was the most wonderful adopted grandmother you could have!" She took a special interest in him and through college wrote him letters of encouragement and friendship.

Grammy Bell had been a Sunday school teacher for fifty years and Sunday school superintendent for twenty-five years; she had also worked as a cook in a boy's reformatory. She loved kids and had a special rapport with boys. Once a boy in the reformatory waved a contraband knife at her. She calmly took the knife and showed him better uses for knives in the kitchen.

Grammy Bell impacted the lives of many young men—men who now are mechanics, businessmen, teachers, lawyers, and college presidents.

Love is the bottom line. God's Word tells us that it is because God loves us that we are able to love. When we give our love back to God, and it has first priority, it makes all the difference in the world.

♥ *Thanks for loving me first, God. Help me love You first, too.*

GOD'S TEACHING STAFF

Moreover, as for me, far be it from me that I should sin against the LORD in ceasing to pray for you; but I will teach you the good and the right way. —1 SAM. 12:23

*G*randmother Marilyn calls her older grandchildren "grandpersons" or "grand-guy" and "grand-gal." When her grand-gal Danielle, now ten and a half, was two years old, Grandma Marilyn told her, "Bye, Darlin'" as she was leaving their house.

After that, every time Danielle saw Grandma's picture, she pointed to it and said, "Darlin'."

Grandma says, "Even now, the cards she sends to me are addressed to Grandma Darlin'—and I love it!"

Marilyn notes that when grandchildren are young they seem to be such little blotters for information, soaking everything up and feeling triumphant when they can actually convey their new knowledge. How right she is! How careful we must be that it is what we want them to learn, and not things they will need to un-learn in later years.

God feels strongly about this, too. His warning to people who cause children to sin is frightening (see Matt. 18:6).

We are part of God's teaching staff entrusted with the precious lives of His children.

♥ *The old hymn says, "Teach me, Lord, that I may teach."*

For this is good and acceptable in the sight of God our Savior, who desires all men to be saved and to come to the knowledge of the truth.
　　　　　　　　　　　　　　—1 TIM. 2:3–4

*T*he night before Cassie's fifth birthday, she was told that it was her last night to be four, and that in the morning when she woke up she would be five.

Cassie said, "Is God going to come and turn my number in the middle of the night?"

Did you ever think about what a puzzling world this must be to young children? Words, concepts, and relationships are among the many things they must sort out as they grow and learn. Children learn early that grandmothers are good solvers of life's puzzles; they may not know all the answers, but they know a lot of them, and they know where to find answers they don't know.

God challenges us to be sure we are giving our grandchildren the answer to life's most important question—how they can be part of God's family forever. So as we help them put together the pieces of information for life, tell them about Jesus who is the only One who can make their life whole and complete.

♥ *Dear God, thank You for the best answer You gave us—Jesus!*

Rejoicing in hope, patient in tribulation,
continuing steadfastly in prayer.
—ROM. 12:12

*J*amie was doing a report for school and called to talk to me about when I had polio. I was nineteen and pregnant with Jamie's mother. I told her how I was put in isolation, given shots that stung for a long time, soaked in hot tubs of water up to my neck, had hot packs applied nightly, and slept in a bed outfitted with ropes and pulleys that I had to use for exercise.

The therapist had told me that I must exercise for ten minutes of every hour I was awake, and exercise past the point of crying for it to do any good. I did it—because I wanted to walk out of the hospital. I did walk out several months later, just before Jamie's mother was born.

I told Jamie the best part of the experience was knowing how many people were praying for me. One person called every night to ask how I was and to say prayer was being offered. I never found out who that person was.

God's plan might not have been for me to be so completely healed, but because people prayed, I was encouraged to exercise diligently, endure uncomfortable treatment calmly, and know that the outcome would be according to God's purpose.

♥ *Dear Lord, I don't need to know what You always have in mind, because I know and trust You.*

. . . Be swift to hear, slow to speak, slow to wrath; for the wrath of man does not produce the righteousness of God.
—JAMES 1:19–20

*O*ne afternoon my granddaughter Angie managed to spill sugar all over the pantry shelves and grape juice on a beige carpet—all within minutes. They were accidents, of course, and she apologized profusely. What was interesting was my reaction; I wasn't upset. We calmly cleaned up the spills and talked about being more careful.

I am ashamed to say my children remember my anger when they spilled things. A favorite family story is about a time when there was a guest for dinner. First, one glass of milk went over, then a second. Even with a guest present, as I was mopping up I said through tight lips, "The next person who spills leaves the table."

When the guest spilled his glass of water minutes later, all eyes fastened on my face. The guest stood and asked, "Where should I go?" We all laughed. I was never angry about accidental spills again.

We need to look to God and His Word for appropriate times and places for our anger. There is always forgiveness and the opportunity to make things right and be more careful the next time.

♥ *Father, thank You for Your constant forgiveness of my mistakes.*

For the word of God is living and powerful, and sharper than any two-edged sword, piercing even to the division of soul and spirit. . . .
—HEB. 4:12

*M*arlene and her family, including Grandma Lavina, were sitting around the dinner table one Sunday critiquing the morning church service. The choir, soloist, and pastor's sermon all received their share of critical comment.

Grandma Lavina sat listening, and finally said in her quiet, soft-spoken voice, "Well, I really think before you speak you should ask yourself three questions. Is this true? Is this kind? Is this necessary?"

Everyone was silent, and then admitted, "You're right, Grandma."

Marlene says that whenever Grandma reprimanded anyone, it was always in a gentle, loving way. But it got the point across. Those three questions were Grandma Lavina's philosophy of life.

Hurrah for Grandma Lavina! She was a shining student of God and His Word. She was quoting what the Bible tells us to do, and in the way God tells us to do it so that it teaches others. We can trust His Word to do its work when our delivery of it is wrapped in genuineness and love.

♥ *Dear God, Your words mean so much to me. Help me pass them on with love.*

*Simon Peter answered and said, "You are
the Christ, the Son of the living God."*
                                    —MATT. 16:16

$\mathcal{D}$etroit Lakes, Minnesota, is where I plan to take my
grandchildren for their next summer grandmother
week. It's a little resort town on a lake where I spent
some of my very young growing up years. An aunt and
cousins still live nearby. I have pleasant memories of
the small town, lazy summers, and maple-nut ice
cream.

The Minnesota trip will be the first "let's see where
Grandma lived" trip for me and my grandchildren. I'll
show them the house where we lived on the lake and
the school where I went to kindergarten. I'll introduce
them to some relatives they don't know they have,
teach them about lake swimming, and treat them to
maple-nut ice cream.

Family history was important in Bible times, too. Remember all those long genealogies? A person's family
line showed whether the person was one of God's chosen people. Jesus' genealogy in Matthew was the best
way for Matthew to show the Jewish people that Jesus
was the Messiah. The carefully preserved ancestry
documented that He was a descendant of Abraham
and David, which fulfilled the Old Testament prophecies about the Messiah.

♥ *Jesus, God's Word about who You are is good enough
for me.*

UNCHANGING GOD

For I am the LORD, I do not change;
Therefore you are not consumed, O sons of
Jacob.
                                        —MAL. 3:6

A grandmother sitting next to me at a college faculty dinner told how she had saved her old typewriter for her grandchildren; she was a bit chagrined when they weren't the least bit interested in it. The reason? They all had computers, and the typewriter wasn't even old enough to be considered an interesting antique. It was just out of date.

I love my computer, but I don't understand it. And I'm amazed at the ease with which my grandchildren, even the very youngest, are able to use one.

Did my grandparents feel this way about automobiles, automatic washers, television, and microwaves? Probably. Change has been constant in the world since the beginning of time. We need to accept and be thankful for these changes and the good things they do for us.

We can also be thankful that we can know and trust God who will never change. His constant, unchanging love and forgiveness are really what makes life the very best it can possibly be.

♥ *I praise You, God, because You are always the same.*

JUST DO IT!

And be kind to one another, tenderhearted,
forgiving one another, just as God in Christ
also forgave you.   —EPH. 4:32

I am always sad when I hear or read about grandmothers who are involved in disputes that lead to law-
suits over their rights to see grandchildren. Usually
they are family fights that have escalated; misunder-
standings that have gotten out of hand.

Saddest of all is when the people involved are Christians. The very people who have experienced the
depth and fullness of Christ's love and forgiveness for
their mistakes and sins are unable to forgive others
who have sinned against them.

I know that sometimes it's hard to forgive; but we
need to forget pride, admit that we are wrong in some
areas, and get over hurt feelings. What would happen
if, when we must forgive someone, we asked ourselves,
"How hard was it for God to forgive me?"

God's forgiveness cost the life of His Son. God loved
us so much, He felt we were worth it. That's a bigger
price than we'll ever have to pay in forgiving someone.
When we receive God's forgiveness, He showers us
with gifts. Among them is His help to follow His example in loving and forgiving others. We can, if we just do
it!

♥ *Thank You, God, for giving me such marvelous gifts.*

GOD'S MAKE-OVER PLAN

*But let it be the hidden person of the heart,
with the incorruptible ornament of a gentle
and quiet spirit, which is very precious in
the sight of God.*

—1 PETER 3:4

*D*o you remember house dresses? They were cotton print dresses of nondescript shape and form. My grandmother always wore them. In fact, my mother wore them, too. On Sundays they wore a little fancier dresses. Most grandmothers looked pretty much alike.

I'm glad that's changed and that we have more freedom for individual style no matter how old we are. Today, grandmothers' wardrobes are no longer limited. And we wear interesting and beautiful jewelry; we have learned how to apply make-up skillfully and color our hair. We've even changed some of our ways of doing things.

God is in the business of changing us, too. He tells us that as we allow Him to shape our hearts and minds we become so beautiful inwardly that it can't help but show on our faces and in the way we walk and talk. It's the best and least expensive make-over plan available.

♥ *I want You to change me, Lord. Inner beauty is more
lasting.*

But it is good for me to draw near to God;
I have put my trust in the Lord GOD,
That I may declare all Your works.
—PS. 73:28

I've been introducing my grandchildren to old movies—especially musicals. It started when I was visiting my California grandchildren. When we went to the video rental store, I rented *The King and I.* Later that day, my grandsons and I sat to watch it. Soon my son and his wife joined us, and we all spent an enjoyable evening with Anna and the King. Now, watching classic musicals is a regular part of Grandma's visits.

We need to promote active grandmothership. That means being involved with grandchildren on as many levels as possible and in ways that they welcome, enjoy, and appreciate.

God meant for us to have close intergenerational relationships. For us to be a part of the younger generation's development in all areas—physical, mental, emotional, and spiritual. It is when we are involved in the first three of these that we have the most impact on the fourth and most important.

♥ *Dear God, help me and my family to draw closer to You as we draw close to one another.*

For a thousand years in Your sight
Are like yesterday when it is past,
And like a watch in the night.
—PS. 90:4

*W*hen Grandma Kary's grandchildren are with her, they don't have to hurry. She says, "When we play games, we take as long as we need. There's time to stop, look at, and talk about the shape of the checkers or whatever—the same with eating, taking walks, reading stories, or just anything we do."

The ability to ignore the clock and know that the object isn't necessarily to finish the game, the meal, the book, or the walk—to know that what's important is what happens during those times together—this is great wisdom.

Grandma Kary's gift is certainly an affirmation of how God views time. We are prone to segment our lives into neat time frames. While this is often desirable and necessary, I suspect we often go overboard and even schedule times for relaxing. I know you have heard, or said, "Hurry; we have to finish this game in fifteen minutes."

The Bible gives us many examples of God's view of time, including the creation of the world. It really isn't important to know how long it took; what's important to know is that God did it. And He did it in His time.

♥ *Dear God, help me to view time more like You do.*
To spend more time on the process.

For we know that if our earthly house, this tent, is destroyed, we have a building from God, a house not made with hands, eternal in the heavens.
—2 COR. 5:1

*T*renna's Grandma Mary took her to church for the first time. Grandma Mary was a tiny, sweet, gentle grandmother who loved the Lord, had a beautiful garden with hollyhocks, and "made soft sugar cookies to die for."

1 c. sour cream	½ tsp. salt
1 tsp. baking soda	2 eggs
2 c. sugar	5 c. flour
1 c. shortening	2 tsp. baking powder
1 tsp. vanilla	

Mix sour cream and soda together and set aside. Mix sugar, shortening, vanilla, salt and eggs together. Alternate adding flour, baking powder and sour cream mixture. Roll out thick. Bake at 375° for 10 minutes. The secret is to underbake.

How many grandchildren will thank grandmas for leading them to know Jesus as their Savior? Grandmothers have a high calling; we are God's ambassadors on earth, showing and telling the way to our eternal heavenly home—all while supplying generous helpings of cookies and milk.

♥ *Father, I'll have cookies and milk ready; help me with the words to tell about You.*

*I will praise You, for I am fearfully and
    wonderfully made;
Marvelous are Your works,
And that my soul knows very well.*
                            —PS. 139:14

*G*randchildren need to know that their grandmothers have a sense of humor. My teenage granddaughter Jamie is alternately puzzled and amused by the things her mother and I find to laugh about.

Bill's Grandma Letitia was, as her daughter admits, "a real character." When he was small, Bill believed everything Grandma said, and she occasionally had fun with him by telling wild stories. One was about how she broke her leg. Actually, she fell down some steps. But the story she told involved a brawl in a bar, the police, and jumping out a window. When Grandma learned the story was Bill's show and tell for school that week, she had second thoughts about future story-telling!

A sense of humor is part of the well-rounded person-in-process we want to show our grandchildren. It's part of the personality God gave us. We can also show and tell our grandchildren that we are willing for God to continue to shape us as we mature. We want to be the people God wants us to be.

♥ *Thank You for including humor in our personalities, Lord.*

But the fruit of the Spirit is love, joy, peace, longsuffering, kindness, goodness, faithfulness.
                                    —GAL. 5:22

*V*icki says her eighty-year-old Grandma Lois doesn't act her age. She says, "When you are around her, the room glows. Her wonderful spirit keeps her young." Then, she added with pride, "My grandma takes care of old people who are sick and bedridden."

Vicki admires her grandma's honesty and straightforwardness. When Vicki's father-in-law died of cancer, Vicki had a hard time accepting it. She called Grandma Lois to talk about it and was helped by the comfort her grandma gave her. Vicki recognizes her grandma knows and is close to God.

God longs to be in us, filling every area of our lives so that the people in our families and all around us know that we know Him and are close to Him. That's one of the reasons He gave us His Holy Spirit. God's Holy Spirit empowers us to serve God in ways that sometimes seem humanly impossible—until we remember that nothing is impossible with God.

♥ *Help me to show people that the God in me is real.*

. . . put on the new man which was created according to God, in true righteousness and true holiness.
                                                    —EPH. 4:24

Sometimes we learn by accident how our grandchildren feel about us and the things we do, and how important these things are to them. Grandma Trenna and her daughter-in-law were talking about where they would have Thanksgiving. Grandson Shawn, overhearing them, said, "Let's go to Grandma Trenna's, she always does everything so special."

Sometimes for fun I call my granddaughter Angie "Angie Pangie." Once, when I didn't add the "Pangie," Angie reminded me by saying, "Aren't you going to say the rest of it?" I was surprised to learn that Angie enjoyed my having a special name for her.

The point is we can never underestimate how much attention our grandchildren pay to what we say and do. This has implications for the kind of Christian life we show our grandchildren.

In Ephesians, Paul challenges Christians, which means "Christ's ones," to live what the name means. We need to ask each day, "Do my grandchildren see Christ in me?"

♥ *Please keep reminding me, Jesus, that my grandchildren need to see You in me.*

*The eyes of your understanding being
enlightened; that you may know what is the
hope of His calling, what are the riches of
the glory of His inheritance in the saints.*
—EPH. 1:18

$\mathcal{N}$ot all grandmothers are the kind grandchildren
want. Some are negative, disagreeable, and complaining. And there are those who don't want to be grandmothers.

One grown-up granddaughter said it was amazing
how negative her grandmother can be and how she is
constantly complaining. When I asked how the family
handles it, she said, "We smile a lot and talk about how
things might not be as bad as they seem."

We probably all know at least one person like this. It
might even be a friend. There really isn't much we can
do about the person, except pray. We can also pray that
the grandchildren find an adopted grandmother, or
that their other grandmother is the "grandma-type."

Prayer comes naturally to most grandmothers. By
the time we are grandmothers, we are abundantly
aware of how talking to God helped us when our children were young. We know our strength and patience
then, and now, is directly related to taking time to talk
with God and read His Word. This may have been what
was missing in our friends' lives. Who knows? When
we pray about them, God may use us to make Himself
known to them.

♥ *Father, use me so that others can know You.*

Let the word of Christ dwell in you richly in all wisdom, teaching and admonishing one another in psalms and hymns and spiritual songs, singing with grace in your hearts to the Lord.
—COL. 3:16

*M*any grandmothers are Sunday school teachers, and I thank and praise God for every one of them. One favorite of mine was Millie. She taught the five-year-old class for more than twenty years.

Millie felt it was important for children to learn God's Word. Each quarter she made a small booklet for each child in her class; the booklet included all the Bible verses to be covered during the next few months. A note was sent home with the booklet, asking the parents to help their children learn the verses. Small prizes were awarded for all good attempts.

When Millie retired from her full-time job, she also retired from full-time Sunday school teaching. But she endeared herself to me by offering to be a willing and ready substitute whenever I need her.

At Millie's funeral, I told how Millie had encouraged children, many who are now adults, to learn Scripture. I also read one of her favorite Bible passages—Psalm 23.

I like to think of Millie now "dwelling in the house of the Lord forever."

♥ *Lord, Your words are precious to read and know.*

Therefore, since we have this ministry, as we have received mercy, we do not lose heart.
—2 COR. 4:1

*M*any grandmothers are caught in the middle between a child and an ex-spouse. It's usually not a pleasant place to be, and the only reason to stay there is because of the grandchildren.

Grandmothers in this position need the wisdom of Solomon, the patience of Job, and a constant supply of God's love. Keeping the grandchildren foremost in mind is what makes it possible.

One grandmother told how she has learned to keep her opinions to herself, listen willingly, talk only to God about everything, and love everyone involved expansively. She sees her priority as grandmother, not marriage counselor or defender. She works to make that relationship in her grandchildren's lives as normal as possible.

The grandchildren are blessed to have such a wise and loving grandmother. Her confidence about her relationship with God allows her to leave her grandchildren's parents in His hands while she fulfills one of the most important roles of ministry God has given her.

♥ *Thank You, God, for the ministry of grandmothering.*

Love has been perfected among us in this: that we may have boldness in the day of judgment; because as He is, so are we in this world.
— 1 JOHN 4:17

*E*ach summer Grammy Rameriz came from California to visit her grandchildren Tracy and Tom. One summer she wasn't able to make the trip. When her grandchildren heard she wasn't coming, they cried. Grammy called and talked with the children to help make it better. Realizing how much the children missed her and she missed them, she asked if the children could come to see her.

They were enthusiastic about the idea and kept saying, "Grammy loves us so much. We want to go. You don't have to worry, Daddy. She'll be waiting for us at the airport. She'll do a good job of taking care of us."

Love has strong bonds and cords—strong enough to reach across a continent and give young children the courage and confidence to make a long journey.

This and our own stories of the strength of love remind us that love is a wonderful characteristic which God has given to us so that we can love as He does. His love for us is the source of our love for others.

♥ *Dear God, help me to love as You do.*

*I will parise You, O LORD, with my whole
     heart;
I will tell of all Your marvelous works.*
                                        —PS. 9:1

*W*hen Grammy Ramirez visited her grandchildren, Tracy and Tom, she always made tortillas. The children loved the freshly made, warm tortillas spread with butter that dripped down their arms. They wanted to share the treat with their friends, and it wasn't long before every time Grammy made tortillas, the yard was full of kids.

Grammy Ramirez quickly saw this as a great opportunity to do some neighborhood evangelism. Before the warm, delicious treat was passed around, she told the waiting children a Bible story. Now, this wasn't an official backyard Bible club or anything like that; it was just a grandmother who loves children feeding them some food from God's Word along with a more earthly treat. She wanted to give children who might not otherwise hear about God a taste, if you will, of His love in an enjoyable, appetizing combination.

Our love for God should spill out from us in words of praise and telling stories about Him whenever and wherever we can. We can trust God to help us find the most natural way for us to do it. We just need to be ready.

♥ *Dear God, I want to be ready to tell others about You.*

This hope we have as an anchor of the soul,
both sure and steadfast. . . .
—HEB. 6:19

*N*an remembers taking her grandmother to the grocery store; she had the feeling her grandmother kind of liked the man who worked there. Nan says, "When we were in the store, Grandmother acted differently. She was like a girl."

When I was dating a gentleman, one of the things my family, including the older grandchildren, noticed and commented on was that I seemed to act differently when the gentleman was around; "younger and girl-ish" was their observation. I didn't ask whether it was a compliment or complaint.

We need to help our grandchildren understand that even though we change physically as we mature, even our more stable emotions might sometimes be very similar to theirs. We can still feel the roller coaster thrills of love and struggle in relationships.

We can show that the constant in our lives is God. He is our anchor when our emotions are buffeted about, just as theirs are. God's Word constantly assures us of His trustworthiness. He does not lie or change.

♥ *Dear God, thank You for Your consistency.*

Therefore we must give the more earnest heed to the things we have heard, lest we drift away.
—HEB. 2:1

*G*randma was half-listening to grandson Ron as she fixed bacon and eggs for both of them. Ron was just two and a half and liked to talk; he always had a lot to tell his grandmother. This time, aware that he didn't have her complete attention, Ron banged his fist on the table several times and said, "Sit down, Grandma, now!"

Grandchildren want and need to be heard, even at that young age. Isn't it interesting that they know exactly when we are not paying attention?

I'm not proposing that we must hang on to every word our grandchildren utter. What we do need is discernment to know when we need to listen closely to what they are saying. If we practice this when they are young, it will become a natural habit as they grow older and benefit them and us.

We all need to be heard—to have someone's complete attention as we talk with them. People who do this are surprisingly called great conversationalists, even though what they do most and best is listen attentively. God is the all-time great attention-payer. He listens, He hears, His attention is on us. How often do I show that courtesy and love to Him?

♥ *Dear God, when I talk to You, help me to give You my complete and total attention.*

GOOD ADVICE

Listen to counsel and receive instruction,
That you may be wise in your latter days.
—PROV. 19:20

*G*randma Patterson was baby-sitting her three-year-old grandson, David. David did not like water and he wouldn't drink it. When he went to bed, he was allowed to have juice, which was put on the table near his bed.

Grandma didn't mind about the juice, but she worried because David wouldn't drink water. She tried to talk him into trying it and ended the discussion by asking him to promise her to take a sip or two of water when he drank the juice. David went to bed an unhappy camper. And the next day he told his parents he didn't want Grandma to baby-sit anymore because she made him drink water.

Grandmothers like to give advice. Of course, grandchildren are not always ready to accept that advice, even when they acknowledge that we are older and could even be smarter or wiser. It doesn't mean we have to stop giving advice, but it may mean we need to take a look at how we give it.

The Bible is full of God's advice for us. It is evident in stories, proverbs, psalms, prophecies, and parables. How would you rate yourself at being able to accept His Words of wisdom?

♥ *Lord, when I read Your advice, help me to accept and do it.*

Bearing with one another, and forgiving one another, if anyone has a complaint against another; even as Christ forgave you, so you also must do.
                                    —COL. 3:13

*G*randmother Adams tells about a time when she knew she had disappointed her teenage grandson by something she did. She immediately wrote to him and apologized:

Please forgive me if I disappointed you—I don't want that. I love you and care what you think about me and also want to set a good example for you and all my other grandpersons, too. I feel I made you angry with me and disappointed you—but remember that no one is perfect, and the best thing we can do is to try to learn from our mistakes. This is a lifelong process, and I don't expect it to be complete in this lifetime. But I do plan to keep trying, as all of us need to. God will help us.

My concordance shows 143 references to forgiveness. The verses fall into two basic categories—God's forgiveness of us, and our need to forgive others. It's hard to miss what God means.

♥ *Dear God, when I am unforgiving, remind me of Your forgiveness.*

INFINITE WORTH

But the very hairs of your head are all numbered. Do not fear therefore; you are of more value than many sparrows.

—LUKE 12:7

I am positive my grandchildren do not mention my cooking among their favorite memories of me. One Sunday, my daughter Gin and granddaughters Jamie and Becky planned to stop by for lunch. I usually keep some prepared food in my freezer for emergency occasions, so before I went to church, I got out my crockpot, threw in some frozen tortellini with tomato sauce, and set out some rolls to thaw.

When my grandchildren came in the house and went to check out the kitchen, they said with surprise, "Grandma cooked!"

Actually this says more about our culture than about us. We are involved in a wider variety of activities outside the home, either in paid positions or volunteer. Our grandchildren see us do well in many roles.

The Bible tells us that when God created people, He made them in His own image. The possibilities for what we are able to do, then, must be countless. Knowing God made us like Him is the reason we can feel positive about ourselves and our abilities.

♥ *Father, You have given me infinite worth. Thank You.*

SYNONYM

To know the love of Christ which passes knowledge; that you may be filled with all the fullness of God.   —EPH. 3:19

*W*hen Judy was a little girl, she went to visit her grandmother who lived on a farm. It was a very different lifestyle for a city girl. Grandma cooked on a wood stove. There was no indoor bathroom or electric lights, and water was carried from the pump and heated for baths. Teeth were brushed on the back step where the bucket of drinking water was kept.

About Grandma herself, Judy remembers two things—she was a fabulous cook and she snored, which kept Judy awake because she slept with Grandma.

Often, what we remember most about people has to do with how they are or what they do relates to us. We think of people, particularly family members, in a very personal way.

God wants this kind of personal relationship with us, too. He wants us to more than know intellectually about His love and forgiveness. God longs for us to feel His love and have complete assurance of His forgiveness. That's what happens when we are part of His family.

♥ *Father, Your name is synonymous with love.*

Whom having not seen you love. Though now you do not see Him, yet believing, you rejoice with joy inexpressible and full of glory.
—1 PETER 1:8

Some grandmothers make really big occasions out of holidays. One granddaughter told of a yearly Christmas Eve party at her grandmother's house following church. The party included a visit from Santa Claus, games, dancing, and singing. At Easter, Grandmother always organized an Easter egg hunt. Her granddaughter remembers that Grandma enjoyed giving parties and everything that went with them—tables set beautifully, room decorations, dressing up, and abundance and variety of people and food. Her grandchildren learned from watching her how to give and enjoy parties. Both are worth passing on to succeeding generations.

There are so very many things that grandchildren can learn from watching us. We hope and pray what they learn will be useful to their lives and usually think along the lines of good working habits, honesty, and kindness. Maybe we think the enjoying part just comes naturally. Maybe it doesn't.

There are many references to joy in the Bible. Some of them have to do with feasts or parties. Most verses link our joy to knowing God. It is the attitude we have and how we respond to the Person who is the source of all joy.

♥ *Lord, does my attitude show that I know You?*

That the sharing of your faith may become effective by the acknowledgment of every good thing which is in you in Christ Jesus.
—PHILEM. 6

*J*eff's grandma and grandpa sold everything they had and bought a recreational vehicle so that they could travel. They have visited each of the fifty states. Jeff and other grandchildren have gone with them on some of the trips, even missing school sometimes.

There are those who would not approve of taking grandchildren out of school for such trips. Others feel there is much educational value involved, not only from the trip, but from the intergenerational exposure as well.

It may not be possible for all grandmothers to take their grandchildren on trips to other states, but it might be possible to manage a short trip, from a few hours to a few days, to a place that would be an informative and fun adventure.

Grandmothers are often the ones who lead grandchildren into the adventure of the Christian life. As children listen to the Bible stories we tell, our own testimonies and daily experiences of God's care, and show interest in discovering things in the Bible with us, we will have started them on an exciting faith journey that will last their whole life.

♥ *Dear God, continue to lead me on my faith journey so that I can show others the way.*

COMMON INTERESTS

Now by this we know that we know Him, if we keep His commandments.
—1 JOHN 2:3

*B*ecky and her Grandma Phyllis are artists. They have taken art classes together and paint together. They look at the world around them with artists' eyes as they collect rocks for painting and stroll along the Mississippi River to feed the ducks.

Becky also likes the stories that Grandma Phyllis tells, even when she tells the same ones frequently.

What joy it is to share a common interest with a grandchild. Sometimes the interest is obvious; sometimes we need to work at looking for one.

One common interest we can enjoy developing with our grandchildren is getting to know God better. God honors this interest. He wants us to know Him better, too. As we continue to grow in our knowledge of Him, we will love Him more and from that love comes obedience to His Word.

♥ *Dear God, I am interested in knowing You better.*

NO STUMBLING BLOCKS

Therefore let us not judge one another anymore, but rather resolve this, not to put a stumbling block or a cause to fall in our brother's way.
— ROM. 14:13

Jim's Grandma Marian was a reporter for the local newspaper for twenty-five years. When Jim was a boy, she took him to the newspaper office and to view parades she needed to write about. Jim says he heard a lot of public relations talk in the newspaper office and among the politicians at the parade.

His grandmother also made him go to church every Sunday. But she did not attend with him every time. He is glad now that she made him go because he values the foundation for his faith and wishes it had been as important for her to go, too.

Grandchildren are quick to spot discrepancies between what we say and what we do. We take a chance that we might be placing a stumbling block in their paths.

As Christians, God has given us much freedom. But He wants us to be careful about what we do and say so that we don't cause a problem for someone who doesn't know Him very well or at all. We handle this best when we try to determine what Jesus would do and follow Him as closely as possible.

♥ *Lord, help me not to misuse the freedom I have in You.*

But encourage one another daily. . . .
—HEB. 3:13 NIV

*F*our of my grandchildren and I were at a resort on a lake in the middle of Iowa. The children ranged in age from six to thirteen. It didn't start out to be a good week. The boy cousins irritated each other, the six-year-old alternately drove us crazy and delighted us, and I was concerned about some problems at work and so wasn't concentrating on having a good time like I normally do.

After a few days, I realized that Becky was the only one who seemed to be consistently content. She got up happy, was happy all day, and went to bed happy. When I needed help with something, she was there to give a hand.

One night as I was tucking her into bed, I told her I appreciated her good disposition. That year she was a big help in making the week go well for all of us. It's important to give honest compliments directly to our grandchildren—rather than indirectly to their parents or our friends.

God calls us to be encouragers. Several verses in the Bible urge us to encourage one another because living as a Christian in this world is not easy (see Heb. 10:25; 1 Thess. 3:2; 4:18; 2 Thess. 2:17).

♥ *Your Words always encourage me, Lord.*

WORDS AND ACTIONS

Pleasant words are like a honeycomb,
Sweetness to the soul and health to the
bones.
—PROV. 16:24

*J*oe says that both of his grandmothers were a joy. The grandmother who lived with his family spoke English and German. As a child, Joe enjoyed learning German words from her. He liked having her around all the time.

His other grandmother lived in a town not too far away. The family went to see her often. Joe says, "Everything was fun when we went there. She was an excellent cook, and we had a great time at dinner. There was a clock in the kitchen that she let me wind."

Joe thinks his grandmother's letting him wind that clock led to his lifelong interest and profession of working on clocks.

We often feel what we say and do has little effect. Who would think that allowing a child to wind a kitchen clock might lead to his profession in life?

The Bible tells us our words have the ability to do many things—pierce, heal, hurt, instruct, please, deceive, and encourage are just a few. The book of Proverbs is God's good advice for us about our words and actions.

♥ *Dear God, I put You in charge of my words and my actions today.*

DIMENSIONS OF LOVE

. . . that Christ may dwell in your hearts through faith; that you, being rooted and grounded in love, may be able to comprehend . . . the width . . . length . . . depth . . . height. —**EPH. 3:17**

One granddaughter confessed that sometimes she didn't want to visit her grandmother because her grandmother wasn't easy to live with—even for a week. The grandmother was very strict, and the granddaughter feared she would do something wrong.

The granddaughter did like her grandmother's house in town, though, with its bay windows, built-in china closets, and stair landings. She also liked working in the garden on her grandmother's farm outside of town. And when they went shopping, her grandmother always bought her a pair of shoes.

Despite her grandmother's strictness, the granddaughter knew her grandmother loved her. She felt that love as they baked together to feed the men who worked on the farm and as they read Bible stories before going to bed.

I'm not against strictness. Sometimes it's needed. But it must be tempered with love as this grandmother's obviously was.

♥ *My mind cannot comprehend the vastness of Your love, Lord. I can only thank You for it.*

He has shown you, O man, what is good;
And what does the LORD require of you
But to do justly . . .
—MIC. 6:8

*P*hyllis's grandma and grandpa owned a paint store. Phyllis tells that she and her siblings would never ask her grandmother for money when they needed it, but that their grandma just knew when they did and would find work for them to do in the paint store to earn it. Phyllis dusted a lot of paint cans.

Rather than just giving her grandchildren money, Phyllis's grandma believed in teaching them the value of earning money. She also believed in being part of her grandchildren's lives and went to all their sporting events. Phyllis has memories of a warm and loving relationship with her grandma.

Grandmothers remember when values were taught pretty consistently at home, school, church, and in the neighborhood. Now our grandchildren can choose from a smorgasbord of values that have changed and keep changing. Often our values are challenged.

We can meet this challenge with the consistency of God's Word. When values are questioned, we must check them against what God has told us. His principles for living will never change.

♥ *Your unchanging Word helps me meet the challenge*
of a changing world, Lord.

Your attitude should be the same as that of Christ Jesus.
                              —PHIL. 2:5 NIV

*P*hyllis says she doesn't know what she would do without her children's Grandmother Bagnall. Each summer the whole family spends three weeks on vacation with her. They enjoy every minute of it. Grandmother Bagnall not only spends the three weeks concentrating on playing games with her grandchildren and reading to them, she also gives good advice to their parents. Phyllis says, "She gives it in an easy-to-take way, never critical."

Grandmothers are natural advice givers. We've had good, valid experience and usually have learned quite a bit by the time our grandchildren come along. The problem is we often share our hard-earned expertise in all the wrong ways. Sometimes it's just a matter of our attitude. I've heard myself and other grandmothers sounding like know-it-alls who couldn't possibly be wrong.

The verse above is the beginning of a passage that tells what a Christian attitude is like. A good question to ask ourselves periodically is, "How does my attitude match Christ's?" Perhaps we should ask those who live around us.

♥ *Father, help me to know when my attitude needs changing.*

REFLECTION

Thus says the LORD of hosts:
"Execute true justice,
Show mercy and compassion
Everyone to his brother."
—ZECH. 7:9

*M*egan's Grandmother Mann has several grandchildren besides Megan. She sends all her grandchildren little notes and cards especially when she knows there's a swim meet or other special activity where they might need a little encouragement.

Megan is the oldest of the grandchildren. Grandma Mann takes her shopping and spends extra time with her to be sure she is getting as much attention as all the little ones get.

Grandmothers are sensitive to the feelings and needs of their grandchildren. They have compassion about what it feels like to be the oldest and gangly while everyone else is little and cute; or receiving clothes you need when you really wanted a new toy.

God wants us to reflect Him in our lives. Throughout the Bible, He tells us in what ways we can be His reflection. Compassion is one of those ways. We must read God's Word and apply it to our lives.

♥ *Dear God, help me to reflect You in all I do.*

*I have taught you in the way of wisdom;
I have led you in right paths.*
—PROV. 4:11

*G*randma Drew gives all her grandchildren their first Bibles. She allows their parents to choose which ones they feel are appropriate, then she purchases them to give at Easter or birthday or other special time.

Her son and daughter-in-law appreciate that she invites her grandchildren to do things that they don't have the financial means or equipment to do, such as going fishing. They also appreciate that she saved all their old games so she can spend hours playing them with her grandchildren.

Grandmothers always seem to be able to know what is just exactly right for them to do with and for their grandchildren.

We know that God is interested in all areas of our lives. He wants us to live effectively. So, if we are talking with Him about our relationship with our grandchildren, we can be sure the good ideas that come to mind are from Him. God's formula for effective living includes knowing and acknowledging who God is, trusting that His Word will lead us, and obeying Him. This is the only way to live.

♥ *I know Your formula for my life is best. I need Your help to follow it, Lord.*

*For I am persuaded that neither death nor
life, nor angels nor principalities nor
powers, nor things present nor things to
come . . . shall be able to separate us from
the love of God. . . .* —ROM. 8:38–39

*M*indy's Grandma Alta spent her hundredth
birthday in the nursing home. There was a big party
with all the family present. After that party, Grandma
seemed to go downhill fast.

Mindy had always been scared of death and didn't
like to be around sick people, so it was hard for her to
visit her grandma. But on her grandma's 101st Christmas, Mindy went to see Grandma.

Mindy tells that it was hard to know that the person
in the bed was her grandma. She knelt down and said,
"Hi, Grandma. It's Mindy." Then she held her grandma's hand and told her what a good grandma she had
been and talked about the things they had done together. When they sang "Silent Night," the line "Sleep
in heavenly peace" held special meaning for both of
them.

That night Mindy thought about her grandma so
close to death—so soon to be with Jesus. She realized
there was no need to be afraid anymore. The next
morning her grandma died.

We are never abandoned by Jesus. Even in death it
is impossible to be separated from Him. There is no
need to fear. We have victory over death!

♥ *Dear God, thank You for the assurance of Your presence in life and in death.*

READING GRANDMA

*For I delivered to you first of all that which
I also received: that Christ died for our sins
according to the Scriptures.*

—1 COR. 15:3

$\mathcal{A}$ letter to Dear Abby from a grandmother told
how the grandma felt bad because her grandchildren's
other grandmother was financially able to take the children shopping to buy toys, clothes, and other things
that the grandchildren wanted. The grandma wrote
that the only thing she could do for her grandchildren
was to read to them. She was the reading grandmother.

A reading grandmother is one of the best kinds of
grandmas to have. Theirs is the joy of introducing
grandchildren to classic favorites and the thrill of discovering new books.

A friend of mine, Diane, is building a library of old
and new books to share with her future grandchildren.
Her daughter isn't even married yet. Part of that library
are the books she and her daughter treasured when
her daughter was young.

The Bible should have a prominent place among the
books you read to grandchildren. Our grandchildren's
knowledge of God's Word will affect their attitude
about their lives. In it they will find God's free gift of
salvation that gives them life everlasting.

♥ *Thank You for letting me take part in helping my
grandchildren discover Your gift of salvation, Lord.*

My mouth shall speak wisdom,
And the meditation of my heart shall bring
understanding.
—PS. 49:3

*T*en things I want my grandchildren to know:

1. God loves them and sent His Son, Jesus, to die for them so that they can be part of God's family.

2. I love them, even when I disagree with them.

3. God forgives us when we ask Him.

4. I like being with them and want them to like being with me.

5. Learn to love God first; then they will obey Him.

6. The adage "This, too, shall pass" is really true. Remember it in tough times.

7. When faced with a problem, list your options and talk them over with God first, then with someone who will just listen and not give advice unless you ask for it.

8. Laugh a lot.

9. Keep on reading and learning.

10. Bitterness, anger, and hatred make you look old and act ugly.

Ask God to help you list the things you want your grandchildren to know. Tuck the list in a gift they want.

♥ *Dear God, thank You for giving us Your wisdom to share.*

MOST IMPORTANT NAME

Nor is there salvation in any other, for there is no other name under heaven given among men by which we must be saved.
—ACTS 4:12

*G*randmother Carol is Baba to her grandkids. She says, " 'Baba' is what came out of our first grandson's mouth when he started to talk. Each time his parents carefully said, 'Grandma,' Dugan smiled and said, 'Baba.' And now to our six grandkids, I'm Baba. It is very nice to be in a mall or at church and hear 'Baba.' I know it's me—and I turn about with great anticipation."

Grandchildren often pick out their own names for grandmothers. Attempts to explain why they chose what they did don't always fit adult logic. Their reasons are really only important to them.

There is importance attached to names in the Bible. In at least two instances an angel told the parents what to name their child. Elizabeth and Zechariah were told to name their son John. Mary was told to name her son Jesus. His name, the name above every name, has power to give eternal life to all who believe.

♥ *O Lord, how majestic is Your name.*

. . . Let the little children come to Me, and do not forbid them; for of such is the kingdom of God. —MARK 10:14

I remember the night my first grandchild, Jamie, was born. Her father called me after midnight to tell me they were on their way to the hospital. I lay in bed praying for my daughter, her husband, and the new little life that was coming into the world. Then, rolling over, I thought, "I'm glad it's my daughter having a baby and not me!"

Anthropologist Margaret Mead, in her autobiography *Blackberry Winter,* wrote about becoming a grandmother, "I suddenly realized that through no act of my own I had become biologically related to a new human being."

We do come to that time when we are happy to give over childbearing to our daughters, and may have come to share Ms. Mead's realization. Though we have finished with birthing and become grandmothers through no action on our part, we are needed to take part in this new human being's world. We may be included in teaching the child about Jesus; we may even have the privilege of leading the child to know and accept Jesus as Savior.

♥ *Dear God, thank You for the part You have given me in my grandchildren's lives.*

Nevertheless we, according to His promise, look for new heavens and a new earth in which righteousness dwells.
—2 PETER 3:13

*W*hen television was available for home purchase, Grandma O'Brien's family was the first in the family and the neighborhood to own a set. Grandma couldn't believe it was real. As she watched, she kept asking everyone, "How are you getting those pictures in that box?"

Even when they told her it was just like radio with pictures, she still insisted for several months that they were somehow putting pictures inside the cabinet.

I'm told that the older we get, the harder it is to accept something new, whether it's ideas or inventions. I'd like that not to be true of me. I want to always, no matter how old I am, be able to listen to new ideas and check them against what I know to be true especially when lined up with God's Word. As for inventions, it's exciting to see what people, with God's help whether they acknowledge it or not, can come up with next.

One day God will give us a new world; He will restore our world to the way He intended it to be. This new world will be filled with goodness.

♥ *Dear Lord, thank You for including me in the plans for Your new world.*

You open Your hand
And satisfy the desire of every living thing.
—PS. 145:16

*E*very single day of her adult life, Grandma McCall wore dress, nylons with a girdle to hold them up, and high heel shoes. No matter what she did—cleaning, cooking, working in the yard—she was dressed up. When she took her grandchildren to the park, she would push them in the swings and get down and play with them in the sand box. But what granddaughter Beth remembers most is her hiking up her dress and running as fast as she could to make the merry-go-round spin for them. Beth says, "She would do anything we asked, but she was always dressed up."

There was a time when dressing up like that was considered normal and proper. I'm sure glad things have changed.

I like the fact that Grandma McCall didn't let what was prescribed apparel for the times keep her from having fun with her grandchildren. Her heart and hands were open.

The theme of Psalm 145 is praise for what God is and for what He does. Everything we have—from necessities such as food and water to the desires of hearts that are committed to Him—comes from His hands, which are spread wide open to give.

♥ *Heavenly Father, open my heart and hands to give as graciously as You have given to me.*

GLORIOUS PRIVILEGE

I will bless those who bless you . . .
—GEN. 12:3

*E*ach summer Grandmother Carol and her family hold an Annual White-Sherbondy & Sundry Relatives Backyard Croquet Tournament. She says it is just croquet in her backyard with whatever cousins, nephews, offspring, aunts, and uncles assemble. It is complete with a traveling plaque that has the tournament winner posted.

Each year the family also has a family portrait taken. One year, thinking it might be a burden to get together to have the picture taken, Grandmother asked everyone, "Do you really want to do it this year?" The response was immediate: "Without a doubt."

These are the kinds of activities that cement our children and grandchildren into the relationship called "family." Next to our relationship with God, it is the most important relationship in our lives. In fact, God uses the family as a picture of our relationship with Him. It is through an understanding of the family structure that children can begin to grasp who God is and His love for them.

♥ *Dear God, thank You for the privilege of being a picture of You.*

*To him the doorkeeper opens, and the sheep
hear his voice; and he calls his own sheep
by name and leads them out.*
—JOHN 10:3

*C*arol tells about the time before their oldest son's child was born and they were pondering boy and girl names. The boy's name was set, but what if it were a girl? Their son, Steve, was driving through the countryside and saw a road sign that said, "Gentle Breeze." He thought what a tender name for a little girl—and a grown woman—a gentle, refreshing, look-what-God-blew-in Breeze. The baby was a girl and they named her Breeze. Grandma says she's a one-of-a-kind, God's gentle gift.

Grandmothers often have grandchildren named after them. This can be very flattering and shows high regard. In our family when the oldest son or daughter marries, the couple gives their first daughter the name Kay as a middle name.

The Bible, in several passages, likens us to sheep who are called by, named, and cared for by the loving Shepherd, Jesus. In Bible times that was the illustration that people understood best. What example might we use today to truly understand the wonderfulness of God knowing all who belong to Him by name?

♥ *Thank You for being my Teacher, Lord.*

*Indeed, You have made my days as
    handbreadths,
And my age is as nothing before You;
Certainly every man at his best state is but
    vapor.*
—PS. 39:5

*T*he *Family Circus* cartoon by Bill Keane showed the little girl of the family asking the grandma, "If I'm only young once, Grandma, how many chances do I get to be old?"

I love the way children think, don't you? But answering their questions is often a challenge. How would you answer that cartoon question? It could very well come from one of your grandchildren.

How do you tell them that we are only old once? And that even though they don't think so now, time goes by much too quickly? That when we were young we thought we'd never be grown-ups, just as they are thinking? That the old adage is true, the older you get the faster time goes?

The Psalm the verse above was taken from reminds us of the frailty, weakness, and littleness of humanity. In *Thru the Bible with J. Vernon McGee*, the commentary states, "Apart from a relationship with God, my friend, it [life] is rather meaningless."

Our answers need to encourage our grandchildren to become friends with God who gives life, at whatever age, the very best meaning and purpose. With Him our chances are eternal.

♥ *Thank You, God, for everlasting life.*

Assuredly, I say to you, unless you are converted and become as little children, you will by no means enter the kingdom of heaven.
—MATT. 18:3

*L*inda credits her Grandma Cripe and Grandma Borge as the ones who allowed her and her sister to be children. At home they had adult responsibilities of caring for several other younger children and doing the cooking and cleaning for the entire household. At Grandma Cripe's house nothing more was expected of them than to enjoy a drawer full of costume jewelry she kept just for them. Grandma Borge let them bake whatever they wanted and taught them how to make her Hot Milk Cake.

It's important for us to allow grandchildren to be children for as long as it is necessary for them, especially in a world that encourages and supports growing up quickly. This is another comment about time but also about the importance of childhood.

Jesus used the illustration of becoming like a little child to show us that we must be born again or start a new life to enter heaven. In that same passage He reminds us that our status in heaven isn't important; the point is to get there. Using children as His example shows how important they are to Him.

♥ *Dear God, I am glad that I am Your child.*

24-HOUR CARE

I will lift up my eyes to the hills—
From whence comes my help?
—PS. 121:1

*J*ohn's Grandma Striemer was bedridden and lived with his aunt and uncle. When you entered her room, you first noticed the glass-topped table covered with cards, notepaper, envelopes, pens, lists, and address books. Grandma Striemer spent her days sending cards and writing to people on their birthdays and anniversaries, when they were ill or had babies, and other important occasions of their lives. As she wrote, she prayed for them, too, and often called to give words of congratulations, encouragement, or sympathy.

Grandma Striemer's favorite passage of Scripture was Psalm 121. John read it at her funeral. This Psalm expresses assurance and hope in God's protection, day and night. It was the testimony of her life, a testimony that she told over and over again with every card, note, and phone call she made to people who needed to hear that God watches over them all the time.

God's round-the-clock help is a promise we can count on. Sometimes we need to be reminded of His availability, and sometimes we can be the reminders to others.

♥ *I need someone to watch over me. I'm glad it's You, Lord.*

THREE GRANDMOTHERS
AND A MINISTRY

Therefore I exhort first of all that
supplications, prayers, intercessions, and
giving of thanks be made for all men.
—1 TIM. 2:1

*E*rcel, Esther, and Nellie are grandmothers who are involved in an intercessory ministry without ever leaving their homes. They are unable to attend worship services, but through prayer, notes, and telephoning they draw wide circles around more people than many of us see each day.

These three grandmothers are thrilled that they are still part of the ministry of their church. Rather than just being on the receiving end of visits, calls, and cards, they are active participants in reaching out and helping others.

Often, these grandmothers spend much of the night praying. Some of the notes they send are for no particular reason and are received by people who needed to be encouraged or to hear that someone was praying for them.

God has given us all the ability to pray, and His Word tells us that we must always pray. No matter how old we are, we can pray—the ability does not diminish with age. Knowing this should call us to a ministry of prayer widening our circle. There is always room for more in this ministry.

♥ *Thank You that I can be part of ministry through*
prayer, Lord.

*That the God of our Lord Jesus Christ, the
Father of glory, may give to you the spirit of
wisdom and revelation in the knowledge of
Him.*
—EPH. 1:17

A well-known radio personality told about finding
a pair of "granny glasses." They reminded him of his
grandmother, who lived to be ninety-nine years old.
She told him often that she prayed for him every day.

A grandson was sent his grandmother's Bible after
she died. In it he read, with tears in his eyes, the prayer
she had written about him on the inside of the cover.

A grandchild calls her grandmother on a regular basis and asks her to pray about difficulties she's having
in school.

A grandmother taught a little boy a bedtime prayer
that he still says regularly before going to sleep.

What are your prayer experiences with grandchildren? The great, good news is that God hears and
answers what must be hundreds of thousands of
prayers. Do we need to be reminded that He does always answer? Of course, we know His answer is sometimes yes, sometimes no, and sometimes wait. Let's be
sure our grandchildren know this principle, too.

♥ *I praise and thank You for answered prayers, Lord.*

A new commandment I give to you, that you love one another; as I have loved you, that you also love one another.

—JOHN 13:34

I saw a sweatshirt in a catalog that said, "If I had known grandchildren were so much fun, I would have had them first!" While many of us would agree, there is another side to the coin.

A letter from a grandmother, asking what to do about her undisciplined grandchildren, who she was planning to take while their parents were away, appeared in *A Better Tomorrow* magazine.

Dr. Gary Roseberg's advice included the following: set ground rules of respect and responsibility; present the boundaries in an upbeat way; keep in mind what works for a three year old probably won't work with a teen.

His final advice was to concentrate on making memories that would last a lifetime. God gives us opportunities to be with our grandchildren that can benefit all concerned. If we approach these times with prayer, God will give us the patience, wisdom, and good ideas that make for a great time together.

♥ *The strong foundation of Your love makes all things possible, Lord.*

Bless the LORD, O my soul;
And all that is within me, bless His holy
name!
— PS. 103:1

*E*dna was grandma not only to her grandson, Randy, but to many children through Backyard Clubs and Sunday school.

When she died, her son's eulogy told that it was only fitting that God took her home on Veteran's Day because she was God's soldier.

Here are some of Grandma Edna's thoughts about her favorite Scripture, Psalm 103:

I praise God with all my being; with love and honor to His holy name.

The Lord is kind and merciful. He has forgiven all my sins. I know of His love for me and His compassion always helps me to be comforted. My Lord gives me the Good things I need, renewing me and refreshing me—so much that I feel like I'm soaring like an eagle. I am renewed with strength from Him.

Let everything everywhere bless the Lord! And how I bless Him too!

Grandma Edna was a treasured link in her family's Christian chain.

♥ *Lord, mold this link with love and make it strong in service.*

And He shall stand and feed His flock
In the strength of the LORD,
In the majesty of the name of the LORD His
    God;
And they shall abide,
For now He shall be great
To the ends of the earth.
          —MIC. 5:4

*W*hen she was a little girl, Vannye lived next door to her Granny Hawley. She and Granny were both early risers, so Vannye would often get up before her family and go next door to eat breakfast with Granny. After school, if Vannye's mother wasn't home, Vannye's first stop was Granny's kitchen.

Granny told Vannye stories of her life and read Bible stories to her; they sang all their favorite hymns together. Thinking back on how secure she felt during that time, Vannye says, "It was a good way to live."

Grandchildren need security. Part of a grandmother's responsibility is to give grandchildren a sense of security. This can range from full-time care to being available to talk, even though you might live in another city or state.

The amount of security our grandchildren feel from us is directly related to how secure we are. As Christians we have all the security we need in Christ. He has chosen us to be His. There is nothing or no one who can change that fact.

♥ *Thank You, God, for the security I feel in knowing that You love me.*

VIVE LE CHANGE!

Behold, I tell you a mystery: We shall not all sleep, but we shall all be changed—in a moment, in the twinkling of an eye, at the last trumpet. —1 COR. 15:51–52

*M*adeleine never got to know her grandmother. A family disagreement before she was born was still festering and her parents and grandparents did not see each other or speak.

When Madeleine's grandmother became ill, her parents took her to visit. It was almost too late. Grandmother barely knew who she was and was hardly able to communicate with her.

But preschooler Madeleine knew it was her grandmother. Since that time Madeleine often says, "I miss Grandma. I'm glad I'm going to see her in Heaven."

Madeleine missed knowing her grandmother, and the family disagreement hardly seems worth it. It doesn't really matter who was right or wrong, and I'm sure everyone involved now wishes they had handled things a little differently. But Madeleine does know she will see her grandmother in heaven.

I like the verse above. It says that we will have new bodies and new attitudes—ones that will not allow us to be at odds with one another. We have to be changed inside so that we can live forever in peace with one another. Then we will truly be like Jesus.

♥ *I fail so often at being like You, Jesus. Some days I long for that "twinkling of an eye" change.*

LOVING WISDOM

Who is wise and understanding among you?
Let him show by good conduct that his
works are done in the meekness of wisdom.
—JAMES 3:13

*J*ack was raised in a home filled with tension. His relationship with his grandmother on his mother's side was not all it should or could have been, which was unfortunate because she took care of him. He didn't have the opportunity to get close to his father's mother, Grandma Wilson (who probably would have been good for him) because she lived in another state.

He remembers that Grandma Wilson came to visit the family once. During the visit, she took the whole family out to dinner at a Chinese restaurant. It was the only relaxing time Jack remembers the family having. It meant a great deal to him because he felt she had done something specifically for him, something he doesn't remember anyone doing before.

The term *dysfunctional* is used frequently to describe families. It must make the heart of God break. He gives families a plan for how to live and we choose to ignore His loving wisdom.

James 3:13–18 includes the verse above. One commentary states that true wisdom can be measured by the depth of one's character. We can evaluate our own wisdom by the way we act. Our children and grandchildren will be able to evaluate us, too.

♥ *Dear God, as a grandmother, help me to seek Your wisdom.*

*Finally, all of you be of one mind, having
compassion for one another; love as
brothers, be tenderhearted, be courteous;
. . . knowing that you were called to this,
that you may inherit a blessing.*
— 1 PETER 3:8–9

I enjoy observing the personalities of my grandchildren. My daughters and son each have two children. In each family, the oldest child is more serious;
the younger ones border on being full-blown comedians. When the serious-minded ones get together they
debate and argue and are very competitive in games.
The comedians just want to have fun.

During one grandmother week we had incidents
where two serious-minded grandchildren got into ex-
changes and the comedians got tired of being around
each other all the time. Grandmother intervened with
a change of activity to give everyone an opportunity to
back off and cool down.

An important aspect of their relationships is that
they really do like and love one another. These incidents help them learn to respect each others' strengths
and accept their weaknesses.

God tells us the elements that need to become part
of our character in the verses above. These qualities
help us and our grandchildren to grow as mature believers. There is a promise attached.

♥ *Dear God, thank You for the promise of Your blessing as we continue to grow in You.*

*And if it seems evil to you to serve the LORD,
choose for yourselves this day whom you will
serve. . . . But as for me and my house, we
will serve the LORD.* —JOSH. 24:15

*W*hen I was collecting grandmother stories, a
friend gave me a charming article that told about two
grandmothers who were as different as they could be.
It told how the one was proper and the other was ec-
centric; then recounted in humorous ways the wide variety of things each taught their granddaughter—from
placing salad forks to sliding down carpeted stairs on a
cookie sheet.

All of this showed the granddaughter that there are
many ways to live and the way she chooses to live will
be up to her.

The verse above is from one of the most well-known
passages in the Bible about choosing. Joshua was an
average person chosen by God to be a leader. He chose
to follow God despite what others might do. His commitment to obey God challenged the people to make
up their minds to follow God.

Now, as then, this is a choice we all make.

♥ *I choose to follow You, God.*

PROMISES THICK AS DAISIES

O Death, where is your sting?
O Hades, where is your victory?
—1 COR. 15:55

𝒢randmother Sunderman lived on a busy street. One day when preschooler Lori was visiting her and went out to play, Grandma reminded her not to go in the street—a car might hit and kill her.

Lori said, "That would be all right, Grandma, I'd go to be with Jesus." Grandma immediately began to search for other ways to explain why the street was a dangerous place for this bright child who had learned early that she needn't fear death.

Henry Ward Beecher wrote, "We have the promises of God as thick as daisies in summer meadows, that death, which men most fear, shall be to us the most blessed of experiences, if we trust in Him. Death is unclasping joy breaking out in the desert; the heart coming to its blossoming time! Do we call it dying when the bud bursts into flower?"

Commenting on the above verse from 1 Corinthians, in *Thru the Bible with J. Vernon McGee* Dr. McGee tells us, "Death has lost its sting, because we are to look way out beyond death. It is a doorway that opens up the vast regions of eternity. It starts us down the hallway, not of time, but of eternity. . . . So like a child I'll put my hand in His nail-pierced hand, and He will lead me to the other side."

♥ *Dear God, thank You for leading me through life . . . and death.*

Rejoice always, pray without ceasing, in everything give thanks; for this is the will of God in Christ Jesus for you.
—1 THESS. 5:16–18

*N*ancy Turk wrote an article titled "Parents Again," published in *A Better Tomorrow*. She gained the following insights on tough times from her own experience of raising a four-year-old granddaughter, when it was necessary for her daughter to leave her husband and separate her four children:

- Be honest with God about how you really feel. He will help you handle it.
- Try to find others in your church or community who are in a similar situation. A support group helps.
- Realize that God has entrusted you with a special ministry.
- Accept and encourage your grandchild's need to talk about his or her past.
- Pray, pray, pray!

Nancy speaks for all "parents again" as well as grandmothers and grandfathers in general when she says, "God has entrusted us with one of His special children. He desires to guide us through this time, but He can only do this when we pray and listen to His voice."

♥ *I trust You for guidance, Lord, as I take part in parenting my grandchildren.*

DEBT OF LOVE

Owe no one anything except to love one another, for he who loves another has fulfilled the law.
—ROM. 13:8

*A*ngela took her Grandmother Kramer's picture to school and put it in the Important Box. When it was time to tell why what she put in the box was important to her, Angela held her grandmother's picture close and said, "Because I love her and she loves me."

Grandmothers are more important to grandchildren than we sometimes think we are. We may think it's just the material things we give them that are important. But there are other measures—measures that have foundations of love. When talking with people about their grandmothers, over and over again they tell of the little things that meant so much to them: the time spent in playing games, reading, taking them places; notes, cards, letters received; food that made them feel special; just talking and listening; the example of lives. Love.

The Bible tells us we owe a debt of love to others because of Jesus' love for us. Our love for Jesus makes this one debt that isn't a burden. Repayment is an opportunity for neverending joy.

♥ *I accept my debt of love, Lord.*

Come and hear, all you who fear God,
And I will declare what He has done for my
soul.
—PS. 66:16

A grandmother asked her friends to pray for her as she attempted to build a relationship with a teenage granddaughter. She was going to ask the granddaughter to go out for breakfast and was worried about what they would talk about. She had always heard about grandmas and grandchildren being close but it had never happened to her. She wondered if it was too late.

The group responded with prayer and promises of further prayer support and offered suggestions for things to talk about with grandchildren, including "where you went to school and the subjects you liked best and why; how you met your husband and about your first date; about any jobs you had and what job she thinks she'd like; about the first thing you bought with your own money." Any of those will start conversation.

Grandmothers and grandchildren have much to tell each other once they start talking. When we talk first to God about these conversations, we might be surprised how often our telling and talking includes God—and we might not be the one who brings Him into the conversation!

♥ *You have done so much for me, how can I not talk about You, God?*

UNIQUENESS

You are worthy, O Lord,
To receive glory and honor and power;
For You created all things. . . .

—REV. 4:11

*A*s a teen, Randy remembers walking into his Grandma Kmieciak's house and hearing her ask, "Did you clean behind your ears? Make sure the door is closed," before she even said hello. He says that it irritated him and other grandchildren for years.

Then Grandma Kmieciak died. It wasn't long before the grandchildren admitted they missed the way she had greeted them. What she had said didn't seem so bad after all. It made her uniquely their grandma.

Do you ever think about what makes you unique to your grandchildren? Do you have a special name they call you? Do you call them by special names? Are there things that only you and they do together? If you answered no, try to think of and begin some small activity that is yours and theirs alone. It can be as simple as a phrase you always say when you see them or as involved as a meal or special food only you can make.

Each of us is unique to God. We do not always understand what God has done or is doing, but we do know He created our world and us and that we are meant to worship Him. He is uniquely God.

♥ *Heavenly Father, I worship You because You are the one and only God.*

GRANDMA DO RIGHT

Trust in the LORD forever,
for the LORD . . is the Rock eternal.
            —ISA. 26:4 NIV

I know many grandmothers who bring their grand-children to church regularly. In fact, many times, if Grandma didn't bring them, they wouldn't be coming.

There may be several reasons why it happens. Parents may work on Sundays, or there is an illness, or it may be that the parents just no longer go to church but are willing to let their children go. Thank God for grandmothers who make a commitment to take them.

I know of one grandchild who attended church and Sunday school with his grandmother for several years. Eventually this helped bring his parents back to God—surely an answer to the grandmother's and grandson's prayers, and affirmation of the grandmother's commitment to do what was right.

It's easy to get discouraged when you are doing what's right. To forget to trust God and His Words that tell us what He will do for us. The key is trusting God because He is Lord of all.

♥ *Dear God, when I'm trusting You, I'm not discouraged. Help me remember that You are my Rock eternal.*

*My mouth shall tell of Your righteousness
And Your salvation all the day.*
> —PS. 71:15

*H*ave you ever told your grandchildren your testimony? Do they know how and when you came to know Jesus as Savior? It's not something that you just sit down and tell them right out of the blue, but it is something they should hear from you.

If you haven't told them, start praying about how and when you can. In fact, if you feel you might have trouble beginning the conversation, you can even ask God to have them bring up the subject. Then, be prepared when He does!

Another way of telling them would be to write it down. You can buy a book that you can write in telling your grandchildren all about yourself—your early life, school experiences, hopes and dreams, and spiritual life. This could be a wonderful written legacy for your grandchildren, one that will grow in value and meaning as they grow older.

Proverbs 20:29 tells us that as we grow older our glory is in our experience. And we are never too old for experience with God in service, prayer, and telling others (especially grandchildren) about what God has done for us throughout our lives.

♥ *Thank You, God, for the many experiences we've been through together.*

*So then those who are of faith are blessed
with believing Abraham.* —GAL. 3:9

*G*randma White kept scrapbooks. Scrapbooks of
people including movie stars, Franklin and Eleanor
Roosevelt, the Dionne Quintuplets, Lindbergh, the
Duke and Duchess of Windsor. A scrapbook of her father's newspaper columns. And one of the church she
attended for several years. And scrapbooks of greeting
cards, stories, poems, and newspaper articles of interest. She also kept many photo albums. We now have a
visual record of family members that includes great-
grandparents, grandparents, aunts, uncles, and
cousins.

Our family has enjoyed looking at the scrapbooks
and albums many times. They often lead to discussions
about family and life. They've even been used to write
school reports. I wonder if Grandma knew how much
her scrapbooks and albums would interest us. Or how
much we have learned about her and her faith through
them.

Abraham believed that God would save him (see
Gen. 15:6). We read of his faith throughout the Bible—
God's family album. God made it possible for believers
everywhere to share Abraham's blessing when He gave
His Son, Jesus Christ, to die for us. It's a promise.

♥ *Thank You for including us in Your blessing, Lord.*

GRANDMOTHER'S BABY

Behold, children are a heritage from
the LORD,
The fruit of the womb is His reward.
—PS. 127:3

I found the following poem in a very old scrapbook that belonged to my grandmother.

Thirty years ago, my baby,
A baby just like you,
With golden fluff in silken rings,
And shining eyes of blue,
Came to fill my life with love;
His dimpled hand was stronger then
Than all the hosts above.

. . . .

Thirty years ago, my baby,
I tell it in your ear.
Another nursling, just like you,
Came from the angels here.
I lost him in the whirlpool
Of the rough world long ago;
And now the angels bring him back—
That's why I love you so!

This grandmother agrees with the psalmist that children are "a gift from God," even a reward. Grandmothers are included as receivers of these precious gifts, whereby they gain the awesome opportunity to help shape the future.

♥ *I praise You for the gift of my grandchildren, Lord.*

LISTEN

*It is written in the prophets, "And they shall
all be taught by God." Therefore everyone
who has heard and learned from the Father
comes to Me.*
                                    —JOHN 6:45

*N*yki was talking to her Grandma Jo while Grandma
was busy doing something. Every time Nyki would say
something, Grandma would ask, "What?"

After several "whats," Nyki said in exasperation,
"Grandma, use your ears. That's what they're for!"

It wouldn't be too surprising if at some time those
very same words had been said to Nyki when she
wasn't paying attention. It's always interesting how the
things we do and say come back to us. Children do pay
close attention.

Grandmothers get busy, and it is easy to do something else while half-listening to what grandchildren
say. It would be worth our efforts to change—not just to
hear but to listen.

The same principle holds true in our spiritual lives.
We talk to God, but do we listen for Him to talk to us?
Throughout the Bible, when God wanted to get His
people's attention, He would begin a message with the
word "Listen!" God created us with ears. He wants us
to use them to listen to Him and others.

♥ *I want to really listen to You and learn, Lord.*

FEELING SAFE

Preserve me, O God, for in You I put my trust.
— PS. 16:1

*W*hen Janet was in the third grade she began spending her summers with her Grandma Frye. During those summers she was given some privileges not allowed at home. At the grocery store, Grandma let Janet pick out the ice cream she wanted—and sugar-coated cereal. During mealtime, Janet always sat next to Grandma so that Grandma would eat the vegetables she didn't like.

Grandma Frye had been a schoolteacher in a one-room school in Kentucky. She had many experiences to tell. Janet grew up to be a schoolteacher, too. They still enjoy comparing notes and sharing stories about teaching. Janet has a comfortable, safe relationship with her grandma.

George Eliot wrote, "Oh, the comfort, and inexpressible comfort of feeling safe with a person; having neither to weigh thoughts nor measure word, but to put them all out, just as they are, chaff and grain together, knowing that a faithful hand will take and sift them, keep what is worth keeping, and then with the breath of kindness, blow the rest away." It is a good description of a friend, who just might be a grandmother.

♥ *Knowing You is all the comfort and safety I really need, God.*

For thus says the LORD,
Who created the heavens, . . .
"I am the LORD, and there is no other."
> —ISA. 45:18

*B*etsy is the Hudgens' family dog who thinks she is a grandchild. When the family goes to see Grandma Hudgens, Betsy begins pawing at the car window as soon as they get near her house. Then, as soon as she is let out of the car, she races into the house to find Grandma and scratches at her knee until she is picked up so she can cover Grandma's neck and face with dog kisses. When Grandma Hudgens comes to visit the family, Betsy goes to the front door and whines until Grandma comes in and pays attention to her.

Our pets do sometimes seem almost human and have a way of becoming members of the family. Genesis tells the wonderful story of the creation of our world and everything in it. Animals were created the day before man. What's most important is God's comment about each creation—"And God saw that it was good."

♥ *God, I praise You for Your creation and thank You that I am part of it.*

*For he that soweth to his flesh shall of the
flesh reap corruption; but he that soweth to
the Spirit shall of the Spirit reap life
everlasting.* **—GAL. 6:8 KJV**

*P*resident Clinton was sworn in on a King James
version Bible received from his grandmother. He re-
quested it be opened to the verse for today. His aides
said the Bible was worn around the edges because the
President carried it to weekly services in Little Rock,
Arkansas, when he was governor.

The President opened his first Cabinet meeting with
a prayer of thanks and a request: "Our Heavenly Father, we thank You for this unique opportunity which
has been given us to serve our country to Thy ends.
Please be with us and guide us. Keep us humble and
eager, and help us to proceed with wisdom. Amen."

Paul tells us we need to pray for our leaders, "I exhort therefore, that, first of all, supplications, prayers,
intercessions, and giving of thanks, be made for all
men; / For kings, and for all that are in authority; that
we may lead a quiet and peaceable life in all godliness
and honesty" (1 Tim. 2:1–2 KJV). Even when we do
not agree with those who are in power, we must pray for
them and remember that it is better to have a govern-
ment we don't agree with than none at all.

♥ *Help me to remember to pray for our President and
others who govern us.*

Now hope does not disappoint, because the love of God has been poured out in our hearts by the Holy Spirit who was given to us.
　　　　　　　　　　　　　　　　—ROM. 5:5

*G*randma Berlew knits slippers and makes dish towels for her stepgrandchildren. Her stepgrand-daughter has more slippers than she'll ever wear, and piles of dish towels. But she doesn't mind. Grandma Berlew's natural grandchildren got caught between parents who divorced; grandchildren and grand-mother lost out. Her stepgrandchildren help her not to be so lonely for them.

A quote from Harry Emerson Fosdick speaks to this and other disappointments.

There is no more searching test of the human spirit than the way it behaves when fortune is adverse and it has to pass through a prolonged period of disap-pointing failures. Then comes the real proof of man. Achievement, if a man has the ability, is a joy; but to take hard knocks and come up smiling, to have your mainsail blown away and then rig a sheet on the bow-sprit and sail on—this is perhaps the deepest test of character.

God knows and understands our disappointment. It is from Him we find the courage that enables us to sail on. He is our hope.

♥ *Father, the hope You give is the wind in my sails.*

. . . Blessed be the name of God forever and ever,
For wisdom and might are His. . . .
He gives wisdom to the wise
And knowledge to those who have understanding.
                                    —DAN. 2:20–21

*M*y grandson Brian and I were driving to visit his aunt and cousins. Brian suddenly said, "Grandma, tell me what my dad was like when he was a little kid."

It was an invitation I was glad to accept. I told Brian how much his dad loved to wear hats, that he had an extremely messy room, and how he started earning his own money by finding jobs to do.

Grandmothers are usually the best people to tell grandchildren what their parents were like. Often it helps grandchildren to hear that their parents had some of the same feelings they do, did some of the same things they've done, and made mistakes like they do—and lived through it. Childhood is not all fun; children have their troubles and problems, too. They are still in the process of gaining the maturity to handle them.

We can be a tremendous help in this stage of their lives because of the knowledge and wisdom we've acquired. We can help our grandchildren know that God's knowledge and wisdom give confidence and peace no matter what happens in our lives.

♥ *I thank and praise You, God, for the knowledge and wisdom You have given me.*

*This will be written for the generation to come,
That a people yet to be created may praise the LORD.*
—PS. 102:18

*B*efore Grandma White was married she was a school teacher in a one-room school in North Dakota. She held the smallest students in her class on her lap to teach them to read and was escorted to square dances by the oldest students in her class, who were often older than she was.

Grandma wasn't a school teacher for very long. She married and had a family. But she continued to use her abilities to teach Sunday school and vacation Bible school. Grandma loved to read, too. One of my best memories of her was seeing tears running down her face as she read a particularly moving part of a book. She often gave books as gifts to grandchildren. Grandma had several well-marked Bibles. I still have one of them.

We are so fortunate to have God's written Word. Written down by godly men whom God chose to inspire so that even though they wrote from their own culture and in their own style it was exactly what God wanted them to write. God was in charge of the writing and of its distribution down through generations, including through grandmothers.

♥ *Thank You for Your written Word, Lord.*

> *Who is a God like You,*
> *Pardoning iniquity*
> *And passing over the transgression of the*
> *remnant of His heritage?*
>
> —MIC. 7:18

*H*aven, age four, was staying with Grandma Stephens and noticed that the family's parakeet had a problem. One of its feathers was sticking out sideways. Haven was very disturbed and told her grandma that she was going to pray and ask God to help the bird. Grandma and Haven prayed together. After they finished, they looked in the cage and saw that the feather had fallen out. Haven was so excited. She told her grandmother, "I need to tell Jesus thank You."

Grandchildren can sometimes be such wonderful examples to us! We need their characteristics of simple trust in God and immediate thankfulness to Him. Too often I've prayed, asking God to grant a request and then, when He did, delayed thanking Him or even forgot to thank Him. How very ungrateful and unloving. And still God forgives.

The question asked in the verse above is asked in other passages throughout the Bible including Exodus, Deuteronomy, Kings, and Psalms. The answer is, there is no one to equal God. We can find those who equal us, but God stands alone.

♥ *I praise You, God, for there is no one like You.*

Come, you children, listen to me;
I will teach you the fear of the LORD.
            —PS. 34:11

*R*andy liked to play jokes on his Grandma Johnson, who was very short. As a teen, Randy could look down at the top of her head; he liked to tease her by saying the part in her hair was crooked. There was no end to the practical jokes he played on his grandmother, and the one he enjoyed most and played the longest before she figured it out was to confuse her by changing television channels with the extra remote control.

There are grandmothers grandchildren can tease and play jokes on, and there are grandmothers they can't. They learn the difference early and adapt to them. In fact, having family members with differing temperaments is good experience in getting along with people. It's another way our grandchildren learn about life by what we teach.

Throughout the Bible, we are told to teach children. It is the greatest textbook for life and will be a guide for every circumstance of their lives. Of most importance is God's message of love and forgiveness. There is also a need for reverence (fear) that is connected to obedience. Many of the gifts of God's promised blessings have conditions. They are all wrapped in love.

♥ *Thank You for our life's textbook, Your Word. Help*
me to learn and teach from it, Lord.

*Likewise the Spirit also helps in our
weaknesses. . . . The Spirit Himself makes
intercession for us with groanings which
cannot be uttered.*
                                    —ROM. 8:26

*R*ed Jell-O always makes Carolyn think about her
grandmother. Her grandma didn't have a phone and
so when Carolyn and her family decided to visit, they
would just stop by. Grandma always had red Jell-O
ready. She would tell them, "I knew you were coming
so I made some Jell-O."

Who can explain grandmother intuition? That special sensitivity alerts us to grandchildren's calls, notes,
or visits and helps us know when they may be troubled
or have a need. I can't help but think that sensing trouble or need is correlated to our praying for them.

I'm sure you have prayed for your grandchildren as
I have—not really knowing what to pray, but placing
them in our Heavenly Father's hands. How marvelous
to know that when we don't have the words, the Holy
Spirit knows exactly what is needed and prays with and
for us. This is one way God helps us to pray. Knowing
this, we can ask the Holy Spirit to intercede for us in
keeping with God's will. God's answer might include
the guidance we need to help them. Or, praying for
them might be all we need to do. It's certainly the best
thing we can do.

♥ *Father, thank You for the help of Your Spirit when I
don't know what to ask You.*

BLESSED MEMORY

The memory of the righteous is blessed. . . .
—PROV. 10:7

*O*ur family enjoys garage sales. While on vacation at the resort near some small towns, my daughter and I saw an advertisement for a whole town garage sale. We left the teens asleep and took the younger grandchildren with us to drive up one street and down the other in this garage sale paradise.

Six-year-old Angie loaded her arms and neck with jewelry and found nearly new coloring books—all for less than two dollars. The ten-year-olds, Becky and Brian, added to their libraries and discovered interesting items to decorate their rooms.

Going to garage sales is an activity that takes less effort and expense than most. It's a fun and interesting way to spend time with grandchildren.

Righteous means doing what is right. For a Christian it implies doing it in a loving way. There are so many right things that we can do with grandchildren; they might even become blessed memories.

♥ *Dear God, I want to be a blessed memory to my grandchildren. Guide me in righteousness.*

When my father and my mother forsake me,
The the LORD will take care of me.

—PS. 27:10

One of my favorite books is *The Summer of the Great-Grandmother* by Madeleine L'Engle. In it the author chronicles the last summer of her mother's life surrounded by her children, grandchildren, and great-grandchildren. Woven throughout the story are the author's frustrations, sadness, terror, and resignation about her mother's illness. Following her mother's death she writes, "The pattern has shifted; we have changed places in the dance. I am no longer anybody's child. I have become the Grandmother."

How quickly it seems we become the older generation. I remember once commenting after I had grown up and married that I didn't necessarily want to ever live with my parents again, but it was nice to know they were always there in case I needed to. All too soon they were gone and I, too, felt a bit like an orphan.

Even though death is not a voluntary action, it can make us feel forsaken because the person has left. God uses the close relationship of parents to assure us that even though people as close to us as our mother and father leave, He will never leave us. Not under any circumstances. Never.

♥ *Father God, thank You for being the only One who can truly say You will always be there for me.*

*Nor as being lords over those entrusted to
you, but being examples to the flock.*
—1 PETER 5:3

Grandmother Maralee feels it takes a little more effort to be a grandmother when grandchildren live two thousand miles away. She was never privileged to have grandparents—they had died before she was born—but she remembers going to her friend's grandparents' house and sensing the love that grandparents had for their grandchildren. Maralee had the feeling that those grandchildren were loved as special children.

When she became a grandmother, she wanted her grandchildren to have that same feeling—that they were special to her even though they lived far away from her.

We may not realize the good model of grandmotherhood we are giving to our own grandchildren and other children. The seemingly insignificant things we do with love for and with our grandchildren—making cookies, reading, playing, or listening—could inspire a child.

When Peter described the characteristics of good church leaders, he could also have been talking to grandmothers. He says we lead best by example. The verse following tells us that Jesus will reward us with a "crown of glory that does not fade away" (1 Pet. 5:4).

♥ *Your example is what I want to follow in leading others, God.*

Do they not go astray who devise evil?
But mercy and truth belong to those who
devise good.　　　—PROV. 14:22

*E*ach time Maralee's grandchildren planned a visit, she would go to garage sales to find toys to entertain them while they were visiting. They were always delighted when they arrived and found "new to them" toys in the old toy box.

One year when they visited, Grandmother Maralee thought it would be fun to take them "garage saling" and let them select their own toy. Five-year-old Robb spotted an electric car you could ride in. It wasn't in working condition, so Maralee said, "No, Robb, that isn't what you want, look over there at the skates!" Robb wouldn't be distracted, and Grandmother ended up pulling Robb to the car screaming, "But I want that car!" From then on Grandmother went to garage sales alone and brought back the surprises.

Sometimes grandmothers' good ideas don't work out. But grandmothers have had years of being resourceful and can always come up with a new idea or simply go back to plan A.

The Bible tells us that the motive behind our plans is what is most important. Even when the good things don't work out, we won't lose trust and respect.

♥ *Lord, keep me checking my motives in everything I do.*

> *And then the lawless one will be revealed,*
> *whom the Lord will consume with the*
> *breath of His mouth and destroy with the*
> *brightness of His coming.*
> —2 THESS. 2:8

*M*ystery trips were the highlight of the day before
Grandmother Stephens' grandchildren went home
from visits. They were each given numbered envelopes. As they pulled out of the driveway, the envelope
numbered 1 would be opened. The directions inside
might be, "Go to the drug store for an ice cream cone."
After the cone was devoured, the #2 envelope was
opened: "Take a ride on the bumper cars," and so on
through the last envelope. The stops were selected according to the age of the child. Some years they included pet shop, bird sanctuary, book store, feeding
the ducks at the park, and buying a balloon. These
mystery trips were never-to-be-forgotten nights to remember—the finale to their visit with Grandma.

Paul explained his relationship with the Thessalonians in family terms, "gentle among you, just as a nursing mother cherishes her own children" (1 Thess.
2:7). His apt words express how we feel as we share
God with our grandchildren in every aspect of our
lives.

♥ *Dear God, it is such a privilege to share You and my*
life with my grandchildren.

*In whom also we have obtained an
inheritance, being predestined according to
the purpose of Him who works all things
according to the counsel of His will.*
—EPH. 1:11

*W*hen Janna was sixteen she came to visit Grandma Stephens for four weeks. Ahead of time, Grandma sent her a questionnaire asking her to write down what she wanted to do and places she wanted to go while visiting. Then Grandma Stephens wrote out an itinerary for their time together. Each day was something special and included big and little outings such as shopping, eating lunch out, a trip to the beach, movies, the fair. Having the itinerary to see and look forward to was fun, even though it was altered as time demanded.

We probably don't put as much thought and planning into the times we spend with our grandchildren as we should—especially for the older ones. And it's wise to find out the things they like to do and plan accordingly. It sure shows and tells our grandchildren how much we care about them.

We have a God who makes plans. When He made the world and everything in it, He had a plan in mind. A plan that included us so that we could live with Him. Some of our plans may fail but God's great plan will never fail.

♥ *I praise You, God, for Your plan for me.*

The Spirit of God has made me,
And the breath of the Almighty gives me life.
—JOB 33:4

One year the Stephens' grandchildren and their parents came to stay with them for fourteen months. Grandmother Maralee says, "That was the year of birthdays. We had eight birthday celebrations!"

Grandma Maralee fashioned a beautiful gold and satin cloak that the honored birthday person wore for the birthday dinner of their favorite food. The person was king or queen for the day.

The family still enjoys the pictures they took of each other decked out in cloak and crown (especially the ones of the adults). At the end of their visit, Grandma secretly stuffed the cloak and crown in their suitcases as a memory of that year of birthdays.

Grandchildren and just about everyone else enjoy birthday celebrations—it is a special time of honor and rejoicing. A celebration of the person's life.

Part of our celebration should be thankful recognition to God for our lives. He gave us life and breath and longs to be included in every area of our lives. Invite Him to the birthday party!

♥ *Dear God, thank You for giving me life here and now, and life everlasting with You.*

DISGUISED BLESSINGS

. . . . there shall be showers of blessing.
—EZEK. 34:26

$\mathscr{G}$randmother Maralee feels another blessing of having grandchildren who live far away is the opportunity for them to attend college near their grandparents. Haven wanted to go to the college her father attended. Her grandparents enjoyed having her close by. Grandma made her favorite foods and often entertained her friends.

Then Janna attended college just a few miles away and they had a houseguest each weekend; they enjoyed attending church together and Grandma Maralee baked goodies every week. The room in Grandma's house is now ready for Robb should he decide to attend college near his grandparents.

Knowing that Grandma is nearby must be a blessing for the parents, too. And what a blessing for grandchildren taking their first steps out alone on life's stage. They have a measure of freedom and independence with a loving grandparent to assist in the wings.

When we look for the blessings in our circumstances, we can usually find them. When we obey Him, He will bless us. And He is not stingy with His blessings. Think how many raindrops there are in a shower.

♥ *Lord, thank You for the many blessings I have received from Your hand.*

Precious in the sight of the LORD
Is the death of His saints.
—PS. 116:15

*G*randma Gert had come home from the hospital to die. She was in a coma. Every day her daughter and granddaughter Rachel would wash her, talk to her, and rub her feet. Rachel's mother had told her to talk with her grandmother because even though she couldn't answer, she was here and maybe could hear them.

The morning Grandma Gert died, Rachel went to say good morning to her. She came to get her mother saying, "I don't think Grandma's here anymore." She knew her grandmother had died.

Some people feel that we should not allow children to be around those who are dying—that it is too traumatic for them. Others feel that children need to know that people do die.

Christians, who know that death in this world means life forever with Jesus, can help children begin to understand what happens when people die and give them opportunity to talk about their fears. This is a subject where grandmothers can express their faith in believing what God says.

♥ *Lord, I want my grandchildren to know that when I am no longer here with them, I am there with You.*

TRUE FRIENDSHIP

A man who has friends must himself be
*   friendly,*
But there is a friend who sticks closer than
*   a brother.*   **—PROV. 18:24**

*G*randma White lived in a mobile home park in Arizona. The park, like many others in the city, had a ratio of approximately ten widows to every widower. The single seniors often went out to dinner together or got together for dessert in each other's homes. Grandma's children and grandchildren used to tease her about marrying one of the eligible men.

Her answer delighted them. "What? Marry one of those old men? I don't think so." She told them she always saw Grandfather as the young man she married. He had never grown old in her eyes, though they were married fifty years before he died.

Remarriages can be wonderful, and are as good a decision as not to remarry. A lot depends on how needs for companionship are being fulfilled. No matter how old we get, we need friends who care about us.

The Bible encourages us to be a true friend to others. Jesus is a friend who always sticks by us. Jesus' way is the best way to have friends. When we are loyal, give help when needed, listen, and show we care, we will never be lonely.

♥ *Father, I am thankful for my friends. I want to follow Jesus' example in being a true friend.*

. . . Whoever receives this little child in My name receives Me; and whoever receives Me receives Him who sent Me. For he who is least among you all will be great.

—LUKE 9:48

O ne time I visited my daughter and grand-daughters, who live in another city. I went to school with granddaughter Becky and was introduced to her teacher and all her classmates. I helped with a project they were working on and listened to a class discussion on reports they would be writing. Then we went to the gym to hear a concert by the junior high band in which my other granddaughter, Jamie, played.

It was an easy and enjoyable way to spend the day. I had a nice time. What surprised me was how much it meant to Becky. She welcomed me into her world with such eagerness and pride that she made me feel very, very special.

Some schools have a grandparents day as a regular activity. It gives everybody a chance to feel special and gives us a look at the world where our grandchildren spend several hours a day.

The welcome or care we show our grandchildren and what they show us can give us a good idea of our real greatness.

♥ *Dear Lord, thank You for making it so easy to show my welcome (care) for You through my grand-children.*

THE DAY GRANDMA PRAYED

Let your light so shine before men, that they may see your good works and glorify your Father in heaven. —MATT. 5:16

One of the most precious memories Terrie has of her grandmother, Alice Mahan, occurred at a holiday time at her parents' home. The entire family had gathered for a big meal—aunts, uncles, cousins, etc. Grandma had deteriorated physically and mentally, and it was hard for the family to see her waste away. On this occasion she was mobile and could talk but was confused and didn't make sense.

At the meal, Terrie's father startled everyone by asking Grandma Mahan to ask the blessing. Terrie couldn't help wondering why he did it. He knew she wouldn't make sense. It would be awkward and everyone would just feel worse.

As they bowed their heads, God gave them a gift. For one brief moment they heard their grandma pray once more. It was a lucid, clear expression to God of thankfulness, faith, and love for her family.

Afterwards, Grandma reverted to the confused, uncommunicative shell of a person that was so hard to accept. But her family had a memory they would all hold close to their hearts and reminisce about. God allowed Grandma's light to shine forth brightly that day to reaffirm to her family that the highest priority in life had been love of her Lord and her family.

♥ *Dear Father, do people see and know that the aim and purpose of my life is to glorify You?*

For whatever things were written before were written for our learning, that we through the patience and comfort of the Scriptures might have hope.

—ROM. 15:4

$\mathcal{G}$randmother Rose came to America from Italy in 1916 when she was twelve years old. She couldn't speak English and was put in the first grade. She had to find her own way of learning the language. When her mother wanted to buy a handkerchief but didn't know how to ask for one, Rose dropped her handkerchief at school on purpose to get someone to say the word for her. Little by little she picked up the words and went to bed at night repeating them to herself.

This story and others about family members have been written down by two of her grandchildren in a homemade book. The book concludes, "Rose carries with her the names and stories of many family members that would otherwise be forgotten. For this reason, we have written it down as best we could, in the hope that others of us can now remember."

Just as it is important for us to know what our family members have done in the past, God wants us to know what He has done. Everything in the Bible is written for our learning and to give us patience and to give us comfort and to bring hope into our lives.

♥ *Dear God, Your Word tells me about the past and gives me confidence for the future.*

SOMEBODY'S GRANDMOTHER

Do not cast me off in the time of old age;
Do not forsake me when my strength fails.
—PS. 71:9

*V*isiting a convalescent home is difficult for me. It is hard for me to see all those "somebody's grandmothers" lying in beds, sitting in chairs, and shuffling along the hallways alone. My head understands that sometimes this is the only way to care for them and that most have families who do come to visit. But still my heart aches. And perhaps I cannot help but wonder if I am seeing my future.

While on a bus with a teen choir tour, one of their young adult sponsors asked me, "As a grandmother, what is the most important lesson you have learned in life?"

I answered almost immediately, "Acceptance."

The sponsor said, "I was afraid you would say something like that."

Visits to convalescent homes remind me of that important lesson. It may be that I will have to accept a place such as this for my future.

Psalm 71 is a psalm for old age. It is a good psalm for senior citizens. In it David says he prays and trusts.

♥ *Dear God, thank You for this wonderful psalm that reminds me of how faithful You are.*

Be hospitable to one another without grumbling.
—1 PETER 4:9

*J*ean still remembers the way her Grandma Ruth smelled "like a homey kitchen, and her hands were always warm. She always welcomed me with a smile and her skin was soft." Jean's mother died when she was nine, and her grandmother became her mainstay and maternal figure.

Grandma Ruth was a good cook and always made the birthday cakes for her family—a dark, rich fruit cake. She was always ready to listen to Jean and liked to tell stories of her own youth, her wedding and the dress that was blue instead of white, her honeymoon trip on a train, and getting lost. Jean's grandparents didn't have much money, and they gave away everything they had. Her grandmother cooked food for all the neighbors.

Grandmothers are often hospitable. They have learned that possessions, status, and power don't mean very much in God's eyes or make a difference in His Kingdom. Our time and the things we know how to do should be used in ways that will make a difference for all eternity.

♥ *Dear God, remind me of what's eternal when I get caught up in the temporal.*

MOST IMPORTANT

*And walk in love, as Christ also has loved
us and given Himself for us, an offering and
a sacrifice to God for a sweet-smelling
aroma.*
                                    —EPH. 5:2

*G*randdaughters Jamie and Becky had come to stay
with me for a few days. They needed shoes to play in,
so we went to the mall. What Jamie really wanted was
a pair of expensive sport shoes like ones her friends
had but her parents couldn't afford.

At the shoe store Becky found what she wanted and
was happily outfitted in no time. After Jamie made her
choice, I asked her to show me the ones like her
friends. She showed me but didn't ask me to buy them.
I thought that showed great strength of character. I
bought them for her, telling myself, "Buying something that parents can't afford is something grandmas
can do sometimes, especially when the grandchild has
not asked for it."

It's certainly not the worst thing a grandmother
could do, as long as things never take the place of what
is more important.

Throughout the Bible, God tells us how important
we are to Him. He loved us so much, He died so we
could live. That's the kind of love we should have for
our grandchildren and others—the kind that goes beyond the affection that prompts the giving of things to
the sacrifice of giving ourselves.

♥ *Dear God, don't let me neglect what's most important in showing love to my grandchildren.*

*I have fought the good fight, I have finished
the race, I have kept the faith. Finally, there
is laid up for me the crown of righteousness.*
—2 TIM. 4:7–8

*W*hen Grandma Mahan died, Terrie wrote to her
cousin who lived in a remote area of Mexico. He was
the only member of the family not able to come for the
funeral. He did not know of his grandmother's death
until he received Terrie's letter and one from his
mother. Terrie included with her letter a copy of the
pastor's notes from the service.

The beautifully detailed letter of their grandmother's final days, service, and testimony of her
strong faith included the following: "She was so proud
of all her family. I find myself wanting to live the rest of
my life so that she is proud of me. I don't remember
her ever not making each one of us feel that we were
special and much loved. She told me once that you
used to say to her when you were a baby, 'I'm Grandma's precious.' That was a memory that was special to
her."

Grandma Mahan's life prepared her for death. She
shared with Paul his confident expectation of meeting
Jesus. Paul's words in the verse above were written to
encourage Timothy and us. Whatever we suffer here
will be worth it all when we see Jesus.

♥ *Dear Jesus, I am eager to see You, my Lord and my
Friend.*

WHEN THAT TIME COMES

*And God will wipe away every tear from
their eyes; there shall be no more death, nor
sorrow, nor crying; and there shall be no
more pain, for the former things have
passed away.*
                                        —REV. 21:4

*G*randmother had been sick for several months before she died. The following excerpt of a poem, signed
by both her and her husband, was among her belongings.

When That Time Comes

Do not allow heroic measures—
  Resuscitation,
  Million-dollar machines
  Wired or hooked up to me—
To prolong life.
Let me die a natural death,
Helped by pain relief.

. . . .

When that time comes
Memorialize me by doing a kind deed.
Remember I am not dead
I am alive in Christ.

The promises in the verse above seem almost too
good to be true. But God said them and we can be sure
that eternity with Him will be much more than we can
ever imagine.

♥ *Dear God, when I wonder what eternity will be like,
I cling to Your promises.*

*But we all, with unveiled face, beholding as
in a mirror the glory of the Lord, are being
transformed into the same image . . . just as
by the Spirit of the Lord.*

—2 COR. 3:18

A beloved grandmother had been sick for several
years. Everyone in the family had questioned at one
time or another why she had to go through all she did.
It didn't seem right or fair.

The philosophy of one of her granddaughters was
that God doesn't insulate His people against tragedy.
He allows things to happen to us, He is with us through
our trials, and good things can come out of them.
Others came to the conclusion that God permitted it
not for Grandma's growth as a Christian but for theirs.

Members of the family had to do things for
Grandma that required a lot of love and servitude. Caring for someone's basic needs requires humility and a
willingness to be a servant. For some family members
is was a time to learn more about sensitivity and compassion.

God wants us to reflect all the things that He is in our
lives. Throughout the Bible He tells us what He expects of His people. Most of the things God asks us to
do aren't hard, but sometimes we need hands-on experiences to show how to become more like Him.

♥ *Dear God, am I a reflection of You to all who know
me?*

Then the dust will return to the earth as it was,
And the spirit will return to God who gave it.
— ECCL. 12:7

*G*randmother Low was explaining the death of a two-year-old granddaughter to a five-year-old grandson. She told him that his sister was with Jesus in His house, but her body was like a little house she had lived in while on earth and it was at a place called a chapel. His sister didn't need it anymore.

When the little boy asked what they would do with his sister's house, Grandmother told him about the service that would be like church. Then, she explained they would take his sister's house, which was in a beautiful box, to the cemetery and put the box in a little place dug in the ground and cover it with earth. Soon, grass would grow over the place.

Death can come at any time to any one of us. The Bible tells us that Christians return to God and "Eye has not seen, nor ear heard, / Nor have entered into the heart of man / The things which God has prepared for those who love Him" (1 Cor. 2:9).

♥ *Dear God, thank You for Your promises that give assurance and hope.*

*May He grant you according to your heart's
    desire,
And fulfill all your purpose.*   —PS. 20:4

I was a grandmother when I graduated from college. When I graduated from high school I was intent on marrying my high school sweetheart; he was in college and we felt his education was more important than mine. In my twenties and thirties I was too busy raising a family, working, being involved in church activities, and writing. Then, in my forties my husband died. My son and daughters were grown and on their own, and for the first time since I was a teen, I didn't have anyone depending on me. Nor was I responsible to another person. I needed full-time employment, and said to God, "I can do whatever You want me to do. You know I need a job. You open the door and I'll walk through it."

I was offered a job halfway across the country—a job I never expected to get, and felt that God truly "opened the door" in a magnanimous way. The company hiring me stipulated that I return to college and receive my degree. I was forty-three.

We can trust God with the desires of our heart. When we do He makes our plans succeed in surprising ways.

♥ *Thank You, Father, for giving me heart's desires that
    are best for me.*

GOOD SPOILING

And now abide faith, hope, love, these
three; but the greatest of these is love.
—1 COR. 13:13

*M*y daughter was sightseeing and shopping in New Orleans when she saw in a gift shop a small wooden sculpture of a grandma with wire glasses; she was perched on a skateboard. It was titled, "Lean, Mean, Spoiling Machine."

It's so easy to do and so much fun to spoil our grandchildren! However, I suppose we do have to admit that there is good spoiling and bad spoiling. Bad spoiling means allowing any kind of behavior without any guidance whatsoever, supplying every request on demand, and absolute blindness to faults and shortcomings. Good spoiling includes undivided attention, surprise gifts, and short-term suspension of some family rules (such as a little bit later bed time and few more treats than are really good for you).

Love motivates good spoiling and love is essential to growth and development all of our lives. It is an attribute of God that He said is the greatest of all.

♥ *Your attribute of love, dear Lord, teaches me love.*

> *And may he be to you a restorer of life and*
> *a nourisher of your old age; for your*
> *daughter-in-law, who loves you, who is*
> *better to you than seven sons, has borne*
> *him.*
> **—RUTH 4:15**

*L*ou often visited her grandma in the small town next to where her family lived. She remembers one snowy night when her grandparents decided to pull her home on a sled. The scene is a picture postcard memory of skimming smoothly over the top of a thick blanket of snow that muffled all sound in the dark, quiet, crisp night and her grandparents pulling the sled while holding hands.

Several years later, after she had grown up, Lou's grandpa died and she began taking Grandma places—shopping, doctor, church, and more. She realizes sometimes as she takes her grandma home that they have changed places.

Life is a cycle. We care for those who are young until they are old enough to care for us when we are old.

Naomi is an interesting character in the story of Ruth. She suffered tragedy in the loss of her husband, sons, and home. Yet she trusted God and was blessed with a daughter-in-law who loved her and gave her a grandson who would take care of her as she grew old.

♥ *Dear God, thank You for the blessings I continue to receive as I trust You.*

THE BETTER WAY

The humble He guides in justice,
And the humble He teaches His way.
—PS. 25:9

*W*hen Lou's daughter died, she decided it would be best for her to adopt her daughter's son, Justin, even though she wondered if she had the energy to parent him through the adolescent years. In order to adopt Justin, both grandma and grandson had to go to court.

Grandma and grandson knew the lawyers would ask them questions. They asked Lou about her job and finances, and she was asked if she loved Justin and wanted to adopt him.

When Justin's turn came, the lawyer asked him if he wanted to live with his grandmother. Justin hesitated and grandma's heart stood still. Then Justin said in all sincerity, "Well, you know, Grandma and I don't agree on everything." Grandma and the lawyers smiled.

Justin, in his own way, understood the seriousness of what was happening. It was important for him to tell the truth so that the adoption was the right thing for him and his grandmother.

We need help in knowing what's right. We begin by thinking and speaking the truth, which includes admitting that we don't know it all. Then, God can teach us His better way.

♥ *Dear God, even when I think I know what's right, show me Your better way.*

COMPUTER GRANDMA

Give her of the fruit of her hands,
And let her own works praise her in the
gates.
—PROV. 31:31

Sara is five and Grandma Billie's youngest grandchild by thirteen years. Grandma has a complete home
computer system and all the programs a child could
wish for, including a nursery rhyme game and one that
can be used to create pictures. When Grandma, Sara,
and the computer get together, they are in their own little world. In fact, there is such a special bond between
Sara and her grandmother that the rest of the family
ignores them when they are having fun and being silly.

I admire any grandmother who understands computers as well as her grandchild does. I love my computer, but it sometimes gives me a headache. The
thought of using it to play games with grandchildren is
beyond my comprehension.

Chapter 31 of Proverbs is said by some commenta-
tors to be advice on how to choose the ideal wife. The
qualities include character, faithfulness, helper,
worker, talented, generous, energetic, wise, and kind.
Sara's grandmother has the qualities of a modern Proverbs 31 woman. One of her rewards is a closeness with
her granddaughter that will continue to grow and last
beyond technology.

♥ *Dear God, help me to continue working on Your list*
of characteristics.

Fear not, for I am with you;
Be not dismayed, for I am your God.
I will strengthen you . . . —ISA. 41:10

*J*im's grandmother was a stubborn woman who married a stubborn man. Together they stubbornly eked out an existence farming on the side of a mountain.

After his grandpa died, Grandma, true to form, stubbornly stayed on the mountain even though she needed cataract surgery. She didn't want to go and have the surgery. Jim, a college student, joined the rest of the family in a campaign to get her off the mountain and into the hospital.

Grandma finally had the first eye done, and then stubbornly refused to go through it again. She had to wear a patch over one eye the rest of her life.

Jim is now an ophthalmologist. He keeps his grandma's picture on his desk, eye patch and all, to remind himself it is sometimes very hard to help others, even those you love.

Does God ever feel frustrated about trying to help us? He tells us in His Word that we can ask Him for help whenever we need it, but too often we think we can handle everything by ourselves. We need to recognize when we are helpless and trust the One who loves us most.

♥ *Dear Lord, keep reminding me that Your help is always available.*

. . . love one another fervently with a pure heart.
                                    —1 PETER 1:22

*G*randmother Lucy's granddaughter remembers the smell of her grandmother's perfume and says her grandmother was a classy lady who always wore dresses and stockings with garters, and had long fingernails. Her home was always filled with fresh flowers. She was an excellent seamstress and made summer, prom, and wedding dresses for her granddaughters.

Every Thursday, a daughter would take her shopping; sometimes grandchildren went along and Grandma would take them for lunch. If the grandchildren mentioned they were looking for something special and couldn't find it, Grandma would find and buy it, except when she knew they were taking advantage of her generosity—and she always knew the difference.

When she died, the family discovered that she had kept everything her grandchildren had ever made for her; she had even written the child's name on the bottom of each item. She had not been affectionate, but they had felt loved.

One of the marks of real love is selfless giving. When we receive God's love and forgiveness, we are able to become less self-centered and more other-centered.

♥ *Lord, I need Your help to exemplify Your Son, Jesus.*

QUALITY OF CHARACTER

*And not only that, but we also glory in
tribulations, knowing that tribulation
produces perseverance; and perseverance,
character; and character, hope.*
—ROM. 5:3–4

*G*randmother Rebecca is described by her son as active, energetic, and vivacious. Her grandchildren are impressed by her lifestyle. At sixty-five her husband went on a river raft trip; she didn't want to be outdone and spent time training so that at sixty-eight she could do it, too, earning the distinction of being the oldest ever to go down the river on a raft.

Later, she went on a second trip to Africa to visit a Bible college in Liberia, which she supports with both money and resources. The family can only guess what might be her next adventure.

We should all have lifestyles that impress our grandchildren, and that doesn't necessarily mean all grandmothers need to go river rafting or take trips to Liberia. What impresses most is our quality of character. How do we handle problems?

The Bible indicates three words that we should associate with trouble or problems—*joy, hope,* and *patience*. Problems should bring out the best in our lives, develop our patience, strengthen our character, and deepen our trust in God. The confidence that results is impressive.

♥ *God, change my response to problems to joy as I trust
You to use them as opportunities to grow.*

September 14 _____

For to me, to live is Christ, and to die is gain.
—PHIL. 1:21

*W*hen Grandmother Susie was eighty-eight, she apologized to her family for living on and on when all her friends and contemporaries were gone. After her husband died she took care of her elderly sister, Mattie. Soon after Mattie died, Susie died. It was as if she felt her work was done. She was ninety-eight.

Dr. J. Vernon McGee wrote in *Thru the Bible with J. Vernon McGee*, "The first time I had cancer surgery, a letter came from a lady that said, 'I know that everybody is praying that you will get well, but I am praying that the Lord will take you home because to be with Christ is far better.' I wrote back and said, 'Would you mind letting the Lord decide about this? I want to stay.'"

There is a reason for our lives and we can believe that God directs the time when He calls us to be with Him. Sometimes we question what God has in mind for us, but we would do best just trusting Him.

♥ *Dear God, I'd like to stay here and be able to work for You as long as I can.*

A man will be satisfied with good by the
fruit of his mouth,
And the recompense of a man's hands will
be rendered to him.

—PROV. 12:14

David's Grandma Hattie owned and worked a newsstand in the early 1940s. Later, Grandma Hattie worked in a department store until she was seventy-seven. She was one of their best salespeople, with more sales than anyone else; she had to be forced to quit. I wouldn't be surprised to learn she found some other work to do.

For years I have quoted a line from one of Peg Bracken's books that says, "Most of the world's work is done by people who don't feel well." She might have added and those who are up in years. Recent statistics show that many people who retire from jobs they have held for years are returning to the work force in different occupations for more than just economic reasons. They like to work. And they are good workers.

The verse above is from a chapter of contrasts in Proverbs. The rewards of work are many and varied. Money often is not the primary goal. Work, ordained by God since the beginning (Adam had work to do in the Garden of Eden), has a lot to do with our well-being.

♥ *Dear God, I want the work I do to please You.*

September 16

WHATEVER YOU ASK

Therefore I say to you, whatever things you ask when you pray, believe that you receive them, and you will have them
—MARK 11:24

*A*nita's Grandmother Carmen was blind. When Anita was a baby, her mother needed to go outside to hang up the wash. She put Anita in the middle of the bed and seated Grandma Carmen on the edge of the bed to be in charge of the baby. Anita was able to roll over, and Grandma was worried she would roll off the bed. She asked God, "Just let me see long enough to keep Anita from rolling off the bed." Whether her "sight" was by eyes or instinct, she was able to keep her granddaughter safe.

A book about all the prayers for grandchildren that grandmothers have made would probably require an entire collection of books—like a many-volume set of encyclopedias. It would be an encouragement to all of us as we pray daily for our grandchildren.

Jesus is our best example for how we should talk to God. Once He prayed, ". . . all things are possible for You. . . . Not what I will, but what You will" (Mark 14:36).

God expects us to ask Him about the concerns we have. And He wants us to have faith that His answer will always be in line with His will, which is always, always, always the very best for us.

♥ *Dear Lord, I trust Your will concerning my grand-children.*

DELIGHTFUL WORDS

How sweet are Your words to my taste,
Sweeter than honey to my mouth!
—PS. 119:103

*G*randma Ivola was with her family for a holiday dinner. They were discussing languages when grandson Matt asked, "Grandma, do you know any Spanish words?"

Grandma thought for a while and said, "Uno."

Matt responded, "No I don't. I asked you."

I love stories like that. They are the kind the family remembers and tells their children. Actually, we should write down the things our grandchildren say that delight us and leave it to them as part of their legacy to share with the following generations.

I think what delights us so much about what they say is that even in their misunderstanding there is almost always a grain of truth or at the very least a different way of looking at something.

God wants us to take joy in His words, too. In the verse above He likens the rules He gives us to live by to something good to eat. In addition, His words give us wisdom. Especially when we allow His words to make a difference in our lives.

♥ *Help me to pay attention to Your words, Lord, so they do make a difference in my life.*

To know wisdom and instruction,
To perceive the words of understanding.
—PROV. 1:2

Grandmother Frony Cappitola James had a big oak table in her kitchen. Her grandchildren liked to gather around it and talk while she was fixing a meal.

Grandmother was a great teaser. Because there was a lot of family and not enough chairs, the children would always ask, "Where will we sit, Grandma?"

Grandma's standard answer was, "Pull up your hands, rest on your fists, and lean back on your thumbs."

Don't you imagine that was a saying that she had heard from her mother or grandmother? What are some of your family sayings? How far in your family history do they go back? Next time you get together it might be fun to talk about them and perhaps write them down for your grandchildren and great-grandchildren.

Some of our family sayings might even be classified as proverbs since they are short sentences drawn from long experience. However, there is a difference between our proverbs and God's book of Proverbs. The book of Proverbs is God's inspired words of wisdom.

♥ *How thankful I am for Your words of wisdom, O Lord.*

LOVE WRAPPERS

But above all these things put on love,
which is the bond of perfection.
— COL. 3:14

𝒢randdaughter Sara was to be in a dance recital. Her grandmother bought her a beautiful outfit covered with hot pink bows. When Sara, who has tomboy tendencies, saw it, she told her mother, "I'm not going to wear it. It makes me look like a poodle." Mother somehow convinced Sara to wear the expensive outfit Grandma had bought.

Grandmothers usually like to buy clothes for their grandchildren. However, sooner or later we come to the realization that our tastes and theirs are different. When we do, it's best either to take them with you and let them pick out what they want, or give them a specific amount of money to buy what they want. Unless you enjoy spending an entire day going from store to store frustrated when what you think looks good your grandchild hates, I suggest the second option.

The verse above is in the middle of a passage that gives guidelines for a holy life. God tells us to wrap our love in compassion, kindness, humility, gentleness, patience, and forgiveness. Letting go, even in little ways, takes that kind of understanding and selfless love.

♥ *I could be more selfless, Lord, especially when I think I know what's best.*

Blessed be the God and Father of our Lord Jesus Christ, who . . . has begotten us . . . to an inheritance incorruptible and undefiled and that does not fade away, reserved in heaven for you. —1 PETER 1:3-4

*J*oe's mother has eight grandchildren. One day she told the family that she had put money aside for the grandchildren to have when she died. "But," she said, "I would really enjoy watching you spend it." So she took them all to Disneyland.

I like that grandmother's spirit! My family knows I have a similar philosophy. There really won't be an inheritance of money. We're enjoying it together now.

After a neighbor down the street died, her family found money squirreled away in drawers, closets, coat pockets, and shoe boxes. Following the discovery of the first $200, they began looking through everything carefully. When my family heard the final amount located was over $3,000, I commented, "Don't waste your time looking when I'm gone."

There is really only one inheritance that we can all count on. What applied to the Jewish Christians that Peter was writing to in the verse above is for us, too. And we, too, should praise God, for His Son, Jesus, who gives us new life, hope, and has an absolutely secure inheritance waiting for us in heaven!

♥ *I praise You, God, for what You did for me in the past, are doing for me now, and will do in the future.*

THOUGHTS AND WAYS

For as the heavens are higher than the
*   earth,*
So are My ways higher than your ways,
And My thoughts than your thoughts.
           —ISA. 55:9

*F*ive-month-old Katherine was very sick. Her family thought she had the flu but she wasn't getting better. Her parents decided to take her to the hospital. When her grandmother arrived just then for a visit, the family asked her to go with them.

At the hospital, the doctors ran several tests and said they couldn't find out what was wrong. They would just have to wait and see. Grandmother wasn't satisfied with the answer and asked if they had tested for dislocation of the intestine. When the doctors said that wasn't necessary, Grandmother insisted. Grandmother was right and her diagnosis saved her granddaughter's life.

How do grandmothers sometimes know things like that? Only God holds that answer. We cannot know now why God allows some things to happen as they do. We can only guess, ponder, discuss, and speculate.

Like the people of Israel, we try to make God fit into a mold of our making. We want His plans and purposes to go along with ours. We need to work on fitting into God's plans—to acknowledge His supremacy.

♥ *I praise You, God, because You don't fit any mold I could possibly make.*

LIFE PATTERN

Brethren, join in following my example, and note those who so walk, as you have us for a pattern.
—PHIL. 3:17

*J*ulie's earliest memories of her Grandma Prokop are of the two of them sitting in the rocking chair in Grandma's bedroom at bedtime. Julie and Grandma rocked and sang "Jesus Loves Me," "Twinkle, Twinkle, Little Star," and other songs. Sometimes on Friday Julie stayed overnight with her grandmother. Then they would brush each other's hair before they went to bed. In the morning, Grandma would French braid Julie's hair, put a big apron on her, and they would bake. Julie had a step-stool to stand on and Grandma would let her pour the ingredients in the mixer, roll out dough, and help do whatever else she could.

Julie wants her daughter to have a close relationship with her own grandmother. And she has a wonderful pattern to follow when she becomes a grandmother, too.

Paul told the Philippians he wasn't perfect (Phil. 3:12); still, he challenged them to focus their lives to be like Christ, just as he was. At that time it was the best pattern they had to follow and said a lot about the testimony of his life. What pattern would people say you follow?

♥ *Lord, following Your pattern is one of my lifelong goals.*

CITY HOME

For our citizenship is in heaven. . . .
—PHIL. 3:20

*W*hen Ron was eight years old, he spent a week with his Grandma Graf who lived three hours away from his home on a farm. He loved playing with the little pigs and helping his grandma mix up the slop to feed them.

Ron regrets that he didn't see much of his grandma as he grew older. She suffered several strokes and the convalescent home she was in was some distance from where he lived. Before he went away to college, he went to see her and because of another minor stroke, she barely remembered him. Grandma died that winter. Ron wasn't able to attend her funeral and tears come to his eyes when he talks about not being able to say goodbye to her. It helps him to know that one day he'll see her again.

The Bible teaches us that we will know our family and friends in Heaven—one writer calls it our "city home." God has waiting for us a new body—one that is resurrected and everlasting—but our God-changed personalities and individualities will be recognizable and wonderfully perfect.

♥ *I can hardly imagine being me and perfect. Only You can do that, Lord.*

*Bears all things, believes all things, hopes
all things, endures all things.*
                                   —1 COR. 13:7

*M*argaret's mother, grandmother, and great-grandmother had marriages that lasted fifty, sixty, even seventy-five years. When Margaret was married, the heirloom willow ware was a special, private gift from her mother.

At eighteen, Margaret didn't realize the specialness of the gift. In fact, at eighteen Margaret didn't realize many things. The marriage was broken within a few years. The willow ware was taken home by a sad and heartsick mother.

Then Margaret married again. A small, quiet ceremony. Family, a few friends, no gifts expected. Margaret could not ask her mother for the willow ware any more than she could put in words that she knew this marriage would last—that she had grown up, matured, was finally ready for marriage.

Margaret received the willow ware again that Christmas. She placed the sugar and creamer on the windowsill as a daily reminder of her second chance and responsibility to future generations.

Only God can help us have the kind of supernatural love characterized in the verse above. As we become closer to God, we love others more.

♥ *Dear God, You have told me what love is, help me
to stop doing what it is not.*

GOD'S WORKMANSHIP

For we are His workmanship, created in Christ Jesus for good works, which God prepared beforehand that we should walk in them.
                                    —EPH. 2:10

$\mathcal{G}$randma Warren calls herself an off-hand or by-the-way cook. Her son, when asked how he rated her as a cook on a scale of 1 to 10, chose 5. Cooking definitely isn't a big thing in her life but she does recognize the need for a homecooked meal now and then and a full cookie jar. Her preferences are reading, writing, shopping, traveling, movies, and theater.

Clearly this is one grandma not known for her good cooking! Her grandchildren will have other warm memories of her, and that's okay.

God created us as individuals. There are obvious and necessary similarities, but when it comes to abilities and talents, the field is wide open. Some focus on one or two things while others have developed a potpourri that dazzles the mind. As we are doing whatever we do, we need to remember that we are created to bring glory to God's Name in everything we do.

♥ *Help me to see the things I do as good works that glorify You, Lord.*

> *Can two walk together, unless they are
> agreed?*
> **—AMOS 3:3**

A favorite story in our family is about Grandma
and Grandpa's tapioca war. Grandpa loved tapioca
pudding. Grandma didn't like to make it. Every time
Grandma made it, Grandpa would say, "It's sure been
a long time since we had tapioca." One day Grandma
decided to give Grandpa tapioca until he hollered "uncle." She served him tapioca for breakfast, lunch, and
dinner. She served it over ice cream and cake, and
alongside pie. Grandpa kept eating tapioca and didn't
say a word. Grandma gritted her teeth and cleaned out
the sticky pan so she could make another batch.

Then Grandpa saw Grandma packing boxes of it to
take with them on vacation. He offered, "If you'll make
tapioca every week or so, I'll never remark about how
seldom it's served again." It was close enough to "uncle" for Grandma.

Even small unresolved conflicts build walls and mar
the joy we have in closeness. God wants us to be close
to Him. The conflict of sin builds walls, separating us
from God and making it impossible to walk together
with Him. Knock down the wall by asking God to forgive and start walking again with Him.

♥ *Keep me walking with You, Lord.*

. . . through love serve one another.
—GAL. 5:13

*T*his story is of a grandmother who, following a stroke, needed to be cared for by her widowed daughter and grandchildren. The grandmother was frustrated by her inability to do things and felt she was a burden to the family. When she prayed, she asked the Lord why He didn't just let her die. She felt she was no use to anyone.

One day when she was feeling particularly depressed, a friend and neighbor came to visit. Her visitor listened to how she felt and asked, "Do you love your daughter and grandchildren? Do they love you?"

At the grandmother's nod, she continued. "Robert Louis Stevenson wrote, 'So long as we love, we serve. So long as we are loved by others, we are almost indispensable.' It's still true."

The grandmother realized that there were many ways she could show and express love for her daughter and grandchildren from her bed or chair.

The first part of the verse above tells us we are free. We can choose to follow our own interests and desires or do the things that please God because we love Him. We please God by loving and serving in the best way we can.

♥ *When I feel discouraged and depressed, show me ways to serve others and You.*

FAMILY RESEMBLANCE

*Now, therefore, you are no longer strangers
and foreigners, but fellow citizens with the
saints and members of the household of
God.*
—EPH. 2:19

*N*ancy didn't meet her grandmother until she was twenty-seven years old. When she was young, family circumstances were such that there was no money for traveling to see Grandmother or for Grandmother to see them. And there was almost no other communication. Only a birthday card or small gift at Christmas.

After she had grown up, Nancy determined to see her grandmother. She realized her dream on her way to accept a job. They spent the week getting acquainted and discovered many family resemblances.

We all have a need to know our families. A few years ago I watched a television show that attempted to re-unite adult children with their fathers. The children all made the same tearful request, "I don't care what happened in the past—what you did or didn't do—please get in touch with me. I just want to talk with you and see you."

There's a children's book titled *Families Are God's Idea.* It's true. God did institute the family. And, as Christians, we are "members of God's very own family." When we meet other Christians there should be a family resemblance.

♥ *Dear Father, I'm glad I'm part of Your family.*

NATURAL COMFORTERS

As one whom his mother comforts,
So I will comfort you. . . .
—ISA. 66:13

$\mathcal{D}$ee was ten when she and her sister went to live with her Grandma Haberkamp for a while after their mother died. It was during the Depression, and the family was on relief. However, Dee said that her grandma did the best she could with what she had and remembers her going to catch fish for them to eat; she also observed that her grandma sometimes didn't eat so that her grandchildren had food.

"She was a comfortable grandma," Dee says. "She loved me and was always good to me."

It would be good to be remembered as a comfortable grandmother. "She's one of the best people in the world to tell my troubles to. Besides that, she's a whole lot of fun. Sometimes I start out moaning and groaning about something to her and end up holding my sides in laughter."

I think it is interesting that God likens the comfort He gives to that of a mother for a child. It says to me that mothers and grandmothers are natural comforters. God made us that way. It's another wonderful way we can be like Him.

♥ *Dear God, help me pass on the comfort I receive from You.*

GRANDMAS AND SELF-ESTEEM

. . . You shall love the LORD your God with all your heart, with all your soul, with all your strength, and with all your mind. . . .
—LUKE 10:27

$\mathscr{G}$randma Ward was a wonderful Christian lady," a daughter-in-law said of her husband's mother, the grandmother to her children. "She was outgoing, helpful and above all, loving—you can look at my husband and see her personality."

Grandma Ward started a church in an area where one was needed and led Sunday school for years with the kind of energy that left most people of her age breathless.

Her daughter-in-law, who had lost her mother at an early age, commented, "She made me feel like somebody."

Grandmothers who are able to build self-esteem in grandchildren usually have good self-esteem themselves. As children they acquired a sense of belonging, competence, and worth from their parents and so are able to help their grandchildren feel loved and competent. They make them feel their ideas, opinions, and uniqueness are of value.

God has told us He wants us to love Him from the inside out—beginning with our emotions and feelings. Then, as we grow more like Him, our self-esteem can't help but grow, too. We are made in His likeness.

♥ *Dear God, I want to love You more completely.*

BLESSING

The blessing of the LORD makes one rich,
And He adds no sorrow with it.
                                   —**PROV. 10:22**

Grandmother Dee has played a significant part in the daily life and Christian nurturing of her grandchildren. She began taking them to Sunday school when they were two years old and rejoiced when one by one they asked her to pray with them to receive Jesus as Savior.

For a report at school, Stacey needed to write down old sayings and then illustrate them. She asked her Grandma to help and giggled with her over "A bee in your bonnet" and "Ants in your pants."

When Grandma had knee surgery, grandson Brian called the hospital every day to see how far she had walked and continued calling her each day when she went home.

Grandma Dee says, "The Lord has blessed us with our grandchildren."

The verse for today reminds us that our relationship to God is more valuable than anything else in our lives. When we recognize that, we realize that all other blessings in our lives come from His gracious hand because He loves us and gives us freely all good things.

♥ *Thank You, Father, I am rich with Your blessings.*

. . . to be absent from the body and to be present with the Lord. —2 COR. 5:8

*W*hen Grandma Young was gravely ill, she repeated the name of Jesus over and over again. It was a whisper of prayer, comfort, and hope for her and her family and a testimony of faith in the One she loved to all who heard her speak that Wonderful Name. As she died, her daughter and granddaughter, Diane, said the verse above and pictured Grandmother crossing over and into the waiting arms of her loving Lord and Savior.

For Diane it was a confirmation of her Christian heritage. Diane's grandmother had raised her mother to know and love Jesus, who raised Diane to know and love Him. Diane, too, was raising her daughter, Amy, to know and love Him so that her grandchildren and great-grandchildren would, too. Because of this she could rejoice with her mother for the freedom from pain and peace in the homegoing of one of God's children.

In *Thru the Bible with J. Vernon McGee*, Dr. McGee says another translation of the verse above might be "at home with the Lord." Death is not the final word. For believers, death ushers us into eternal life with God. It is our passage home.

♥ *Thank You, Father, for the promise of going home to You.*

THE ANSWER

He heals the broken-hearted
And binds up their wounds.
—PS. 147:3

*D*iane's first baby was stillborn. Because Diane was so ill she was unable to see her baby daughter or attend the funeral. Diane's mother felt not only the loss of her first longed-for grandchild but the burden of not being able to help her daughter. Years later, mother and daughter found this poem by Margaret Gerner, which expressed Diane's mother's feelings:

I am powerlessness. I am helplessness.
I am frustration.
I sit with her and cry with her.
She cries for her child; I cry for mine.

. . . .

Where are the answers?
I should have them.
I'm the mother.

Diane's mother knew she could not fix her daughter's hurt; she had to trust God to do that.

We cannot escape the pain of grief, sorrow, and loss. We can count on God's promise to be our source for the power, courage, and wisdom that will help us through it. He is the answer.

♥ *Lord, thank You for Your presence in my sorrow.*

*Praying always with all prayer and
supplication in the Spirit, being watchful to
this end with all perseverance and
supplication for all the saints.*

—EPH. 6:18

*A*my's great-grandmother suffered with migraines. At two years old Amy was a pray-er. When Great-grandma had a migraine, Amy prayed. Once Amy walked into Great-grandma's house, went to her bedroom and said, "Jesus is going to come up through my mouth to help you!" Amy knew Who to ask for help when nothing else would.

The prayers of children delight and encourage us. They believe so completely. Their minds are not cluttered with all the logic, reasoning, and arguments that get in the way of our faith when we pray.

Adults can find all the verses in God's Word that tell us that God hears and answers prayer, and we know He always answers. Still, we often pray with such little faith.

The habit of praying short prayers to meet every situation in your day can be learned. When prayer is your life and your life a prayer, you are really living!

♥ *Dear God, I need to talk to You more and others less.*

TRUE STORY

All Scripture is given by inspiration of God, and is profitable for doctrine, for reproof, for correction, for instruction in righteousness.
—2 TIM. 3:16

Lynne's Grandmother Daisy Dell loved to take jaunts in the car. One time when she was visiting with Lynne's family, she asked Lynne's father to take her for a ride. While they were on the drive, Lynne's father pointed out all the things the car could do. He added, with a smile, that the car had a new device that caused the lights to get brighter as the car approached a store. As they drove along, he would hit the bright switch whenever they were near a store.

Grandmother kept saying, "My stars, well, my stars. How did the car do that?"

The memory is a pleasant one for her and her grandchild of a pleasant time taking a ride together. From such memories we create family stories to tell from one generation to another.

I wonder what stories Adam and Eve told their children about Eden. Did Adam tell how he decided on names for the animals? Did they describe how beautiful it was? What did they say about their walks with God? How did they handle the part about the snake and the reason they had to leave?

We have the whole story, from the beginning, told by people whom God chose and inspired to tell us His truth.

♥ *I'm glad we have Your true story to help us live, Lord.*

October 6 ⸺

*Therefore do not worry about tomorrow, for
tomorrow will worry about its own things.
Sufficient for the day is its own trouble.*
                                      —MATT. 6:34

*O*ne time Lynne's mother and grandmother made
Lynne a bed. They worked on it in the basement.
Grandma held it together as Lynne's mother nailed it.
After several hours, they finished the bed and pro-
ceeded to carry it upstairs, but it was too big to go up
the basement steps. They had to take the bed apart,
carry it up in pieces, and reassemble it in Lynne's bedroom. They have laughed about the experience many
times since then.

Children are keen observers of how family members
handle the frustrations and troubles of life. Mothers,
watching a preschooler play house, often feel uncomfortable when they hear their words coming from their
preschooler's mouth, or when they see their actions
and attitudes mimicked with doll families.

It is also easy for children to take on the same wor-
ries we express. God advises us not to be anxious about
things. Anxiety causes attitudes, actions, and words
that express frustration in negative ways. Trust in Him.
We might find ourselves fretting less and laughing
more.

♥ *Dear God, help me move from frustration and worry
to planning and trusting.*

IMAGINATION

Now to Him who is able to do exceedingly abundantly above all that we ask or think, according to the power that works in us, to Him be glory in the church by Christ Jesus throughout all ages, world without end. Amen.

—EPH. 3:20–21

*L*ynne remembers, as though it were yesterday, a large weeping willow in her backyard and the wonderful times with her grandmother under it. The tree was a wonderful house for playing dolls with Grandma; it provided shade for Monopoly tournaments and a canopy for tea parties and luncheons with triple-decker sandwiches.

Our grandchildren's imaginations know no bounds. Their favorite play sometimes begins with "Let's pretend" and we are off to a land filled with princes or princesses; we might even be the fairy godmother or wicked witch.

God gave us our wonderfully imaginative minds. He encourages our creativity because He is a creative God. But we are limited by our humanness and cannot even begin to imagine what wonderful blessings He is prepared to give us. And they aren't pretend.

♥ *Dear God, how good You are. I join others in praising You through endless ages.*

The righteous shall flourish like a palm tree. . . . They shall still bear fruit in old age. . . .
—PS. 92:12, 14

*C*arolyn's mother has no memories of her grandparents. They came from Czechoslovakia and left all their family behind. They must have had great courage to leave so many they loved knowing they would probably never see them again. Carolyn's mother feels she has had a good life but feels deprived of grandmothering.

Because of different circumstances, Carolyn's sister-in-law also has no memories of her grandmother. In her case it was a broken family situation. She had met her grandmother only once.

As Carolyn thinks about situations where there are no grandmothers, she realizes how blessed she has been to be with her own grandchildren. It encourages her to continually develop a good relationship with her grandchildren so they will have a memorable grandmother heritage.

Grandmothers might desire to be like palm trees. These trees are known to be solid and strong and live long lives that produce much fruit. Our lifetime of living with God is the best thing we have to share in our relationship with grandchildren.

♥ *I will honor You, God, as long as I live.*

And of His fullness we have all received,
and grace for grace. **—JOHN 1:16**

*B*abi and Deda were Carolyn's names for her Czechoslovakian grandmother and grandfather. They all lived in a small, two-bedroom bungalow in Chicago. One bedroom was the grandparents', and the other was shared by Carolyn's mom, her sister, and her two brothers. A long narrow hallway connected the living room and kitchen. In the hallway was a china cabinet with Babi's few prized possessions and a squeaky rocking chair.

The sound of a squeaky rocking chair still evokes memories of Carolyn's grandmother rocking and singing Bohemian songs to her. Carolyn knew she was loved.

Helping grandchildren know they are loved is one of the very best memories a grandmother could possibly give grandchildren. Its value cannot be measured. We might be surprised by the ways our grandchildren feel loved. It is often through the simplest things we do.

God's love for us is true love; the model for all our love relationships. When we willingly give up our self-centered interests, our actions will more clearly show others God's love.

♥ *Dear God, guide my actions to show Your love to others.*

. . . Ask, and you will receive, that your joy may be full.
                                    —JOHN 16:24

*F*ran and Carolyn loved being with their grandparents and can still describe the rooms of their small house in detail. They were fascinated by the tiny bathroom with a claw foot bathtub. The kitchen was very plain, antiseptic-white and shiny. There were no kitchen cabinets, only a metal cabinet with a couple of drawers and a space under the sink.

Fran and Carolyn would sneak into the kitchen and open the top left drawer next to the sink. In the drawer were two glasses filled with water—and their grandparents' teeth! Grandmother usually wore hers, but Grandfather wore his only on special occasions. Later Fran and Carolyn learned that all the cousins remember going to see if the teeth were still there.

The world is often puzzling to young children. The things we accept as natural might even seem frightening to them. We need to give grandchildren the freedom to ask about the things they don't understand.

God has given us that same freedom through His Son, Jesus. We can talk with God personally and directly about the things we don't understand and trust Him to hear us and answer. We just need to be sure we are listening.

♥ *Lord, I'm good at asking, help me to be better at listening.*

ULTIMATE GOAL

I press toward the goal for the prize of the upward call of God in Christ Jesus.
                                        —PHIL. 3:14

*A*llione plans to graduate from high school about the same time as her great-grandson. She is ninety-one years old. Her lifelong goal for a high school diploma has been filled with obstacles. She immigrated from Italy when she was seven; when she was in third grade, she had to leave school to work and help the family make ends meet. Her job scrubbing floors in a hospital began her career in nursing. She studied nursing through mail courses and took classes at the hospital.

At nineteen, when she married, her husband discouraged further schooling and state law wouldn't allow her to sit with children in regular classes. Allione took night classes and studied while caring for seven family members. By the time she reached ninth grade, the law had changed so that she could attend daytime classes in a regular classroom with her youngest daughter. Then World War II intervened delaying her expected 1942 graduation. Four decades later, she will receive her diploma and achieve her goal.

Paul describes a goal for Christians in the verse for today. It is to know Christ, be like Him, and be all that Christ wants us to be. It is the ultimate goal.

♥ *Dear God, help me to reach my goal by living for You.*

I thank my God upon every remembrance of you.
—PHIL. 1:3

*F*ran's grandma was good at making doll clothes on her treadle sewing machine. One Easter Fran's mother made Fran a dress. Then, they took the leftover material to Grandma, who made a matching outfit for Fran's Tiny Tears doll. She also made a Czechoslovakian outfit for another of Fran's dolls. Fran still has the dolls and outfits.

Grandma's clothesline was on a pulley from an upstairs window. So, washing doll clothes and hanging them up to dry was always fun.

Fran remembers that her grandmother was never too busy to stop what she was doing and sit with her grandchildren in her rocking chair. As they rocked and sang, Fran used to wonder what her grandmother was thinking about.

What do you think about as you hold your grandchildren? Are you remembering a son or daughter who was once the same age? Are you talking to God about the child you hold? Are you thanking Him for the child?

Not only when we hold our grandchildren, but every time we think of them, we should thank God for them.

♥ *God, every time I think of one of my grandchildren, remind me to thank You for him or her.*

For this reason I bow my knees to the Father
of our Lord Jesus Christ, from whom the
whole family in heaven and earth is named.
—EPH. 3:14–15

$\mathcal{G}$randmothers like to introduce their grandchildren to their friends. It is almost as if grandchildren are the precious pearls in a necklace to be displayed and admired. We introduce them in pictures and in person whenever possible. One granddaughter remembers sitting on her grandmother's porch and being introduced to all her grandma's friends as they strolled by. To each friend, Grandma repeated, "Isn't she beautiful? She looks like me!"

The resemblances please us. When we look at our grandchildren and see ourselves or some other family member when they were younger, we feel assured of the continuity of our family.

There is another family we know will continue. It is the great family of God which includes all those who believed in Him in the past, all who believe in the present, and all who will believe in the future. God is our Father. His love for us made it possible for us to be part of His family. When we love God, others can see our resemblance to Him. And that pleases God!

♥ *Dear God, help me to resemble You so that others*
can see I belong to Your family.

*A friend means well, even when he hurts
you.* —PROV. 27:6 TEV

$\mathcal{G}$randma Jeanne has "dates" with her grand-children Bethany, Joshua, and Kristin. One "date" with Kristin took them to a resale shop where three-year-old Kristin was allowed to pick out any dress she wanted.

Four-year-old Joshua said to Grandma Jeanne on one of their dates, "Grandma, you love me so much you wish you could keep me, don't you?"

Grandma Jeanne wondered how to answer, then said, "Yes, I do love you very much and so does your mommy. She loves you even more and she'd be so sad if I kept you, so I get to borrow you every so often."

Grandma Jeanne feels that if you want your grand-children to be your friends when they are adults, make friends with them as children.

We need to be the kind of friend to our grand-children who can tell them things they do not want to hear. If we have invested time in a relationship and friendship with them, they will be able to take it from us knowing it is in their best interest. In fact, they may come to appreciate that it is one of the purposes God has for us in their lives.

♥ *Lord, show me the best way to be friends with my grandchildren now and as they grow up.*

Blessed is every one who fears the LORD,
Who walks in His ways. —PS. 128:1

$\mathscr{D}$ear Abby's column included the following letter.

A little girl gave a wonderful explanation of the final years and death of her grandmother. She said to her mother, after the funeral, "Mom, you always said that Grandma walked and talked a lot with God. What I think happened is that one day God and Grandma went for an extra long walk, and they walked on and talked on, until God said to Grandma, 'You are a long way from home and are so tired, you had better just come home with me and stay.' And Grandma went."

What a beautiful way to tell a child about the death of a grandmother! And how wonderful for a grandchild to know that a grandmother walked and talked with God! Psalm 128 tells us we all should walk in His ways.

♥ *I want to walk in Your ways. Help me to listen to You*
so I will stay on the right path.

INCENTIVE PLAN

The counsel of the LORD stands forever,
The plans of His heart to all generations.
> —PS. 33:11

*J*have enjoyed the book *Funny, You Don't Look Like a Grandmother* by Lois Wyse. In the book, there is a poem titled "Grandmothers Are to Love," which talks about the unique love a grandmother can pass on to her grandchildren. It ends with these poignant verses:

> *You're a very special trust.*
> *Remember this . . . please do,*
> *The love of generations*
> *Is handed down to you.*
> *So if you have a grandma*
> *Thank the Good Lord up above,*
> *And give Grandmama hugs and kisses,*
> *For grandmothers are to love.*

God's plan for families to love each other was set when He created people, and it has continued through every generation since then. The hugs and kisses are all in God's plan too. His great love for us makes it possible for us to take part in handing down "the love of generations."

♥ *Thank You, God, for letting me be part of Your plan.*

> *. . . For what is your life? It is even a vapor*
> *that appears for a little time and then*
> *vanishes away.* —JAMES 4:14

*B*rian had come from California to go with his cousins for his first Grandmother Week. We were headed for a resort in the woods that had a swimming pool, miniature golf, boats, and horses. After two days of sleeping in, all-day fun and games, pizza, late-night movies, and more pizza, Brian greeted his dad on the phone with the words, "Dad, I'm with the wild side of the family now!"

When I took the phone to speak to my son, he was still laughing about the idea that his son thought his grandmother was wild!

We sometimes do present a different picture to our grandchildren than we did to our children. It must be because we are mature, stable, and more relaxed. Or maybe it's because we have finally learned what's important—spending time with the people we love and enjoying things together.

As the old saying says, "Life is short no matter how long we live." The Bible urges us to live according to God's will. We find out about His will by reading His Word and talking over our plans with Him—including the ones for good times with grandchildren.

♥ *Dear Lord, keep me talking to You about what is important to do with my life.*

The LORD God is my strength;
He will make my feet like deer's feet,
And He will make me walk on my high
hills.
—HAB. 3:19

*W*hen Kristen was a freshman in high school she learned that she had Hodgkin's disease. During the years following she battled the disease with treatments that could only be described as horrid. Her grandmother became her source of strength as she nursed Kristen through that time.

Kristen was cured and went to college to become a pediatric oncologist so she could help children who have cancer. While at college, she learned that her grandmother had cancer and refused treatment because it would be similar to what Kristen had gone through and she didn't think she could stand it.

Kristen began calling and talking with her grandma, writing letters and sending cards until her grandmother recognized that it was Kristen's turn to be a source of strength to her.

Kristen and her grandmother know God. They trust in His strength. And because they can draw on His strength, they have been able to be a source of strength to each other.

Sometimes God gives us some of the strength we need through others. The result is that everyone involved becomes stronger as they learn more about trusting God.

♥ *Give me opportunities to learn more about trusting You, Lord.*

NEW GRANDMA PRAYER

But certainly God has heard me;
He has attended to the voice of my prayer.
—PS. 66:19

$\mathcal{T}$erri is about to become a grandmother for the first time. She is filled with an assortment of feelings from joy to dismay.

While looking forward to making little clothes and doing some knitting, Terri is thinking of the kind of grandmother she'll be. She wants to be available when needed and not intrusive; she wants to do things with her grandchild that she didn't have time to do with her children. She has already begun praying for her grandchild's spouse as she did and does for her children.

One of the best things grandmothers do for grandchildren is to pray for them. It's at the top of the list right next to spending time with them, hugs, and cookies. An inspirational speaker challenging Sunday school teachers to pray for the students in his or her class by name each day, assures them of amazing results. Can we do any less for our grandchildren?

Read Psalm 66 to remind yourself that you belong to a great and marvelous God who loves you and hears your prayers.

♥ *I praise You God because You don't reject my prayers*
or withhold Your love.

O LORD, You have searched me and known me.
　　　　　　　　　　　—PS. 139:1

*T*he following excerpt was taken from a poem found among the possessions of an elderly Irish woman who died in a geriatric hospital.

What do you see, what do you see?
What are you thinking when you look at me?
A crabbed old woman, not very wise,
Uncertain of habit, with far-away eyes.

Who dribbles her food and makes no reply
When you say in a loud voice, "I do wish you'd
　　try."
. . . .
But inside this old carcass a young girl still
　　dwells,
And now and again my battered heart swells.
I remember the joys, I remember the pain,
And I'm loving and living life over again.

So open your eyes, my friend, open and see
Not a crabbed old woman—look closer—see me.

The poem is the heart's cry for us always to see one another as individuals. We must remember that God knows who we are. He sees us through eyes of love and He calls us by name (Isa. 43:1).

♥ *Dear God, I'm glad You know me and that I am learning to know You more each day.*

And forgive us our sins,
For we also forgive everyone who is indebted
*   to us. . . .*
                                        —LUKE 11:4

I once committed what I felt was an unpardonable grandmother sin. I forgot a grandson's birthday. To this day, I really don't know how it happened except that I often let myself get much, much too busy.

Can you imagine how I felt? I couldn't think of anything I could do that would make it right. Even calling to apologize, asking forgiveness, and sending a belated card and gifts didn't seem good enough.

Alex was very young and doesn't remember the incident. His forgiveness was swift and complete, and includes forgetting.

This is God's kind of forgiveness. Jesus talks quite a bit about forgiveness in the Gospels. He tells us in several passages that because we receive forgiveness from God for the wrong we do, we must forgive others. It is at the center of our relationship to God as it was when Jesus taught the disciples how to pray. We are even given a symbolic picture of how God forgives: "As far as the east is from the west." Our sin is not only completely gone; it is forgotten. This is the only way to be forgiving.

♥ *Dear God, teach me how to always truly forgive.*

Understanding is a wellspring of life to him who has it.
　　　　　　　　　—PROV. 16:22

*G*randmother Beth wore a wig after her two brain operations. Several months later her hair grew back and she was able to fashion it nicely. When she went to visit her grandchildren, she didn't have on her wig. Three-year-old Kit took one look at her and asked, "Grandma, where is your other hair?"

Grandma explained that she didn't need her wig anymore because she had her own hair, but the little girl insisted on seeing it until Grandma promised to bring it the next time she visited.

Hair that can come off, teeth that come out, and other removable parts are fascinating to our grandchildren. And the fact that we are now able to talk about and explain these things alleviates possible fear and promotes acceptance. The more we are able to talk and explain, the clearer will be their understanding.

The Bible tells us frequently to go after wisdom and understanding. God's wisdom is a fountain of life that can make a person happy, healthy, and alive forever. We gain understanding by God's wisdom when we live according to His Word. This is reality.

♥ *Thank You, Lord, for life that comes from Your real and living Word.*

Let your speech always be with grace,
seasoned with salt, that you may know how
you ought to answer each one.

—COL. 4:6

$\mathcal{G}$randma Barrett was talking with her eight-year-old grandson Alex about his baby-sitter. Alex said he liked her adding, "But Grandma, she says the 'S' word."

Grandma wasn't sure how to respond and finally asked, "What is the 'S' word?"

Alex said, "Shut up!"

Every grandmother in the world must have a grandchild language story. Words that are mispronounced, misunderstood, or misplaced in sentences, along with the words that children are told not to say under any circumstances. Of course, we need to educate the parents (and grandparents) not to use those words, either.

The Bible tells us the way we talk is important. The words we use tell more about us than the way we look. Especially as we tell others about Jesus, our words and lives must match so that the message makes sense and people will listen to what we say.

♥ *Take charge of my conversation, Lord, so people*
know I belong to You.

He gives power to the weak,
And to those who have no might He
increases strength.
　　　　　　　　　　　　　—ISA. 40:29

*O*ne grandmother confesses that while she savors the freedom of older years, she is more than willing to give it up for the special times she spends with her grandchildren. Her empty nest is occasionally filled with grandchildren at her table, under her feet, and in her bed.

This grandmother has recycled her time, money, and energy back into her grandchildren by being available whenever needed. She feels energy is the hardest to come by and goes the fastest.

I am reminded that even as young mothers, my friends and I used to wonder at the unending energy of our children. There was always mention of wishing we had some of it. Things only got worse as we aged. Luckily, there is usually time to recoup in between.

There's more about strength in the Bible than there is about energy. The Webster definitions are similar, talking of force and vitality. We get tired. God never tires. We can ask God to renew us, to replenish our strength and energy from His never-exhausted supply.

♥ *Dear God, You are my strength. Thank You for the*
energy You give me each day.

If I say, "My foot slips,"
Your mercy, O LORD, will hold me up.
—PS. 94:18

$\mathcal{I}$t is difficult to become a grandmother before a daughter is ready to be a mother. An article I read recently told the heartbreaking story of a single mother and her fourteen-year-old pregnant daughter. Their decision to keep the child resulted in a steady deterioration in the relationship between mother and daughter and was compounded by financial stresses. Finally, the daughter went to live with her grandmother and mother raised the child for several years.

The article advised that families finding themselves in similar circumstances develop a plan of action, have a firm sense of practical matters such as day-care costs and how medical expenses will be paid. It is also advisable to consult an attorney concerning the advisability of becoming the baby's legal guardian in order to be covered by the grandparent's health insurance. A support group is also helpful.

In family crisis we need good advice and we need support. The advice of experts or those who have the same experience and the support of friends who comfort and encourage is absolutely necessary. Knowing we have the support of a loving Heavenly Father keeps us going when we feel we might fall. Even in difficult circumstances there can be joy.

♥ *I have often felt Your support, Lord. Help me to trust You more so I can feel joy when things are difficult.*

*But without your consent I wanted to do
nothing, that your good deed might not be
by compulsion, as it were, but voluntary.*
—PHILEM. 14

*M*ary Martin loved to be remembered as Peter
Pan. One morning her grandson Matthew knocked on
her bedroom door at six in the morning and asked if
he could bring some friends in to meet her.

Being an obliging grandmother, Mary asked when,
to which Matthew responded, "Now." Several little
boys marched into the bedroom, and Mary Martin sat
up and smiled while her grandson made the introduc-
tion, "This is my grandmother, Peter Pan."

Young grandchildren, especially, often have no
sense of time or place. This results in some interesting
situations, such as the one above.

Spontaneous is a great word. It means "moved by a
natural feeling or impulse." Paul used the word when
asking Philemon to accept Onesimus as a brother in
Christ—a member of God's family.

This passage helps us remember there are no dis-
tinctions among believers. We are all equal in Christ
(Gal. 3:28). Our acceptance of God's family members
often could stand some spontaneity.

♥ *Lord, make me uncomfortable when I don't accept
some of Your family members.*

*For prophecy never came by the will of man,
but holy men of God spoke as they were
moved by the Holy Spirit.*

—2 PETER 1:21

She loved to watch her grandmother make cookies without a recipe. Grandma just threw them together with pinches of this and handfuls of that. Then she mixed it all together with her hands and placed mounds of dough on a cookie sheet to bake. They were the most wonderful cookies in all the world.

The granddaughter had watched this process hundreds of times and thought she knew it by heart. When Grandma died, she tried to make the cookies just the way her grandma did but was never able to get them to taste the way they did when Grandma made them. She wished the recipe had been written down.

God used forty men to write His Word. He didn't change their styles or interfere with their personalities, but His message comes across. They wrote down exactly what God wanted to say so the generations would have an accurate plan to follow. God knew we would need to have His Word written down to get it right.

♥ *Thank You, God, for Your written down Word. Help
me to do what it tells me.*

> *But those who wait on the LORD*
> *Shall renew their strength;*
> *They shall mount up with wings like eagles,*
> *They shall run and not be weary,*
> *They shall walk and not faint.*
>
> *—ISA. 40:31*

A book by Shirley K. Morgenthaler, *Right from the Start,* should be a gift to all new parents. The book, subtitled *A New Parent's Guide to Child Faith Development,* helps parents discover practical ways to lay the foundation for Christian growth in the first three years of a child's life—the formative time in a child's spiritual and emotional growth.

Dr. Morgenthaler once saw a plaque that said, "Two things you need to give to your children. One is roots. The other is wings."

The plaque became especially valuable after she visited where her great-great-grandfather was born. Dr. Morgenthaler said, "How exhilarating, what a feeling of freedom, what a soaring of spirit to think that, because of who they were—my parents, grandparents, great-grandparents, and great-great-Grandpa Johann—I am rooted in Christ and can try my own wings to become the person God wants me to be!"

It is our very rootedness that helps us continue to grow and nurtures our grandchildren's roots while encouraging them to try their wings and soar with us.

♥ *Thank You, Lord, for the roots and wings in my life.*

*One generation passes away, and another
    generation comes;
But the earth abides forever.*

—ECCL. 1:4

*J*anet was a shy, insecure young woman, an excellent student who was the first one in her family to go away to college. Following her first semester, Janet returned home with a grade report of straight A's. Everyone was happy—except Grandma Rachel.

Grandma looked at the report and commented to Janet, "You'll never get married if you continue to make grades like these."

Her grandmother loved her and wanted her to be happy; they were just from different generations.

We are different from those in the past and will be different from those in the future. The continuity of people is through births, but we are transitory creatures. And if we look at life in terms of this life only, we are the most colossal failure in God's universe. We've actually only been around for a short time when compared to the earth. This should give us perspective about the things that are said and help us look for the underlying motives and purposes.

♥ *Thank You, that in Your view, we are not failures.*

GRANDMA'S PORCH

The silver-haired head is a crown of glory,
If it is found in the way of righteousness.
—PROV. 16:31

*F*or the last twelve Halloweens, Oak Crest, a senior residence, has hosted a Grandma's Porch for three hours each Halloween afternoon. The people who live in the residence invite children under twelve to trick-or-treat on their porch. The children come in costume, and the residents give out suckers, and serve cider and apples.

The children love to go there because everyone is so happy to see them. The parents are happy because it's safe. The residents enjoy seeing and spending some time with the children. It's a good mixing of generations.

Have you ever noticed that most children have no trouble at all addressing older people as Grandma or Grandpa? That's because we have a special place in the hearts of children.

Perhaps children intuitively perceive something of the splendor in our gray hair. But there is an explicit condition for the honor; we are called to be righteous, to live the way God wants us to live. When we do, everyone knows it!

♥ *Help me to live so that everyone knows I love You.*

EMULATING LOVE

As the Father loved Me, I also have loved you; abide in My love. —JOHN 15:9

$\mathcal{T}$he following is an excerpt of an article my grandmother had in a scrapbook.

Grandmothers are the best of all people because they want you so much. They're always glad to see you. . . .

Grandmothers let you do just about anything—have pillow fights, jump on the bed, make tent houses out of chairs and blankets, slide down banisters, stay up past bed time, drink another root beer! . . .

Grandmothers give you things—old jewelry, World Fair souvenirs, silver dollars, money for the movies and stuff like that . . . and sometimes toys when it isn't even Christmas. . . .

Grandmothers are best to talk to because they understand and always have time to listen. . . .

Best of all about a grandmother is her lap—the most comfortable place in the world. Big or small, it is always upholstered with sympathy and forgiveness.

God's love for us comes wrapped in understanding, forgiveness, and comfort. The example we give of those attributes can give grandchildren a desire to know God.

♥ *Dear God, can my grandchildren see You in the ways I love them?*

For if there is first a willing mind, it is accepted according to what one has, and not according to what he does not have.
—2 COR. 8:12

$\int$ome of the gifts Lois Wyse recommends for grandmothers in her book *Funny, You Don't Look Like a Grandmother,* include a personally designed card with Grandma's name featured prominently (spelled or misspelled—who cares?); the latest photograph of Darling Grandchild; a frame to hold the latter; a leaf, flower, acorn, or dandelion picked by Darling Grandchild; cookies, cupcakes, or Anything Else made by D.G.

The verse above is from a passage that is really talking about giving for God's work—so I am stretching the point somewhat, but the principle remains. Giving is a natural response of love. We express love for people when we want to give them time, attention, and gifts.

Grandmothers really understand what God was getting at here. Like Him, we are more interested in the how than the what.

♥ *Dear God, I want to use this same principle when I give to You.*

And He took bread, gave thanks and broke it, and gave it to them, saying, "This is My body which is given for you; do this in remembrance of Me." —LUKE 22:19

*E*very Christmas, Grandma Riker's children and grandchildren received booties that she crocheted for them. They came in all sizes and colors, and everyone, from the youngest to the oldest, wore them around the house, during stays in the hospital, and off to college. Since they didn't wear out in a year, it was possible to collect a few pair and have them available to give to friends to wear at home, in the hospital, or away at school.

In fact, when Grandma Riker died, her family found boxes of booties that she had made up ahead of time. They divided them among themselves to wear and give for years to come. Grandma Riker is missed, but her booties are a warm remembrance.

Warm remembrances can be those things we make such as slippers, sweaters, and scarfs that warm physically, or they can be the feelings we have been able to give our grandchildren; they can even be a combination of both.

Jesus told us to do something in remembrance of Him. It's called the Lord's Supper. This remembrance will warm our hearts with gratitude and anticipation of joy.

♥ *At Your Table Lord, I remember what You did for me and thank You again for Your love.*

November 3

Now may the God of peace Himself sanctify
you completely; and may your whole spirit,
soul, and body be preserved blameless at the
coming of our Lord Jesus Christ.
                                   —1 THESS. 5:23

*W*riter Helen Steiner Rice tells that of all her grand-parents only Grandma Bieri has a special place in her heart. She lived with Helen's family from time to time and is remembered by Helen for her wonderful spirit, Christian faith, and big lap.

Helen tells of heading straight for her grandma's room after school to tell her about the day. She often found her grandma bent over her large German Bible. Even after living in America most of her life, Grandma Bieri didn't speak English well and, according to Helen, "got by with a few words of approval, a wonder-fully accepting smile, and a love that was irrepress-ible."

Three essentials for grandmothering—approval, smiles, and love. From infancy to adulthood, we need those three things to be healthy, whole people. God de-signed us to need them and to give them.

When God made us, He gave us a spirit, soul, and body—all integral parts of us as persons. God intends for us to nurture one another with approval, smiles, and love so that we can grow into the strong Christians we are meant to be.

♥ *I want to nurture others and You continue to nurture*
me, Lord.

A LITTLE KINDNESS

Love is patient, love is kind. . . .
—1 COR. 13:4 NIV

*B*ibianna and her many brothers and sisters called their grandmother "Mother"; they called their mother "Mom." When Bibianna was eighteen, she worked at a bank and bought a car. One of the first things she did was drive sixty-six miles to see her grandmother.

Bibianna and her grandmother had a very special relationship, and Bibianna felt she really got to know her grandmother better without all the rest of the family around. She remembers especially how happy her grandmother always seemed to be for her and how she encouraged her.

Bibianna says, "She was always so kind, and I needed someone to single me out and be kind to me. A little kindness goes a long way."

Love cannot exist without kindness. They go together like cookies and milk, sunshine and flowers. When we know and love God, our love becomes more unselfish and our actions expand in kindness. God will help us look beyond our own desires to give love and show kindness without expecting something in return.

♥ *I want to follow Your most excellent way of love, Lord.*

Therefore receive one another, just as Christ also received us, to the glory of God.
—ROM. 15:7

She was nineteen, pregnant, and unmarried. Her mother was upset; her father was furious; her grandmother was sad but accepting. The decision was made to give the baby up for adoption, and daughter, mother, and grandmother spent a day together just before the baby was born.

The granddaughter still can't get over her grandmother's attitude about the situation. She told her granddaughter the baby would be born soon, gave her opinion about whether it would be a boy or girl, and was encouraging about the hard decision for the adoption of her great-grandchild.

The granddaughter said, "Despite what had happened, she made me feel accepted. Never did I need it more."

God loves and accepts us on the simple acceptance of Christ. Nothing else is required. He asks us to do the same thing with others. It doesn't mean we have to agree totally with them about everything; it does mean that we understand that when we are with God, our differences won't matter any longer. We will all be changed to be like Him.

♥ *When I am unaccepting of others, remind me of Your acceptance of me, Lord.*

You comprehend my path and my lying down,
And are acquainted with all my ways.
—PS. 139:3

*W*hen I asked Scottie what she enjoys about being a grandmother, her immediate answer was, "Having my two-year-old granddaughter run toward me with arms outstretched saying, 'Gammaw, Gammaw.'"

Scottie went on to tell that she was present and helped when her daughter chose home delivery and gave birth to her second grandchild, a grandson. For Scottie and the doctor and nurses who assisted, it was an experience that can only be described in words such as ethereal and awesome as they rejoiced together over the new life they helped bring into the world.

There was a time when Grandmother's presence at the birth of grandchildren was as normal and everyday as the sun rising and setting. But while birthing is a natural part of life, it is almost always described in terms of the miraculous by those who are present. We are filled with wonder in the presence of God's creation.

The Bible tells us that from the time we are conceived we are in God's presence. He thinks about us constantly (Ps. 139:17–18).

♥ *Keep reminding me, Lord, that I am made in Your image.*

CHARACTER ATTRACTIVENESS

She opens her mouth with wisdom,
And on her tongue is the law of kindness.
—PROV. 31:26

*G*ramma Dorothy always talked to Steve like he was an adult. When he was eight, Gramma told him, "Every day your life is going to go faster."

Steve thought that bit of wisdom was hilarious and laughed so hard he rolled off the couch he was sitting on when he heard it. Now an adult, he realizes the truth of his Gramma's words.

As grandmothers we are eager to share with our grandchildren all we have learned in life. Sometimes they are not so eager to hear what we've learned and prefer to find out for themselves. While I don't recommend that we beat grandchildren over the head with all our wisdom, I do propose that we slip in small slices of accumulated knowledge in our normal conversation. Sometimes we live long enough to hear that they really listened to what we said and discovered it was true!

Proverbs 31 is a picture of a woman who loves God. It doesn't say she is a grandmother, but she could be. Her qualities are outstanding and cover every aspect of life. It's interesting to note that the Bible doesn't tell about her appearance. What makes her attractive is her character.

♥ *Dear God, help me to be more concerned with my character than my appearance.*

*I can do all things through Christ who
strengthens me.*   —PHIL. 4:13

$\mathscr{P}$am's Gramma Margaret was raised on a farm
and was very self-sufficient. She could do everything
and nearly everything was homemade. Pam and her
brothers spent a month at a time with Gramma. One of
the things they did was mash grapes for making jelly.

Pam's family raised chickens. Once when Gramma
Margaret came for a visit, it was time to eliminate a
rooster. So Gramma went out and very capably and
coolly caught the rooster, cut off its head, and pro-
ceeded to teach her grandchildren how to pluck the
rooster.

"Gramma was lots of fun," her grandchildren say
remembering canning, chickens, and working with her
on the farm.

This grandmother had a great attitude; she also had
the ability to make even work seem like fun to her
grandchildren. Attitude has a lot to do with making a
person self-sufficient.

One way to change our attitude is to look at things
from God's point of view. When we focus on what we
are supposed to do, we are able to get our priorities
straight. Attitude based on God's power is unbeatable.

♥ *Dear God, when my attitude gets out of line, show
me Your view of things.*

Yet I will rejoice in the LORD,
I will joy in the God of my salvation.
—HAB. 3:18

Sean and Tricia liked to go to Grandma Dannenfeldt's house, where they could ride a mattress down the staircase. When Grandma went to live in a retirement home, they tried to visit her each week. She enjoyed being taken to the bowling alley to watch the bowlers.

Their Grandma Jacob was even more fun than Grandma Dannenfeldt. She let her grandchildren do more things and often joined in. Every morning they were at her house, they would eat cereal with her and a huge, brown, stuffed Scooby-Doo toy with a green collar.

We often hear of perfectly ladylike grandmothers joining in activities with their grandchildren—activities they would never have dreamed of participating in with their children. What happened between motherhood and grandmotherhood? Maybe we learned to take ourselves less seriously. We're probably having more fun.

The Bible tells us we have much to be happy and joyful about. Even in difficulties, we need to take our minds off of our troubles and look to God for help and strength. Some of us haven't learned this yet; others have and are sliding down staircases with their grandchildren.

♥ *When I get caught up in worry, Lord, turn my thoughts to You.*

TEACHING PRINCIPLES

Thus says the LORD, your Redeemer, . . .
"I am the LORD your God,
Who teaches you to profit,
Who leads you by the way you should go."
—ISA. 48:17

*N*anny devoted her life to her only grandchild, Debbie. Debbie describes her grandmother as Irish, round, and jolly as can be. Nanny had a tremendous sense of humor and delighted in playing pranks on friends and family members. She was also a devout Baptist and lifelong Democrat. With Nanny, there was no question about what would get you to heaven—accepting the Lord Jesus Christ into your heart and voting a straight Democratic ticket!

Debbie learned much from Nanny. She says, "I felt so loved. She instilled in me the thought that I could do anything I wanted if I put my mind to it. I was always included in their conversation, and Nanny was constantly bragging about me."

It is amazing how much we can learn when we feel the teacher cares about us and respects us. This is what God meant to have happen. We begin learning from birth and our first teachers should be our families. Their love, care, and respect for us as persons help us learn with confidence. Love, care, and respect are God's teaching principles. He wrote a Book about it!

♥ *Thank You for Your Book, the Bible, that teaches me what I need to teach others.*

Having predestined us to adoption as sons by Jesus Christ to Himself, according to the good pleasure of His will.   —EPH. 1:5

*W*hen Debbie was in the seventh grade, her grandmother decided she should have a new piano. Debbie says, "I will never forget the day we went to buy it. It was a rainy spring morning and my mom, Nanny, a cousin, and I drove to Paducah, Kentucky, to the piano store." Debbie and her mother, the church organist, picked out the piano and then began looking around the store. Her mother sat down at an organ and began to play.

Nanny said, "We will take both the piano and organ. Now what kind of discount will there be for paying cash?" Nanny and the owner dickered back and forth until finally Nanny said, "I will let you pay the sales tax on these two items if you find the song, 'Oh, My Papa'."

The owner found the song, gave it to Nanny, and said he would love to pay the tax. The day left a great impression on Debbie. She still feels it was a major demonstration of love—her grandmother shared what she had because she got pleasure from it.

The Good News Bible ends the above verse with the words, "this was his pleasure and purpose."

♥ *Your great and wonderful love is more than I can comprehend, Lord. But I am so thankful for it.*

FAITH'S ACTIONS

. . . add to your faith virtue, to virtue
knowledge, to knowledge self-control, to
self-control perseverance, to perseverance
godliness, to godliness brotherly kindness,
and to brotherly kindness love.
                                    —2 PETER 1:5–7

A grandmother and I were talking about today's
grandchildren and how so many of them have more
than the usual number of grandparents. In fact, one of
her grandchildren has seven grandparents.

Rather than clicking our tongues and shaking our
heads over the reasons for the numbers, we should
eventually, after the sadness and hurt, be able to rejoice and be happy for all the grandparenting our
grandchildren will receive—the benefits of additional
time, attention, and care. There is no place for jealousy
or other negative feelings. This is a time to see the
larger picture—what is best for the grandchildren. It
calls for all our forbearance (a good old-fashioned
word meaning self-control or refraining from doing or
saying).

Our faith must be much more than what we believe
about the facts of God and Jesus. There must be action
to show that our lives are truly changed. The verses
above are Peter's list of faith's actions. God doesn't
give us a choice about these. They need to be incorpo-
rated into our lives on a continuing basis.

♥ *I couldn't work on all those actions without You,*
God. Thank You for helping me learn Your way.

November 13 _____

And I will pray the Father, and He will give you another Helper, that He may abide with you forever.
                                        —JOHN 14:16

*W*hen I was a young mother, I remember traveling with my mother to see my grandparents who were both in the hospital at the same time. Grandma died shortly after we got there, and my grandfather was still in the hospital and couldn't attend the funeral. In fact, they did not tell him of her death for several days because he was so ill.

I remember thinking about how close they had been and how sad it was that during her last days, Grandma had not had the comfort of her husband beside her. This, of course, is not unusual. Except for accidents or other unusual circumstances when a couple dies together, someone has to die first. The one left will not have the comfort of the other. I am in that position. My husband died several years ago. There is a possibility that I will not remarry. However, we who know God and have similar circumstances are not comfortless.

The disciples didn't want Jesus to leave them. They didn't know what they would do without Him. Jesus promised them help. He promises the same help to us.

♥ *Thank You, Father, for giving us the help and comfort we need for all of our lives.*

*But indeed I also count all things loss for
the excellence of the knowledge of Christ
Jesus my Lord, for whom I have suffered the
loss of all things, and count them as
rubbish, that I may gain Christ.*
                                    —PHIL. 3:8

*G*randmothers' houses should contain books for
grandchildren. I recommend *Just in Case You Ever
Wonder* by Max Lucado, which shows children that
some things will always stay the same. One part reads,
"I'll always love you. / I'll always hug you. / I'll always
be on your side. / And I want you to know that . . . /
Just in case you ever wonder."

Grandmother Time, by Judy Gattis Smith, contains
dozens of creative ways to share with your grandchildren your love and energy and your faith in our
Lord. The book includes both "old-fashioned" and
"new-fangled" ideas to make your grandmothering
unique and includes some special ideas for out-of-town
grandparents.

I'm glad that God set the precedent for the need for
books by giving us His Book. He has also given us good
advice on how to choose the things that we read and
watch. What we put in our minds or the minds of
others, including our grandchildren, has a lot to do
with the words and actions that come out.

♥ *Keep Your advice about the things I read and see
clear in my mind, Lord.*

November 15 ————————————————

*. . . the Holy Spirit has made you overseers,
to shepherd the church of God which He
purchased with His own blood.*
—ACTS 20:28

*A*ll of her young life, the girl had been sexually
abused. One day her mother took her to her grandmother's house in another state. The little girl saw the
small, round, aproned woman and thought, "Here's
someone who will be kind and love me." But her
mother told the grandmother that the child was not
hers, that she was watching her for a friend. When they
returned home, the sexual abuse continued.

We need to recognize the signs of abuse that might
show up in children. The signs include consistently
poor hygiene, consistently inappropriate clothing for
weather, fatigue, inattention to medical problems, lack
of supervision at home, unusually passive or aggressive
behavior, expression of pain in genital area, masturba-
tion, unusual interest in genitals of others or animals,
not wanting to be with a particular person, regressed
behavior, age-inappropriate expression of affection.

We can be sure Jesus' tears mingle with ours over
what is happening to many children in our world. God
calls us to be watchful and to care for our family in
Christ—like a Good Shepherd.

♥ *Make me more aware, Lord, of things I might not
want to see.*

This is love, that we walk according to His commandments. This is the commandment, that as you have heard from the beginning, you should walk in it. —2 JOHN 6

$\mathcal{G}$randma Jenny was born in Sweden. She and her three young children came to America in the early 1900s. Her granddaughter, Jennifer, still has the basket that held their belongings when they landed at Ellis Island.

As Grandma Jenny grew older, she developed Parkinson's disease, which made her voice shake, and osteoporosis. The family took turns taking care of her. From time to time she was with her granddaughter Jennifer's family. Jennifer couldn't talk with her grandmother, who never learned English, but she could sing and dance for her. So Jennifer mimicked a popular comedian of the time, and sang and danced for her grandmother. Grandma would laugh and laugh and have Jennifer do it again and again. Jennifer remembers the delight in her Grandma Jenny's eyes as they communicated in the only way they knew how.

What we feel deeply can find a way to be expressed when words fail us. Love always finds a way to communicate—usually through actions. The New Testament repeatedly tells us that we should love one another. The emphasis is always more on actions than on words. God's actions always speak love to us.

♥ *Help my actions show the love my words tell, Lord.*

GOD TALKING

Give ear and hear my voice,
Listen and hear my speech.
—ISA. 28:23

*G*reg was fifteen when his grandfather died. The family decided to take turns staying with Grandmother for a while. The night Greg stayed with her, he asked how he was related to another family member. Gramma Lottie talked for four hours! She filled him in on family history, down to details such as the colors of dresses people wore on special occasions.

Many grandmothers are talkers. We've been around for a while and have a lot to say. Certainly we have opinions about everything. But God wants us to just listen sometimes so He can talk to us.

Even when we ask God questions, we don't always listen before we begin talking again. Listening is one of the hardest things to do. One way of listening to God is reading His Word. Another way is to be silent during our prayer time with Him. When you read the Bible, when you are quiet during prayer, does some truth become evident to you, do you realize an answer to something that has been troubling you, do you have a sense of peace? Keep listening. That's God talking!

♥ *Dear God, help me to be quiet and listen to You more than I do.*

. . . This same Jesus, who was taken up from you into heaven, will so come in like manner as you saw Him go into heaven.
—ACTS 1:11

Three-year-old Wes only sees his Grandma Mills about four times a year. At the end of one visit, his grandma told him she was sad to see him go. Wes responded, "Don't be sad. I'll be back."

Wes was echoing the words he hears when he visits the grandparents who live near to him. At the end of each visit, when he doesn't want to leave, they tell him, "Don't be sad. You'll be back soon." (By the way, these grandparents are called, Grandma and Grandpa Ding Ding because, when Wes was little he would point to the big clock in their house and say "Grandma, ding, ding," whenever it would chime.)

The disciples must have been feeling sad when Jesus left them. God sent angels to comfort them with encouraging words that gave them hope for the future and motivated them to continue the work Jesus gave them to do.

We can also be encouraged by those words, not by standing around looking into the sky, but by being ready for Jesus to return at any time.

♥ *I'm glad You told us You were coming back, Jesus.*

To be made new in the attitude of your minds.
—EPH. 4:23 NIV

*C*hris says her grandmother had an attitude, but she was funny. She meant her grandmother looked at life and reacted to it in mostly negative ways. The fact that Chris found her grandmother's attitude funny is a good response. Reacting to an attitude with an attitude can cause a lot of trouble.

When Chris lived with her grandmother for several months, her grandmother made her breakfast every morning. No one had made her breakfast since she had become old enough to feed herself. This helped Chris see more than her grandmother's negative attitude.

Have you had an attitude check lately? There really should be a difference in attitude between Christians and non-Christians. But even with our new nature, there's still work to be done on our thoughts, actions, and attitudes. Perhaps someone close to us might be a better evaluator.

Don't be discouraged if the change is slow. Keep trusting God to do the changing until one day you have the only attitude to have—one like Jesus Christ.

♥ *Dear God, I'm glad You're willing to keep working on changing me.*

Moreover the law entered that the offense might abound. But where sin abounded, grace abounded much more.

—ROM. 5:20

A young mother divorced her husband and gave up her two daughters to him. She promised not to see them until they were grown up and married. She further promised not to intrude in their lives even then: she would not expect to participate in holiday get-togethers or special occasions, such as grandchildren's graduations or weddings. It was a hard and merciless, self-imposed sentence that has not been altered by time or compassion.

The mother matured and reunited with her daughters when they married. She has now become a grandmother but honors her original decision concerning holidays and special occasions. Sometimes it is painful, but God is good and gracious. Her daughters have forgiven her, her grandchildren love her, and she sees them as much as she can. She accepts the consequences of her actions and is thankful for God's mercy.

God forgives us when we make bad choices, but we still must live with the consequences of the decisions we make. God can be counted on to help us, though, for His grace, as the old hymn says, is "greater than all our sin."

♥ *Dear God, I am overwhelmed by the magnitude of Your forgiveness and grace.*

November 21 _____

Therefore I will look to the LORD;
I will wait for the God of my salvation;
My God will hear me.
— MIC. 7:7

*O*ne Thanksgiving it seemed to take longer than usual to make dinner at Grandma McCall's. While they were waiting, someone asked, "Grandma, are you hungry?"

Grandma who was hard of hearing replied, "No, I'm from Denmark."

Stories like this aren't as amusing to me as they once were; sometimes I don't hear things as clearly as I once did. I find myself asking people to repeat things or sometimes, not wanting to admit I didn't hear, I simply smile and nod my head. I suppose one day my grandchildren will tell stories about how Grandma Mona smiled and nodded her head when they made up totally inappropriate questions to ask her because she didn't want to admit she couldn't hear! Maybe I'd better begin taking up lip-reading.

Several passages in the Bible ask us to hear God when He talks to us and ask God to hear us when we talk to Him. Too often we suffer from spiritual hearing loss and don't hear what He tries desperately to tell us. Fortunately, God is never hard of hearing; He always hears us when we talk to Him. It's a promise.

♥ *Dear God, remove my spiritual deafness so that I hear You clearly.*

*Judge not, and you shall not be judged.
Condemn not, and you shall not be
condemned. Forgive, and you will be
forgiven.*
                                    —LUKE 6:37

*M*y sister-in-law has become a grandmother without being a mother. When she married my brother after his first wife died, she immediately gained two daughters, a son, and seven grandchildren. She appears to handle instant grandmotherhood well, and the grandchildren accepted her quite easily as their new grandmother.

I love the adaptability of children. Unless they are swayed by adult inferences, they are able to do a good job of knowing if people like them and will usually give them a chance without pronouncing judgment.

Jesus asks us to be discerning instead of negative and to be sure that we examine our own lives more than criticize others. It is very human that the things we don't like about others are often the very things we dislike about ourselves—it's just easier to see in other people. One grandmother told her grandchildren, "If you want to change something about someone else, you'd better check first to see if you do the same thing."

The bottom line is always forgive. Forgive yourself and others. God did, and He is the only One who has any right to judge.

♥ *When I am prone to criticize, Lord, help me to take a look at myself.*

SURPRISE PLANS

For I know the thoughts that I think toward you, says the LORD, thoughts of peace and not of evil, to give you a future and a hope.
> —JER. 29:11

*M*artha was diagnosed with polio when she was ten days old. As she grew, it became increasingly difficult for her to walk, even with the help of crutches and a back brace; a wheelchair became a necessity. Then, when Martha met and married a young man, they made the painful decision that it would probably be best not to have children—until Martha learned she was pregnant.

There was concern because, along with the complications left by polio, Martha was now forty-one. Despite all these things, Jason Dale was born, healthy and weighing over nine pounds. His birthday is appropriately near Thanksgiving Day. Mother, baby, father, grandmother, and the whole family are doing fine.

Even though God has given us the freedom to make decisions and choices, He sometimes helps us change our minds in surprising ways. I believe it's because He has a better plan for us. We may not understand what that plan is, and that's fine. God just asks us to accept what He has for us. He will reveal everything we need to know when we are ready to know it.

♥ *Dear God, help me remember that Your plans are always better than mine.*

CORD OF LOVE

I drew them with gentle cords,
With bands of love . . .
—HOS. 11:4

*J*ill's grandparents had a cottage in Michigan. Her grandmother loved to cook and often gathered berries, mushrooms, and other edibles from the woods to use in her cooking. Jill remembers coming back to the cottage after an afternoon of swimming to find a wonderful meal her grandmother had prepared while they were gone.

When Jill was in her teens, she admired how well her grandmother could sew and loved to watch her stitch wherever the family gathered. One of the things she watched her grandmother make was a cathedral quilt. Jill has the quilt, and when she looks at it can pick out the pieces of material from aprons and dresses the family once wore. The quilt is stitched with love stronger than thread.

Napoleon is credited with saying, "Charlemagne, Alexander the Great, and other generals have built up empires, and they built them on force, but Jesus Christ has millions of people who would die for Him, and He built an empire on love." God draws us to Him by love. It is stronger than any other cord.

♥ *Dear God, I feel Your strong love for me in so many ways. Thank You.*

MAIL CALL

Grace and peace be multiplied to you in the knowledge of God and of Jesus our Lord.
— 2 PETER 1:2

I am a grandmother pen pal to a young man named Rodney. The teacher of his class at school asked several grandmothers and grandfathers at church if we would be willing to write to the children in her class to help them learn about writing letters. I enjoy Rodney's letters to me. He tells me about school, his hobbies, his pet, and asks questions such as, "What kind of car do you drive? Do you have any pets? What kind of job do you have?"

Whenever I travel, I send Rodney a postcard from where I am and tell him a little bit about it. I'm glad that someone is helping children learn about writing letters. It's becoming a lost art.

Letter writing was one of the ways God used to give us His Word. Those letters written by Paul, Peter, John, and others through the inspiration of the Holy Spirit give instruction, comfort, encouragement, and hope. God's letters to us are meant to be read often, the message is always Good News!

♥ *Your Word is like a packet of letters from Home, Lord.*

And Jesus said to them, "I am the bread of life. He who comes to Me shall never hunger, and he who believes in Me shall never thirst."
        —JOHN 6:35

*M*ary's grandmother lived on a farm in Michigan. When the family went to visit her, she always had freshly baked bread for the week, seven loaves, sitting on the table cooling. After the family had been there for a while, she would serve them warm bread and butter for a snack.

The smell of the bread, the melting butter on the warm slices of soft bread, and the crisp crust has lingered in Mary's memory as practical evidence of her grandmother's love for her and her family.

Bread was an absolute necessity of life in Bible times, and Jesus repeatedly referred to Himself as bread so the people would understand that He was a necessity of life. Jesus said, "I am the living bread which came down from heaven. If anyone eats of this bread, he will live forever; and the bread that I shall give is My flesh, which I shall give for the life of the world" (John 6:51).

The bread we eat daily is physical and doesn't last. Jesus is our spiritual Bread. We need Him for complete satisfaction and eternal life.

♥ *Dear God, thank You for the Bread You sent to give us life.*

Remind them to be subject to rulers and authorities, to obey, to be ready for every good work, to speak evil of no one, to be peaceable, gentle, showing all humility to all men.

—TITUS 3:1–2

*D*ebbie's grandfather was a fur trader. The trappers and their families would come in old, beat-up trucks to bring pelts and hides to sell at all hours of the day and night. Many times her grandfather, whom she called "Papa," would have to turn down the fur because it wasn't a high enough grade or it was torn or he just didn't need that particular species. When this happened the trappers would often get angry and dangerous, because they counted so much on the money.

Just when things would be getting tense, Debbie's grandmother (Nanny) would appear on the back porch with an armload of Debbie's old clothes or things she had purchased at sales. She would call the trapper by name and say, "I was hoping your wife and children would be able to get some use out of these clothes. I was thinking about you all just the other day and put these aside just for your family."

Nanny knew how to keep the peace with the traders. The verses above show us how to be responsible Christians and citizens—through peaceable service and living.

♥ *Dear God, help me with my Christian responsibility in the world today.*

GROWTH CYCLE

*As newborn babes, desire the pure milk of
the word, that you may grow thereby.*
—1 PETER 2:2

*S*andy was afraid to remove the eggs from under the
chickens at her Grandma Luthy's chicken farm, but
Grandma patiently instructed her and demonstrated
how to do it until she was able to gather eggs like a regular farm hand.

Grandma laughed at all Sandy's jokes. Once, when
Grandma asked Sandy to get a pair of tongs to lift the
corn-on-the-cob out of the pan, Sandy went outside
and brought back the big ice block tongs. This made
Grandma laugh and made Sandy feel good.

Sandy felt as nurtured by her grandma as the hundreds of plants that started out as seedlings in con-
tainers in the dining room and moved eventually into
the garden to produce food for family and others.
Grandma Luthy knew what it took to make things and
people grow.

Children want to grow up. They want to be like the
grown-ups in their lives. And they need help to do so.
When we accept Jesus as Savior we are spiritual babies
that need to grow. We need spiritual milk to begin and
a steady diet of God's Word to continue growing as believers. Is there someone helping you grow as a believer? Are you helping someone in their spiritual
growth?

♥ *I want to increase my spiritual appetite, Lord.*

Therefore, if anyone is in Christ, he is a new creation; old things have passed away; behold, all things have become new.
—2 COR. 5:17

*S*andy says when her first child was born, it wasn't until her mother held the baby and began to show her how to care for him that she felt comfortable with her child.

One day when Sandy was visiting her mother, a grandson named Mark was there. During the morning she told Sandy it was time for her to go out on the porch with Mark to eat a muffin. It was part of their daily ritual.

Grandmothers are counted on for a variety of things. Our children often come to us for guidance, support, and encouragement as they learn to raise their children. Our grandchildren look to us for cookies and money and even daily muffins on the porch. To both generations we're a resource.

The dictionary defines a resource as "something that lies ready for use or can be drawn upon for aid," and "ability to deal effectively with problems." Sounds accurate to me, with one addition—how well we fit the definitions is related directly to our relationship with God, the source of everything we are and can be.

♥ *I praise You, God, for giving me new life. I want to be a good resource for my family.*

TREASURE HOLDER

But we have this treasure in earthen vessels,
that the excellence of the power may be of
God and not of us.   —2 COR. 4:7

*A*re you familiar with the book *Stories from Grandma's Attic*? The author, Arleta Richardson, remembers her grandma's big old farmhouse as a storybook with a story to be found everywhere she looked. The stories begin with the magical words, "Tell me about when you were a little girl, Grandma"—words that unlock the stories behind all the treasures in Grandma's attic.

To grandchildren, our houses, apartments, and mobile homes, with or without attics, can seem to be filled with treasures—treasures usually have a story involved with them. One of our greatest pleasures should be relating those stories when interest is expressed.

The greatest treasure we have to tell is the valuable message of salvation in Jesus Christ that God has given us to share. We carry God's priceless power in us enabling us to do His work. This power is able to let the Good News of God shine through us so brightly that our grandchildren and everyone we meet will want to know His story.

♥ *Praise God for His priceless power which gives me*
the courage to make Him known.

December 1 ———————————————

VALUABLE READING

My tongue shall speak of Your word,
For all your commandments are
righteousness. —PS. 119:172

A grandmother gave the old family Bible to her grandson and suggested that he would find it valuable to read. In the middle of the Book she had hidden a fifty-dollar bill.

That's certainly one way to try to motivate grandchildren to read God's Word. There are other, less expensive ways, though. One is to keep the Bible in a place where grandchildren can see it—and use it. I'm not talking about a coffee table Bible; the message of a coffee table Bible is *"Don't touch!"*

Another way is to begin reading short passages to them when they are small. And, to help grandchildren understand the place of esteem the Bible has in our homes, let them see us using the Bible.

Instilling a love for the Scriptures in our grandchildren begins with our feelings about His Word. The Book of Psalms has several great verses about God's Word. "Your word I have hidden in my heart," and "Your word is a lamp to my feet / And a light to my path" (Ps. 119:11, 105) are two of the most familiar. These verses express a love for God's Word that should prompt us to use the Bible as one way to introduce the ones we love so much to the One who loves them more.

♥ *Dear God, help me to pass on my love for Your Word to my grandchildren.*

GRANDMA SONG

*Speaking to one another in psalms and
hymns and spiritual songs, singing and
making melody in your heart to the Lord.*
—EPH. 5:19

*L*orraine wasn't able to talk with her grandmother
because her grandmother spoke only Spanish. But
grandmother taught Lorraine how to sing "Jesus Loves
Me" in Spanish and took her to church with her. When
Grandma was bedridden, Lorraine would play the guitar and sing Christian songs for her. Her grandma was
able to understand that Lorraine truly knew that Jesus
loves her.

Sometimes music communicates when spoken
words can't. When members of the early Church met
they spoke to one another from the Old Testament
Scriptures, especially Psalms, and composed and sang
hymns. This is one evidence of the presence of the
Holy Spirit in a believer's life—God is present, and He
brings joy.

Have you ever made up a song to sing to God? It's
easy if you use a well-known tune such as "Jesus Loves
Me" or "Happy Birthday." It's especially fun if you
share the song with your grandchildren. They'll love to
sing the song Grandma wrote.

♥ *Thank You, God, for music and what a wonderful
way it is to communicate with You and others.*

December 3 _____

WANTED: ONE GRANDMOTHER

. . . God is love, and he who abides in love abides in God, and God in him.
—1 JOHN 4:16

*O*ur small group was talking about grandmothers. One by one we told our happy, funny, warm, inspiring "grandma stories" until one woman said, "I never had a grandma, and my mother died when my daughter was a baby. She doesn't have one either." Then she added, "When my daughter marries and has children, I've asked God to let me still be living so that I can be the kind of grandma I always wanted."

Older women in the group immediately offered to be adopted grandmothers to both her and her daughter. Grandmothers are necessary links between generations. When there isn't a grandmother available, we miss being in touch with people who lived when we didn't. Wherever there aren't "natural" grandmothers we should be willing to fill those positions. Grandmothers have the capacity for loving a great many grandchildren. Especially when they know and love God who is love, and who is the reason we are able to love one another.

♥ *Is there a grandmother position open that I can fill?*

. . . The harvest truly is plentiful, but the laborers are few. —MATT. 9:37

*N*ot all grandma remembrances are warm and loving. Some are painful. The following story was told to me by a granddaughter.

My dad and his sister were abandoned by their unmarried mother when he was three and she was one. His sister was adopted, but my dad lived in a variety of places and homes. When he learned where his mother was, she had married and adopted two children. Years later, after my father married and I was born, I became curious about my grandmother. My father knew where she lived and we drove to see her. He went to the door while I sat in the car. I couldn't see the door, but I could hear clearly. First, I heard a scream. Then I heard a voice ask, "What do you want?"

My father asked, "Would you like to meet your granddaughter?"

I heard my grandmother say, "I don't want to meet nobody." And the door slammed. My father came back to the car a sad and broken man.

We can only imagine what had brought this grandmother to this miserable, God-forsaken place in her life. If you know anyone like this, pray for her and reach out in God's love. This could be the mission field where God has asked you to serve.

♥ *Dear Lord, am I seeing the field where You want me to work?*

CHOSEN PEOPLE

*But you are a chosen generation, . . . His
own special people, that you may proclaim
the praises of Him who called you out of
darkness into His marvelous light.*
—1 PETER 2:9

In 1983 Dale Evans Rogers, with Carole C. Carlson, wrote the book *Grandparents Can*. The book is drawn from her long, hard experience as a mother, grandmother, and great-grandmother. It talks about building friendships with grandchildren, taking time to listen and communicate, creating a sense of roots, becoming role models, and providing security in the face of a changing, unstable world.

Her book ends with this challenge: "We have been called by God to do things no one else can do. How privileged we are to be such chosen people. Come on, grandparents, join us in prayer to change the world we touch with the magic of love."

Do you feel and act like a chosen person? You should! The Bible tells us that God decided a long time ago to make us His own. Through Jesus, we are gifts to God and He accepts us with joy. As grandmothers and grandfathers, we can multiply God's joy by being among the ones who bring our grandchildren to Him. The best way is with love.

♥ *God, I praise and thank You for choosing me. Help me show my grandchildren they are chosen, too.*

But God demonstrates His own love toward us, in that while we were still sinners, Christ died for us.
—ROM. 5:8

*W*hen Lisa visited her Grandma Beckman in her tiny Chicago apartment, Grandma always gave her ice cream in little cups to eat with a wooden spoon. She also had pop in little paper cups, and shoestring potato chips. After this treat they would watch "Family Classics" on television.

The things we do with grandchildren that are remembered are so very often such simple pleasures for them and us. It is always amazing to me the detail to which those things are remembered. Also, what I think my grandchildren will remember is not at all what I remember! When I visit my California grandchildren, I usually bring a number of small presents. What my grandson comments on is how he remembers and likes the smell of my perfume. Another grandchild says, "I like it that you smile and laugh a lot."

When Jesus ate the Last Supper with His disciples, He asked them to remember Him. What do you think they remembered most about Him? What do you remember about Him when you take communion?

What Jesus wants us to remember most is that He gave His life for us. The communion service is a celebration of our being saved from sin by Jesus' death.

♥ *Dear God, thank You for using the simple things to remind us of Your priceless gift.*

That you would have a walk worthy of God who calls you into His own kingdom and glory. **—1 THESS. 2:12**

*L*isa called her Grandma Rita a "doing-things-with grandma." Lisa said, "She took her grandchildren shopping, to lunch, and on the only out-of-state trips I took when I was a child." And she always called Grandma Rita with questions about nursing her children because Grandma had nursed all her children, too.

But more than the shopping, lunch, trips, and advice, Lisa loves her grandma for the way she has always supported her, thought the best of her, and encouraged her—no matter what.

We might be surprised if we knew how much our grandchildren depend on our support and encouragement. Perhaps some grandmothers have taken the attitude that this is their parents' responsibility. Nothing could be further from the truth. Children need all the support and encouragement they can get from parents, grandparents, teachers, and any other significant adults in their lives.

God calls us to be encouragers. Our words and lives can encourage our grandchildren to live in ways that will bring joy to them, you, and God. Our support (or comfort) keeps them going when things are rough.

♥ *I praise You, Lord, for Your total dependability.*

Then they brought young children to Him,
that He might touch them.
                                        —MARK 10:13

*T*he family had just taken Grandmother to a nursing
home. It was hard to see her lying in bed; she had always been active, always doing things for other people.
Her hands, which had never stopped moving as they
made and served food, cleaned house, sewed and
mended, dressed and undressed children and grandchildren, and a million other things, now lay still on the
folded-down sheet. Her granddaughter felt helpless
and, not knowing what to do with her own hands,
shoved them in the pockets of her skirt.

A few days later the granddaughter had a minor accident. In the emergency room, a friend assured her
that she would be all right. The friend took her hand
and held it gently. The granddaughter's eyes filled with
tears of gratefulness. It was then she knew what to do
when she went to visit her grandmother again.

A touch can be more comforting than words; something as simple as holding a person's hand speaks vol-
umes. The New Testament gives several examples of
Jesus touching people for healing. Many of us have experienced Jesus' touch in our lives. The peace, blessing, and comfort it brings is indescribable.

♥ *Dear Lord, like the children You touched so long*
  ago, I come to You for your touch.

Therefore we also pray always for you that our God would count you worthy of this calling, and fulfill all the good pleasure of His goodness . . . —2 THESS. 1:11

*B*illy Graham's mother wrote in *They Call Me Mother Graham,* that she often wonders "if we, as mothers, recognize how much our prayers have influenced our children's choices through life. It is something we should contemplate seriously." If every grandmother in the world was praying on a regular basis for her grandchildren, this would be a changed world beginning with changed families. Think about the ways you might do this. You might pray as you look at their pictures on your table or wall; pray after you talk with a grandchild on the phone; pray for them as you purchase a gift, send a letter, or card, or get a gift ready to mail; pray for them whenever you are sitting and waiting, such as in a doctor's office.

You might pray the above verse in the Living Bible version: "And so we keep on praying for you that our God will make you the kind of children he wants to have—will make you as good as you wish you could be!—rewarding your faith with his power." There is no greater loving legacy.

♥ *Father, thank You for my grandchildren. It is a privilege to talk with You about them.*

HIDDEN TREASURES

*That their hearts may be encouraged, being
knit together in love, . . . both of the Father
and of Christ, in whom are hidden all the
treasures of wisdom and knowledge.*

—COL. 2:2-3

*A*nother grandmother and money story. Debbie
tells about looking through a book at her Nanny's
house one day and finding several hundred dollar bills
pressed in the pages. Nanny just smiled and said, "We
might need that later and now you can help me remember where I put it."

Debbie said her family didn't know why her grandmother hid money in the house (they found thousands
in the pantry and a drawer of the sewing machine when
she died); perhaps it was because of memories of her
impoverished childhood.

I understand about keeping things that might be
needed later. Whenever I need extra supplies for a
children's craft project, a drama presentation, or other
special program at church, I call a friend and ask her
to check her "basement outlet" for what I need. She
usually has it.

The verse for today tells us that all we really need is
Jesus, "in whom are hidden all the treasures of wisdom and knowledge."

♥ *God, I praise You for the treasures of wisdom and
knowledge You've made available to me.*

*If you then, being evil, know how to give
good gifts to your children, how much more
will your Father who is in heaven give good
things to those who ask Him!*

—MATT. 7:11

*M*y pen pal, Rodney, wrote me a letter about his grandmother. This is what he wrote:

Dear Miss Warren,
    I like my grandma because she brings me toys. It is fun to go shopping with her. She used to have two dogs. They died. Their names were Fred and Buster. They were old, though.

Love, Rodney

When I ask young grandchildren about their grandmothers there are two things that are usually mentioned—toys and food. (Grandmas who have pets get extra points.)

As a giver of good gifts, we are following God's example. We need to remember that the kindness we show in giving can't compare with how kind, generous, and wise God, the Creator of those characteristics, can be.

♥ *Dear God, Your standard of wise generosity is my goal.*

CONSTANT COMPASSION

*The LORD is gracious and full of
  compassion,
Slow to anger and great in mercy.*
—PS. 145:8

$\mathcal{E}$very Sunday morning for several weeks Rachelle prayed and asked her Sunday school class to pray for her grandmother, who had gone to live in a convalescent home. It was hard for Grandma to go and hard for Rachelle and her family to let her go. Grandma had lived with the family for three years. Rachelle liked going to Grandma's room to look at pictures and try on her grandmother's jewelry. Her little brother, Nick, missed Grandma, too, and worried about her and her new home.

Rachelle's prayer was that Jesus would help her grandma be happy and like where she was living.

I love the tenderheartedness and compassion of children. It must be a sorrow to God that this characteristic of His, which children exhibit so openly and easily, is not as evident in adults—especially since we can read God's Word and have seen in our own lives His constant compassion.

David praises our compassionate God in the Psalms (see Pss. 86:15; 103:8; 111:4; 112:4; and today's verse). David received and felt God's compassion. It motivated him to have God's compassion for others. It should be our motivation, too.

♥ *Dear God, when I am not compassionate, remind me of Your ongoing compassion toward me.*

December 13 ―――――――――――――――――

*And have put on the new man who is
renewed in knowledge according to the
image of Him who created him.*

—COL. 3:10

In another of my college speech classes, the students' first impromptu speech was about their remembrances of their grandmothers. The students told about grandmothers who drive speed boats; have big gardens and cook everything from scratch; like to go fishing at 4:00 A.M.; are energetic and good listeners; are in better shape than most college students; have a young attitude and like rock music; are generous; knit and are easy to talk to; love arts and crafts; and have Christmas ornament collections. All of these grandmothers were over seventy, and several were in their eighties.

Do you ever wonder how your grandchildren would describe you to a friend or a teacher? Actually, we don't really have too much to worry about. Most grandmothers have pretty good images!

This shouldn't be too surprising. We are told in Genesis 1:27 that God created us in His own image. When we become Christians we are enrolled in God's continuing education program. The lessons bring about changes that make us more and more like Him. Commencement takes place in Heaven.

♥ *God, I'm glad You are teaching me how to be like You. I want others to see how You have changed me.*

Moreover it is required in stewards that one be found faithful. —1 COR. 4:2

Cheryl's grandmother had beautiful hair; everyone said so. And Cheryl, who is a hairdresser, was the only one who could do it for her the way she wanted it done. When Grandma died, Cheryl's mother was upset with the way her mother's hair was arranged for the funeral. She called Cheryl and asked her to come and help her explain what needed to be done. When Cheryl saw her grandmother, she became upset, too, and decided to fix her grandmother's hair herself. As Cheryl cut, curled, and arranged her grandmother's hair, she thought about what her grandmother had meant to her and how her grandmother had always trusted her to do it. Cheryl felt it would please her grandmother to know that her granddaughter was able to do this one last thing for her. She had been faithful to her grandmother's trust.

Faithfulness is more important to God than how talented we are. In what ways do you show trust in your grandchildren so that they may learn faithfulness? In what ways are you faithful to their trust in you? What a pleasant way to receive a reward from God!

♥ *Dear God, I want to be faithful to You in everything I say and do.*

We are bound to thank God always . . . because your faith grows exceedingly, and the love of every one of you all abounds toward each other.

—2 THESS. 1:3

*A*ndrea loved tomatoes. She liked to eat them whole, like apples. And Grandma grew tomatoes in her garden. One day the family was gathered at Grandma's house for dinner. Grandma had cut two large tomatoes into wedges and put them in a dish that was sitting right next to Andrea's plate. When Andrea, a preschooler at the time, saw the dish full of tomatoes, she thought her grandmother had put them there just for her and ate every single wedge before dinner even started.

Preschoolers feel that everything in the world revolves around them. They understand the world as "the world is me." When they are about five years old they begin to be willing to add, "and you, too."

This is part of the natural growth and development; yet sometimes we see grown people who still evidence a "the world is me" outlook on life. It is God's plan for us to grow in all areas: physical, intellectual, emotional, and spiritual. We can't grow toward God without growing toward others in love. How we've grown will help us teach our grandchildren that the world is all of us.

♥ *Help me to grow toward You in more knowledge and faith, Lord.*

Therefore we make it our aim, whether present or absent, to be well pleasing to Him.
—2 COR. 5:9

*T*he grandmother I sat across from at the mother-daughter banquet told me she still saw friends she had made when she was a preschooler. This grandmother had always enjoyed painting and one of her friends liked to write. When they married and had children, they set aside their painting and writing to raise their families. As grandmothers they have time to pursue these interests again.

These grandmothers continue to be interesting people because they are actively involved in doing more than sitting around waiting to get older. Who knows? There could be another Grandma Moses or Eudora Welty in the making. What an encouragement we can be to grandchildren who need to see models of older adults stretching themselves to accomplish goals.

We should all have a first goal in common—to please God with our lives. It could well be the only goal that might lead to accomplishments beyond our dreams.

♥ *Dear God, help me to keep my goals in the right order with pleasing You first.*

Then you will know that I am the LORD;
those who hope in me will not be
disappointed. —ISA. 49:23 NIV

I arrived at my daughter's house with Christmas gifts for everyone. Six-year-old Angie met me at the door, surveyed the packages, and said, "I wanted a Dalmatian puppy for Christmas and I thought *you* would bring me one, Grandma."

Angie had been talking Dalmatian puppy to her family for weeks and had received no encouragement or hope of getting one. Her last hope had been Grandma, and I had failed her.

It's hard to disappoint grandchildren. We want to give them the things they want. There's pleasure in it for them and for us. But Angie needed to learn that Grandma will not always be able to supply all she wants, and I needed to be reminded that I cannot do everything and I do sometimes disappoint people.

This is part of God's plan to grow us. As God leads Angie to understand that people sometimes disappoint us and me to understand that I can disappoint people, He's developing in her and deepening in me a trust in Himself, the only One in whom there is no disappointment.

♥ *Thank You, Father, for never disappointing me.*

MAKING MEMORIES

. . . May you see your children's children.
—PS. 128:6

*B*ette's grandmother had a big wood stove in her kitchen. When Bette visited before Christmas, her grandmother gave her a sheet of paper on which to write what she wanted for Christmas. Then she showed Bette where to put the paper in the back of the stove so her list would go straight to Santa Claus in the smoke that curled up the stove pipe and out into the sky!

Some grandmothers find they are more creative and playful with their grandchildren, perhaps because there isn't the constant weight of responsibility that was part of rearing their own children. As one grandmother said, "My grandchildren and I have fun together, and then they go home."

Grandchildren do go home eventually, and they take with them memories of their time with us. They may be quiet times sitting together, reading, and talking; or they may be attending a three-ring circus. What's important is being together.

♥ *Thank You for my family and the companionship of my grandchildren.*

DISAPPOINTMENT

These things I have spoken to you, that in Me you may have peace. —JOHN 16:33

*M*y California grandchildren (and their parents) were coming for Christmas for the first time in many years. The children were eager to see snow.

The boys walked off the plane in big snow boots, carrying heavy jackets, woolen hats, and mitts. They were ready for winter. The only problem was Illinois was having a brown Christmas. There was no snow, and the temperature was in the 50s. Each day we listened hopefully to weather reports. Except for a light dusting of snow early one morning, we were disappointed. Yet, when asked about one of the best Christmases they ever had, they all agree, "the one we were all together."

Disappointments are inevitable. No snow wasn't a biggie; the way we dealt with the disappointment about it was. We didn't let it affect our time together.

God tells us in the Bible that we will have trouble. He also tells us what to do about it: He tells us not to be discouraged because we belong to the Overcomer!

♥ *Help me feel Your peace when I am disappointed. Do not let it affect my relationship with You or others.*

GIFTS

Thanks be to God for His indescribable gift!
—2 COR. 9:15

*J*ust about every grandmother struggles to choose gifts to give grandchildren for Christmas, birthdays, and other occasions. One grandmother gives each child three things at Christmas—something to wear, something to read, and something to play with. Another grandmother feels parents should buy the toys and books, so she gives a savings bond; still another tells her grandchildren a price range and takes them shopping.

Giving gifts is one of the more joyful aspects of grandmotherhood, especially when we are able to give that one thing a grandchild needs or desires. My daughter Bev once complimented me on knowing what kinds of gifts her preteen son, Rob, liked.

We choose gifts to meet our grandchildren's interests, desires, and needs as we get to know and respect the ways they are different from one another. God's gifts to us are always exactly what we need and desire, beginning with His gift of salvation and continuing through our life with Him. He provides never-failing love, joy, peace, continuing forgiveness, comfort, mercy, guidance, daily presence, etc.

♥ *These are gifts from You that I am most thankful for today.*

December 21 _____

*The Lord is not slack concerning His
promise, . . . but is longsuffering toward us,
not willing that any should perish but that
all should come to repentance.*
—2 PETER 3:9

*G*inger's grandmother was her piano teacher. Ginger enjoyed going to her Grandma's house; it was filled with interesting things to look at and play with from the years her grandparents and her mother lived in China. At Christmas, when the whole family gathered for a big dinner, it wasn't until the meal was over, the dishes were done, and Grandma came into the living room to sit down that any presents could be opened by impatient grandchildren.

Patience is hard for everyone, not just grandchildren, to learn. I am convinced that the hardest thing God asks us to do is wait, and it doesn't help that we are living in a world that glorifies doing more things in less time.

Perhaps the best way to help us learn to be patient is to constantly and consistently remind ourselves about God's patience with us (see 1 Tim. 1:16). He waits patiently for us to come to Him for forgiveness and salvation and then continues in loving patience with us as we falter and fail in following Him. It's part of His definition of love.

♥ *Dear Father, I am so thankful You are patient with me.*

Beware lest anyone cheat you . . .
according to the tradition of men, according
to the basic principles of the world, and not
according to Christ.   —COL. 2:8

*G*randma Carol and her grandchildren go caroling every Christmas. When they first began, they went just to the neighbors' houses. Now they visit neighbors, church members, and shut-ins. The grandchildren make ornaments to give to those they carol to, and their mothers make cookies to give away and to enjoy at Grandma's after the event.

It is sometimes easy to let the busyness of a season crowd out meaningful traditions such as caroling. I propose not to lose what's really important in the rush. This will be different for each family and requires a family conference of some sort, but will be worth the effort. Be sure to do it early—perhaps during a picnic in July. If your family doesn't have any Christmas traditions, have fun deciding on some together.

Traditions were important to Bible families, too. We know they had many that were part of their faith. Those are the best kinds of traditions because they are based on truth given by a living God.

♥ *I praise You because You are a living God.*

THE GREATEST STORY

And she will bring forth a Son, and you shall call His name JESUS, for He will save His people from their sins. —MATT. 1:21

*C*arol began a story tradition with her three sons and continues it with her grandchildren. When the grandchildren stay overnight, she tells a story that begins, "There was a little boy (or girl)." The story then recounts what this little grandchild did that day. When grandchildren are asked if they want Grandma to read a story or tell a "There was a little boy" story, they always opt for "their" story.

Carol tells a postscript to this delightful idea. For many years Carol's youngest son read the Christmas story prior to opening Christmas gifts. The year her two oldest grandsons learned to read, she began the festivities with, "There were two little boys who learned to read so they could read a story about another little Boy." Then the grandsons read the Christmas story.

The Bible begins with the story of Creation and continues through Old and New Testaments with story after story telling us everything we need to know about God and His Son. Jesus' story has been called "The Greatest Story Ever Told" and it begins with, "There was a little boy. . . ."

♥ *Dear God, You tell wonderful, life-giving stories. Thank You.*

BETHLEHEM PERSPECTIVE

For my eyes have seen Your salvation . . . A
light to bring revelation to the Gentiles,
And the glory of Your people Israel.
—LUKE 2:30, 32

*C*hristmas Eve at Fran's grandma's house included all the aunts, uncles, and cousins. The children would play in the living room and the adults would visit in the kitchen. There was a little, tiny Christmas tree with bubble lights on the mantel.

After dinner, everyone gathered in the living room and her grandparents passed out the Christmas envelopes. Everyone knew what was in the envelopes—$2.00 for children, $5.00 for adults—but they always acted surprised. Fran says the way they handed out the envelopes made everyone feel special.

We need to return to Christmases where there is more giving of self and less giving or expecting of material things. More gathering together of families with visiting as the primary focus. More emphasis on people rather than things. We need more Bethlehem perspective.

God's gift to us came wrapped in everyday, ordinary strips of cloth displayed on a bed of straw. But it was a gift given by a Heavenly Father to let us know how special we are to Him. It is the best Christmas present ever.

♥ *Dear God, when I think of the gift of Your Son, I realize how much You love me. Thank You.*

December 25 _____

*. . . you . . . have carried out the mission
the LORD your God gave you.*
—JOSH. 22:3 NIV

$\mathcal{G}$randma Jean has a large globe in her house. When grandson Stephen comes to visit, he likes to look at the globe and ask questions about the names that are taped on it. Grandma explains that the names are of people who went to those countries to tell the people about Jesus and that she and Grandpa help them with prayers and money. What a great way to interest grandchildren in missions! And a beginning step in helping them hear a possible call to become a missionary.

When we become Christians, God gives each of us a mission. For some it is in their homes and families. For others it is their neighborhoods or the places where they work. For still others it is somewhere in another city, state, or country.

Our mission is described in what we call the Great Commission in Matthew 28:19–20. The way we perform the mission God gives us has a powerful effect on our grandchildren. It can be life-changing.

♥ *Dear God, help me to use my gifts in the mission
You've given me.*

As each one has received a gift, minister it to one another, as good stewards of the manifold grace of God.

—1 PETER 4:10

*J*ean's grandmother, she called her "Babi," always preferred the "old ways." What she called new-fangled inventions were hard for her to learn to use and she was perfectly happy with an old-fashioned toaster that had sides that flipped down; a cloth covered cord.

Jean says, "If I gave Babi a gift, I was sure to get it back. One Christmas I bought her a nightgown and a new toaster. She preferred her old flannel nightgown and out-of-date toaster. I got both gifts back as wedding presents!"

I've heard of grandmothers who put the gifts they receive in dresser drawers and closets to be discovered years later, unopened and unused. Gifts are meant to be enjoyed and used. So it is with the gifts that God has given each of us. When we find out what gifts God has given us, we must be willing to use our gifts generously, not hide or hold them back.

How are you using your gifts as a grandmother?

♥ *Thank You, Lord, for the gifts that You have given me.*

The LORD your God in your midst, . . .
He will quiet you in His love,
He will rejoice over you with singing.
—ZEPH. 3:17

*O*ne Thanksgiving, Keri and her sister watched their grandmother whip cream for the pumpkin pies. They decided to help and whipped it some more. They whipped so well, it turned into butter. Their grandma didn't scold, though; she just announced that there would be no whipped cream for the pies that day.

Another time, Keri and her grandmother made bread dough and put it in a bowl to rise while they went shopping. Grandma kept saying, "We'd better hurry or the dough will rise too much." Grandma had Keri believing that when they got home the dough would have risen until it overflowed the bowl and came to meet them. They laughed about the picture that created in their minds as they enjoyed the bread.

Grandmothers can be sensitive to what can happen when grandchildren are trying out things. This verse in Zephaniah makes the point that there is great happiness when we have God with us—happiness for us and for God as He rejoices about us in song. It sounds like the kind of relationship we'd like our grandchildren to have with us and with God, too.

♥ *Father, I praise You for being happy about me because my happiness comes from You.*

COMFORT REMEDY

*T*he night Mollie and her sister were able to admit that their grandmother wasn't going to recover and would die, they stopped to eat dinner at a pizza place on the way home. As they ate, they held hands and talked of their memories of their grandmother and what the future would be like without her. Mollie said, "As two who love food would do, we drowned our sorrow in that entire pizza, with not a piece to take home."

I think a grandmother who wants her granddaughters to be comforted would appreciate and approve of this way to alleviate their sorrow. We all have our own remedies for comfort. Special foods (my preferences are ice cream or chocolate), things we do, or places we go to ease the pain and help us regain perspective.

God promises us a day when there will be no more sorrow. Sometimes in the depths of our present sorrow, we long for the fulfillment of His promise and can hardly wait. That's when we need to take comfort in His Words, the good memories we have, and generous portions of pizza, ice cream, chocolate, or you name it.

♥ *When sorrow comes, Lord, help me to find comfort in You.*

INVITATION TO REST

There remains therefore a rest for the people of God. For he who has entered His rest has himself also ceased from his works as God did from His.

—HEB. 4:9–10

*V*irginia says her grandmother was quite a lady. When Grandfather went to fight in the Civil War, Grandmother went to live near where he was so she could be with him. Her house was always full of grandchildren; those she was raising and others who lived with her on and off throughout the years. She always took them with her to Sunday school. And in her house, Sunday was truly a day of rest when no one did anything but go to church, eat, and take a nap.

I personally advocate that kind of schedule for Sunday and guard my naptime with passion—to be interrupted only by calls or visits from grandchildren.

The Bible tells us about entering God's rest. In the Old Testament this rest for Moses and the Israelites was the land God had promised them. God's rest for us is the peace He gives now and our eternal life in the new earth to come. His rest is available to us daily and continues until we go to be with Him. It is available to everyone who receives Him as Lord. He especially wants us to make sure our grandchildren have the opportunity to receive His invitation.

♥ *Thank You, Lord, for Your wonderful invitation to eternal life and rest, open to everyone.*

*Walk in wisdom toward those who are
outside, redeeming the time.*

—COL. 4:5

"I was proud of my grandmother," Becky said. "She was a mother of thirteen children, grandmother to thirty or forty, and she still had time for me—to love me."

Becky's grandfather was a farmer, and the farm where her grandparents lived had huge, long barns with lots of chickens that were free to roam. Becky went to her grandparents' farm several times a week and always tried to talk her grandmother into letting her help gather eggs. She loved to climb between the bales of hay where her grandmother couldn't go and find the hidden nests. Becky still has one of the baskets she collected eggs in. It sits in her kitchen to remind her of her busy grandmother who took time to love grandchildren.

We all have twenty-four hours each day; it is how we choose to use them that is significant. The time we spend with grandchildren has far-reaching results. In today's verse, the phrase "redeeming the time" means when you see an opportunity, ask God to lead you in what to do and say. When you let God be in charge of your mouth and actions, people respond more positively.

♥ *Dear God, if You want me to talk to someone today about You, let them begin the conversation.*